westermann

FiNALE Prüfungstraining

2025

Niedersachsen

Zentralabitur Englisch

Liebe Schülerin, lieber Schüler,

sobald die Original-Prüfungsaufgaben zur Veröffentlichung freigegeben sind, können sie unter **www.finaleonline.de** zusammen mit ausführlichen Lösungen kostenlos heruntergeladen werden. Gib dazu einfach diesen Code ein:

EN4A7B1

Einfach mal reinschauen: www.finaleonline.de

Autoren: Anne Böker und Karolin Hofmann
sowie: Isabel Wagemann-Steidel, Ortrud-Christine Rotzoll und Thomas Lehnen

Bildnachweis:
|CartoonStock.com, Bath: 151.1. |iStockphoto.com, Calgary: chekat 1.2, Titel; DeanDrobot 2.1. |stock.adobe.com, Dublin: leonidkos Titel, 1.1.

Druck A[1]/Jahr 2024
Alle Drucke der Serie A sind im Unterricht parallel verwendbar.

Redaktion: Federlese GbR – Christina & Boris Kühne, Grevenbroich
Kontakt: finale@westermanngruppe.de
Layout: LIO Design GmbH, Braunschweig
Umschlaggestaltung: Janssen Kahlert Design & Kommunikation GmbH, Hannover
Umschlagfoto: stock.adobe.com, Dublin, leonidkos; iStockphoto.com, Calgary, chekat
Druck und Bindung: Westermann Druck GmbH, Georg-Westermann-Allee 66, 38104 Braunschweig

ISBN 978-3-07-**172537**-9

FiNALE online.de

Wissen, was drankommt

FiNALE online.de ist die digitale Ergänzung zu deinem FiNALE-Abiturband. Hier findest du eine Vielzahl an Angeboten, die dich zusätzlich bei deiner Prüfungsvorbereitung in Englisch unterstützen!

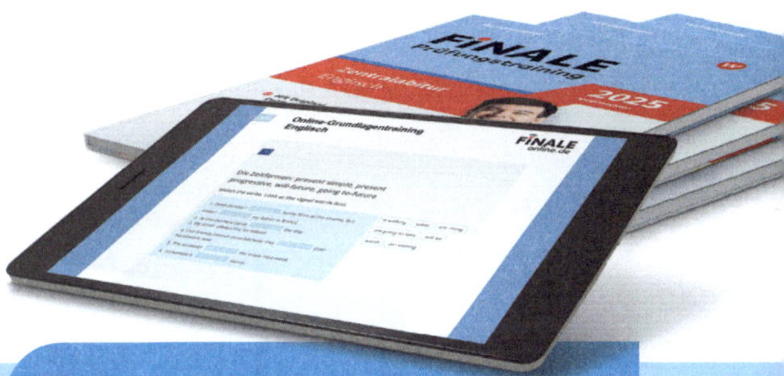

Original-Prüfungsaufgaben mit Lösungen

Schalte dir mit dem Code auf Seite 4 die aktuellen Original-Prüfungsaufgaben frei.

Audiodateien Englisch

Passend zu deinem FiNALE-Arbeitsbuch kannst du dir die Audiodateien zu den Hörverstehensübungen anhören.

Tipps zur Prüfungsvorbereitung

Mit unseren Tipps zur Prüfungsvorbereitung entsteht Lernstress erst gar nicht.

Abi-Checklisten

Mit den Abi-Checklisten ist die Vorbereitung auf die Englisch-Abiturprüfung noch einfacher. Einfach als PDF oder in beschreibbarem WORD-Format herunterladen und den eigenen idealen Zeitplan erstellen. Hake in der Checkliste ab, was du kannst und noch nicht kannst, um deinen Wissensstand zu überprüfen.

Die **Abi-Checklisten** helfen dir, den Überblick über den Prüfungsstoff zu behalten.

www.finaleonline.de

Inhaltsverzeichnis

Textgestaltung

Ausdrucksvermögen / Verfügbarkeit sprachlicher Mittel

Beispiele für Prüfungsaufgaben

Aufgaben mit Beispiellösungen

Aufgaben mit Bewertungskriterien

Aufgaben zur Sprachmittlung mit Beispiellösungen oder Bewertungskriterien

Original-Prüfungsaufgaben 2022/2023 und 2024

Arbeiten mit FiNALE

FiNALE Prüfungstraining Englisch möchte Ihnen eine praxisnahe Hilfe zur Vorbereitung auf die Abiturprüfung sein. Im Praxis-Teil finden sich daher – neben den Original-Prüfungsaufgaben 2023 – zu allen geforderten Themenbereichen weitere authentische Aufgaben, die in ihrer Form den Vorgaben entsprechen. Wir verzichten hier auf eine Differenzierung nach Kursen mit grundlegendem beziehungsweise erhöhtem Anforderungsniveau. Im Abitur unterscheiden sich die Aufgaben einerseits durch den Textumfang, andererseits durch den Schwierigkeitsgrad des Textes. Auch als Schülerin oder Schüler in einem Kurs mit grundlegendem Anforderungsniveau sind Sie durch den Englischunterricht mit längeren und komplexeren Texten vertraut. Als Schülerin oder Schüler eines Kurses mit erhöhtem Anforderungsniveau können Sie eine Textanalyse auch an kürzeren, einfacheren Texten üben.

Zwei Aufgaben im Kapitel „Beispiele für Prüfungsaufgaben“ werden kleinschrittig erarbeitet und schließen mit einer Musterlösung. Dies soll für Sie eine exemplarische Hilfe sein auf dem Weg vom Ausgangstext über das Textverständnis, die Methodik der Textanalyse und die Evaluation hin zur Gliederung und sprachlichen Darstellung des Zieltextes. Den weiteren Aufgabenbeispielen folgen Bewertungskriterien ganz in der Form, wie Ihre Lehrerinnen und Lehrer sie zur Korrektur der Abiturarbeiten an die Hand bekommen. Sie dienen Ihnen zur Selbstkontrolle in Ihrem fortschreitenden Prüfungstraining. Geschrieben wurde dieses Buch im Jahr 2024, damit es frühzeitig zur Vorbereitung auf das Abitur 2025 beitragen kann. Die zu diesem Zeitpunkt aktuellen Abituraufgaben 2023 werden jeweils mit Musterlösung angeboten, wobei aus rechtlichen Gründen zwei Prüfungsteile von den entsprechenden Aufgaben aus dem Jahr 2022 ersetzt werden. Sobald die Original-Prüfungsaufgaben des Jahres 2024 freigegeben sind, können Sie sie unter www.finaleonline.de abrufen.

Das Kapitel „Basiswissen“ bietet Ihnen eine kompakte Übersicht über die für das Zentralabitur vorgegebenen Themen. Es hilft Ihnen, das im Unterricht erworbene Wissen zu strukturieren und in seinen Grundzügen abzurufen. Um den Umgang mit dem thematischen Vokabular zu vertiefen, ist dieser Teil in englischer Sprache geschrieben und wird durch Glossare zum thematischen Vokabular ergänzt.

Die sprachliche Leistung spielt in der Fremdsprache bei aller inhaltlich-thematischer Kompetenz immer noch die herausragende Rolle. Ein sicherer Umgang mit den Strukturen und Wörtern der englischen Sprache ist also unabdingbar. Deshalb haben wir in FiNALE ein ganzes Kapitel zur sprachlichen Leistung aufgenommen.

Wir wünschen Ihnen viel Erfolg!

Informationen und Tipps zur Prüfung

Prüfungsteile im Abitur 2025

In der Abiturprüfung wird es zwei Prüfungsteile geben:
1. a) Hörverstehen (30 Minuten)
   b) Sprachmittlung (60 Minuten)
2. Textaufgabe (195 Minuten gA / 225 Minuten eA)
   Für die Textaufgabe besteht die Wahlmöglichkeit zwischen zwei Vorschlägen; die Auswahl der Textaufgabe ist in der Prüfungszeit inbegriffen.

Die für den Prüfungsteil zur Textaufgabe angegebene Zeitdauer beinhaltet sowohl die Auswahl- als auch die Bearbeitungszeit. Sie können also sofort mit der Bearbeitung der Aufgaben beginnen. Der abgewählte Themenvorschlag verbleibt bei Ihnen. Machen Sie keinesfalls den Fehler, sich nach einer halben Stunde oder sogar noch später umzuentscheiden! Am besten legen Sie den nicht genutzten Themenvorschlag außerhalb Ihres Sichtfelds (zum Beispiel auf dem Boden) ab, um dieser Versuchung und Verwechslungen aus dem Weg zu gehen.

Als Hilfsmittel stehen Ihnen über die gesamte Prüfungsdauer einsprachige und für den schulischen Gebrauch geeignete zweisprachige Wörterbücher der Allgemeinsprache (Deutsch–Englisch/Englisch–Deutsch) sowie eine Liste aller Operatoren zur Verfügung.

Hörverstehen

Im Abitur 2025 wird es einen Hörverstehensteil geben, der 30 Minuten in Anspruch nimmt. Sie sollten dabei imstande sein, wesentliche Inhalte eines authentischen Hörtextes zu verstehen.

Als Material für die Prüfung können Hörvorlagen z. B. aus Radiosendungen, Reden, Interviews oder Gesprächen sowie Hörspielen und Hörbüchern herangezogen werden. Die Länge der einzelnen Vorlagen überschreitet fünf Minuten in der Regel nicht. Das Hörverstehen wird mittels geschlossener und halboffener Aufgabenformate überprüft, wobei die folgenden Aufgabenformate denkbar sind:
- Multiple-Choice-Verfahren mit drei oder maximal vier Alternativen pro *item*
- Zuordnungsaufgaben
- Kurzantworten (mit ein bis fünf Wörtern)
- gelenktes Notizenfertigen (Vervollständigung von Sätzen, Tabellen, ...)

Richtig/Falsch-Fragen zum Ankreuzen kommen nicht vor, da hier die Wahrscheinlichkeit, die Lösung durch Zufall richtig zu erraten, zu hoch ist.

TIPP zum Punktesammeln

Wichtig: Sollten Kurzantworten gefordert sein, zählen Rechtschreib- und Grammatikfehler nicht, solange erkennbar ist, was ausgesagt werden soll. Die geforderte Wortzahl ist jedoch unbedingt zu beachten!

Die Datei mit den Höraufgaben läuft bis zum Ende, ohne angehalten zu werden. Sie enthält daher auch alle Zeitintervalle, die zum Lesen der Aufgabenstellung benötigt werden. Die Texte werden zweimal angehört.
Um 5 Punkte zu erreichen, müssen 45 % der items richtig gelöst werden, für 11 Punkte mindestens 75 %.

Sprachmittlung (Mediation)

Im Abitur 2025 wird im ersten Prüfungsteil auch die Kompetenz Sprachmittlung geprüft. Hier kommt es darauf an, den Inhalt eines deutschsprachigen Textes sinngemäß, zielgruppengerecht und kontextgebunden in englischer Sprache wiederzugeben. Die entsprechenden Merkmale der geforderten Textsorte müssen beachtet werden. Die Adressatin bzw. der Adressat muss in die Lage versetzt werden, den Text für ihre/seine Zwecke nutzen zu können. Je nach Text kann es sinnvoll sein, kulturelle Besonderheiten zu berücksichtigen, indem man zusätzliche Erläuterungen anfügt. Unbekannte Wörter und Wendungen müssen gegebenenfalls umschrieben und sprachliche Strukturen vereinfacht werden. Die Mediationstexte beziehen sich häufig auf Alltagserfahrungen bzw. kulturelle Besonderheiten aus dem deutschsprachigen Raum.
Sprachmittlung (*mediation*) darf also keinesfalls mit Übersetzung (*translation*) verwechselt werden. Entscheidend ist für die Sprachmittlung allein die korrekte Wiedergabe wesentlicher Inhalte in sprachlich angemessener und idiomatisch richtiger Weise.
Für den Prüfungsteil Sprachmittlung gilt als Bewertungsgrundlage: Der Inhalt wird mit 40 %, die Sprache mit 60 % bewertet.

Schreiben

Ausschlaggebend beim Schreiben ist die sogenannte kommunikative Absicht; es muss deutlich werden, welchem Zweck der Text dienen soll. Es wird erwartet, dass die Schülerinnen und Schüler selbstständig Texte verfassen, die zielgruppengerecht und sinnvoll strukturiert sind. Die Abiturklausur wird aus einer großen Bandbreite möglicher Themen ausgewählt, die sich auf fachliche oder auch persönliche Fragestellungen beziehen können. Hierbei müssen Planungsstrategien, beispielsweise die Mindmap, ebenso bekannt sein wie Vorgehensweisen zur Gliederung, Bearbeitung und kritischen Beurteilung der eigenen Texte. Die Grundlage der schriftlichen Abiturprüfung können auch sogenannte mehrfach kodierte Texte sein. Hierzu zählen zum Beispiel Karikaturen, Bilder, Statistiken oder Diagramme. Die Aufgabenstellung deckt zudem in ihren drei Teilaufgaben alle drei Anforderungsbereiche ab. Die Teilaufgabe für den Anforderungsbereich 3 bietet dabei zwei Auswahlaufgaben (3.1 / 3.2), von denen nur eine zu bearbeiten ist.
Auf die Bewertung der sprachlichen Leistung im Rahmen der sogenannten **integrativen Sprachentwicklung** wird später noch eingegangen (s. S. 123).

Leseverstehen

In der Abiturprüfung 2025 wird es keine Aufgaben zum Leseverstehen geben, da man sich bundesländerübergreifend auf das Aufgabenformat „Sprachmittlung“ verständigt hat. Dennoch müssen die erworbenen Kompetenzen auf der Niveaustufe B1+ während der Qualifikationsphase auf das Niveau C1 erweitert werden, um selbstständig einen längeren, anspruchsvolleren fiktionalen oder nicht-fiktionalen Text zu verstehen, ihm gezielt Detailinformationen zu entnehmen und unbekanntes Vokabular zu erschließen. Die Arbeit mit einem Wörterbuch muss also beherrscht werden, ebenso wie die unterschiedlichen Arbeitstechniken etwa des intensiven und extensiven Lesens. Sie müssen außerdem in der Lage sein, sprachliche und gestalterische Merkmale eines Textes zu erfassen und somit die Wirkungsweise eines Textes analysieren können.

Den Erschließungstechniken wie *skimming* (globales Leseverstehen, Erkennen der Hauptaussage des Textes), *scanning* (detailliertes, genaues Lesen) und *careful reading* (Suchen nach spezifischen Informationen) kommt dabei große Bedeutung zu. Weiterhin sollten unbekannte Wörter auch ohne Zuhilfenahme eines Wörterbuches erschlossen werden können.

Sprechen

In einer P5-Prüfung (oder mündlichen Nachprüfung im schriftlichen Prüfungsfach) werden sowohl monologisches als auch dialogisches Sprechen geprüft. Beim monologischen Sprechen muss man über einen Zeitraum von ca. zehn Minuten frei und zusammenhängend über ein vorgegebenes Thema reden, das auf der Grundlage von Prüfungsunterlagen, zumeist eines Textes, zu erschließen ist. In der Regel wird zunächst eine kurze Zusammenfassung des Textmaterials erwartet, bevor die weiteren Aufgaben abgearbeitet werden. Hierbei soll laut KC korrekt und flüssig gesprochen werden. Die Schülerin bzw. der Schüler soll im anschließenden Prüfungsgespräch zeigen, dass sie/er flexibel und spontan auf die prüfende Person reagieren und eigene Argumente begründen kann.

Insgesamt soll das Prüfungsgespräch so natürlich wie möglich und idiomatisch korrekt geführt werden, wobei der/die Schüler/-in zeigen soll, dass sie/er Verständnisschwierigkeiten in der Zielsprache ausräumen und Wortschatz- und Grammatiklücken überbrücken kann. Die mündliche Prüfung dauert in der Regel mindestens 20 Minuten.

Die Präsentationsprüfung im 5. Prüfungsfach

- Die Präsentationsprüfung ist eine Form der mündlichen Abiturprüfung und unterliegt den Vorgaben der mündlichen Abiturprüfung.
- Das Anforderungsniveau der Prüfungsaufgabe ist mit dem einer konventionellen mündlichen Prüfung vergleichbar.
- Die konventionelle mündliche Abiturprüfung bezieht sich auf die Inhalte von mindestens zwei Kurshalbjahren, dies gilt auch für die Präsentationsprüfung.
- Die Präsentationsprüfung darf nicht die gleichen Inhalte haben wie die schriftlichen Abiturprüfungen (P1–P4).

- Nach der Meldung zur Präsentationsprüfung und erfolgreicher Zulassung zum Abitur sollte ein informelles Vorgespräch über die organisatorischen Aspekte der Prüfung mit der Lehrkraft erfolgen.
- Thematische Vorschläge können durch den Prüfling gemacht werden, es besteht jedoch dazu keine Pflicht. Stellt der Prüfling eigene Themenvorschläge, so sollten diese **bis spätestens eine Woche vor Aushändigung der Aufgabenstellung** mündlich oder schriftlich bei der Prüferin / dem Prüfer eingegangen sein.
- Die Lehrkraft stellt **zwei Wochen vor dem Prüfungstermin** eine Prüfungsaufgabe auf Basis eines übergeordneten Themas.
- Die Prüfungsaufgabe muss in Teilaufgaben gegliedert sein und in der Zeit von der Aufgabenstellung bis zum Prüfungstermin zu bearbeiten sein.
- Der Prüfling wählt, in welchem Medium (Tafel, Flipchart, Microsoft PowerPoint etc.) die Präsentation erfolgt.
- Die Prüfungsaufgabe kann materialgestützt oder materialfrei gestaltet sein.
- Der Prüfling muss die Aufgabe eigenständig bearbeiten.
- Der Prüfling erstellt eine schriftliche Dokumentation, in der sie/er die inhaltliche Struktur und die Lösung der Aufgabenstellung skizziert. Sie enthält zudem alle verwendeten Quellen sowie eine Angabe zur gewählten Präsentationsform. Die Dokumentation gibt der Prüfling e**ine Woche, nachdem sie/er die Prüfungsaufgaben erhalten hat,** ab.
- Neben der auf Englisch zu haltenden Präsentation erfolgt am Prüfungstag ein längeres Prüfungsgespräch zum Prüfungsthema in der Fremdsprache.

Verknüpfung der Themenfelder und Lektüren

Die curricularen Vorgaben für die Oberstufe sehen die Behandlung von **verpflichtenden Themenfeldern** vor, die im jeweiligen Abiturdurchgang durch verbindlich zu behandelnde Materialien ergänzt werden. Die obligatorischen Materialien sollen vor einem thematisch breiteren Hintergrund erarbeitet und in diesen eingebettet werden.
Die folgende Übersicht hilft, dies zu veranschaulichen.

Verbindliche Themenfelder für 2025

Auf alle genannten Themenfelder muss im Laufe der vier Semester eingegangen werden.

Beliefs, values and norms in society: **Tradition and change** – Britishness – the American experience – postcolonial/neocolonial experiences – migration effects on the world of work	**Individual and society** – identity – ethnic, cultural and linguistic diversity – gender and sexual diversity	**Globalisation** – effects on the world of work – impact on personal lives – global responsibility concerning e. g. politics, the environment, economy – English as a global language

Erhöhtes Niveau (eA) **Shakespeare** – the world that made him – modern adaptations	**Die Lektüren/ Materialien müssen mit diesen Themen verknüpft werden.**	**Science and technology** – chances and risks – visions of the future – the media, e.g. the influence of the media on public opinion and personal life – the digital revolution

Das Curriculum ist vor allem auf eine Vernetzung der Themen ausgelegt, wie sie sich durch die jeweiligen literarischen Texte, Sachtexte, Songs, Filme oder Dokumentationen ergibt. Im Folgenden werden die verbindlichen Texte für den Abiturdurchgang 2025 aufgelistet und thematisch verortet, sodass Sie in der Lage sind, die sich anbietenden Vernetzungen nachzuvollziehen. Die jeweiligen Niveaustufen werden mit gA (grundlegendes) und eA (erhöhtes) Anforderungsniveau abgekürzt.

Verbindliche Materialien für 2025

Die Reihenfolge, in der die Materialien behandelt werden, ist nicht festgelegt. Auch gibt es keine feste inhaltliche Bindung der Lektüren an die Themenfelder. Die hier genannten Verknüpfungen sind daher nur Vorschläge.

Material	**inhaltliche Schwerpunkte**	**thematische Verknüpfungen**
Autobiographie: Sarfraz Manzoor, *Greetings from Bury Park* (2008)	– growing up – (ethnic) identity – Britishness and multicultural Britain	The Individual and Society Politics, Culture, Society – Between Tradition and Change (Bezugskultur: UK)
Kurzprosa: Camille Acker, „Cicada“ (2018)	– ethnic identity – discrimination	The Individual and Society Politics, Culture, Society – Between Tradition and Change (Bezugskultur: USA)
Nafissa Thompson-Spires, „Fatima, the Biloquist: A Transformation Story" (2018)	– ethnic identity – discrimination	The Individual and Society Politics, Culture, Society – Between Tradition and Change (Bezugskultur: USA)
Film: *Pride* (Regie: Matthew Warchus, 2014)	– coming of age – sexual diversity – tolerance and discrimination	The Individual and Society Politics, Culture, Society – Between Tradition and Change (Bezugskultur: UK)
Kurzdrama: Jasmine Lee-Jones, *seven methods of killing kylie jenner* (2019/2021)	– ethnic identity – the influence of social media on personal life and public opinion	The Individual and Society The Media

zusätzlich für erhöhtes Anforderungsniveau		
Roman: Ian McEwan, *Atonement* (2001)	– Britishness – innocence and guilt perception(s) of reality	The Individual and Society Politics, Culture, Society – Between Tradition and Change (Bezugskultur: UK)
Kurzprosa: Nafissa Thompson-Spires, „Heads of the Colored People: Four Fancy Sketches, Two Chalk Outlines, and No Apology" (2018)	– ethnic identity – discrimination	The Individual and Society Politics, Culture, Society – Between Tradition and Change (Bezugskultur: USA)
Kurzprosa: Camille Acker, „Mambo Sauce" (2018)	– ethnic identity – discrimination	The Individual and society Politics, Culture, Society – Between Tradition and Change (Bezugskultur: USA)
Film: *Boy Erased* (Regie: Joel Edgerton, 2018)	– coming of age – sexual diversity – tolerance and discrimination	The Individual and Society Politics, Culture, Society – Between Tradition and Change (Bezugskultur: UK)
Drama: *William Shakespeare, A Midsummer Night's Dream* (ca. 1595/1596) Film: *A Midsummer Night's Dream* (Regie: Michael Hoffman, 1999)	– dream and reality – love and marriage – gender roles	The Individual and Society Shakespeare

Hinweis

Die Lektüren werden in diesem Band an der Stelle thematisiert, an der sie inhaltlich am naheliegendsten zu verorten sind. Grundsätzlich bietet jedes der Materialien verschiedene Zugangsmöglichkeiten an, sodass es unter unterschiedlichen Gesichtspunkten behandelt werden kann.

Basiswissen

Das folgende Kapitel gibt einen Überblick über die curricularen Themenfelder des Oberstufenunterrichts ohne konkrete Semesterzuordnung. Das Ziel dieses Vorgehens ist es, einen Gesamtüberblick über die inhaltlichen Kenntnisse zu bieten, die im Zentralabitur z. B. auch für Hörverstehen und Mediation vorausgesetzt werden. An geeigneten Stellen wird darauf hingewiesen, wie die verbindlichen Lektüren thematisch im größeren Kontext verortet werden können. Die Zuordnung in fünf große Themenfelder entspricht den Vorgaben für das Abitur 2025 (s. S. 12). Fast alle Unterkapitel in diesem Buch entsprechen dem geforderten Basiswissen für beide Jahrgänge. Darüber hinaus wird auf weitere Lektüren, Filme und andere Materialien hingewiesen, die in vorherigen Abiturdurchgängen relevant waren und/oder sich als „Klassiker" zur näheren Auseinandersetzung mit dem Thema eignen.

Politics, Culture, Society – Between Tradition and Change

Britishness

People outside of Britain often refer to the British as the English – two terms which are often falsely regarded as being synonymous. This stereotypical perception may have its roots in the history of the British Isles as well as the history of the British Empire. Here, the dominance of English culture can certainly still be seen. In the following chapter a general overview will be given with regard to the correct terms to use when speaking of "the British" as well as the main cultural values and norms which have shaped British society.

Common Stereotypes

British people, but in particular the English, are considered to be well-mannered and polite. A common example named in this context is that British people apologise both when they accidentally run into someone and when they are run into. The British are also renowned for their sense of irony and for their small talk, which they usually begin by talking about the weather, especially when they meet someone they don't know. Some consider the English to be snobbish and arrogant but also very hospitable. Both the British and the Irish are famous for their pub culture. More stereotypes could be listed, but being what they are – clichés –, all of them must be carefully examined.

TIPP Further reading

The peculiar ways of the English are humorously depicted in *Watching the English* by Kate Fox (2004), a sociological approach to (stereo)typical English behaviour and "Englishness".

Geographical and Political Distinctions

There are several phrases commonly used to refer to the English-speaking area in Europe. They are explained here.

- **Great Britain:** refers to the main island including England, Scotland and Wales
- **The United Kingdom** (of Great Britain and Northern Ireland): the political term meaning England, Scotland, Wales and Northern Ireland; the terms "Britons" and "The British" are commonly used synonymously to describe the nation and its people
- **Scotland, Wales and Northern Ireland** were and are centrally governed by London but have all gained rights of self-government (S & W: 1999, NI: 2006)
- the **Republic of Ireland:** independent from the United Kingdom since 1921; as a result of the Anglo-Irish Treaty, the island of Ireland was divided into Northern Ireland (which still belongs to the UK) and the Republic of Ireland
- The **Commonwealth of Nations** is a political association of 56 member states, nearly all of which are former colonies of the British Empire. The Commonwealth was founded in 1931 and its members share political frameworks, a certain extent of history and the use of English as a main language. Elizabeth's II successor King Charles III is king of 15 member states (known as Commonwealth realms), the rest are republics (36) or have a different monarch (5).

English Cultural Dominance and its Historical Roots

- The **name "England"** is derived from the Angles, a Germanic tribe which settled the island during the 5th and 6th centuries.
- On the island of Great Britain, England gained dominance over Welsh and Scottish territories, which had been settled by Celtic tribes; over the centuries, all three parts of Great Britain became a political union which still bears traits of its cultural diversity (this can be observed in language, cultural heritage and political concessions).
- At the beginning of the 16th century, England gained worldwide influence during the **Age of Discoveries:** English merchants followed the great explorers and English settlers founded colonies in North America and other newly-discovered parts of the world, while the British East India Company set out to exploit the wealth of the newly established Asian colonies economically.
- The growing territorial expansion during the 16th and 17th centuries led to the development of the **British Empire,** which – at its height – included approximately one quarter of the world's landmass.
- The Empire lost its influence as the former colonies began to seek independence.
- The earliest colonies to obtain independence from Britain were the thirteen northern American colonies, which in 1776 formed the United States of America.
- During the 19th and 20th centuries, most of the other colonies gained independence by peaceful or violent means (the most important ones being India, South Africa, Australia and the Republic of Ireland); some former colonies joined the Commonwealth of Nations – an organisation which promotes trade and cultural relations between its members.

Because of the long history of Britain as the world's ruling colonial power, British culture has influenced societies worldwide. Its cultural effects can be observed in many nations: Australia recognises King Charles III as King of Australia, represented by the Govenor-General; driving on the left is the rule in many former colonies and many still use English as their official language, etc.

On 8 September 2022, Queen Elizabeth II died of old age. Her distinctive rule, marked by international respect, neutrality and adaptiveness, felt timeless. In fact, she acted as a steady unifying force for more than 70 years, a time in which Britain faced multiple fundamental challenges. One of them is its colonial legacy, with its detrimental effects on local economies as well as individual and national traumata persisting to this day. Hence, the Queen's death has been met with international mourning and condolences as well as a surge of criticism addressing her complicit role in an empire built on genocide, slavery and exploitation. An overdue discussion had been prevented so far by Elizabeth II's extended reign and popularity. Her successor, King Charles III, will be struggling to replicate the impact and reputation of her rule. The task of transforming the British monarchy would therefore adversely affect Charles's reign, especially since it will likely require the involvement of politics and change many of the traditional institutions of British society.

Democracy and Monarchy

Despite being a monarchy, the United Kingdom has a long history of parliamentary structures; indeed, first attempts to assert popular power date back to the Magna Carta of 1215 and the Bill of Rights of 1689. Britain has no written constitution, and its legislature is based on laws passed by parliament. Parliamentary sovereignty is the leading norm and the monarch accordingly no longer plays an active role in legislative processes. Parliament constitutionally consists of the Crown (the monarch formally heads Parliament), the House of Lords (the aristocracy) and the House of Commons. Parliament, however, is controlled by the Prime Minister and his or her cabinet. The Prime Minister and his or her government have therefore gained the executive powers of the monarch and act in his/her name.

The Issue of Class

Britain is generally considered to be an extremely class-conscious society. The definition of "class" can very generally be put as a distinction in social standing, which developed in feudal times and became more diversified during the Industrial Revolution. Social differences can be defined in terms of heritage (aristocratic vs. common birth), educational, professional and financial standing. Class distinctions into upper, middle, lower and, since the Thatcher Era of the 1980s, a new upper and an underclass have their origins in the emergence of new working and entrepreneur classes during the Industrial Revolution.

The British class system is no longer "closed", meaning that it offers chances for upward or downward movement (social mobility). Education or professional success allows members of lower classes to move upwards on the metaphorical "social ladder". Thus, people are no longer bound to the class they were born into.
Class is generally associated with certain stereotypical traits. The various classes differ with regard to habits and attitudes, as can be observed in everyday life, for instance, in where people live, what they eat, the way they dress, spend their free time, which media they consume, which schools their children attend, the vocabulary they use and what accent they speak with. British people are very aware of these class differences.

Class differences are most easily observed in the British educational system, which is still divided into public schools (which are, in fact, privately funded) and state schools. British public schools control admission by means of tuition fees and application procedures, but grants and scholarships can in theory be applied for by anyone. Attending one of these schools is still to some extent a requirement for admission to the so-called "Oxbridge" universities. Thus, social mobility is essentially a matter of financial background.

Britain and the EU

The UK was a member of the EU from 1973 to 2020, but during this period the scepticism of certain political and public circles towards Europe never ceased.
On 23 June 2016, a referendum was held about Britain's membership in the EU: 51.9 % voted to leave the EU, 48.1 % to remain. The UK finally left the EU after long and complex negotiations on 31 January 2020. Brexit is the UK's attempt to break free from unwanted EU rules and regulations in order to re-establish national sovereignty. Its supporters hope the UK will shed what they see as its EU-regulated and hampered shell in order to negotiate free trade agreements with other countries that will provide it with a better economic and social future.
Others fear that there will be significant economic drawbacks, as the UK is no longer a member of the European single market. This may lead to higher prices of goods on both sides of the Channel, despite the new EU-UK Trade and Cooperation Agreement.
Another problem is the question of Northern Ireland. The Republic of Ireland is still part of the EU, but the Brexit deal avoids a "hard border" between the Republic and the six counties of Northern Ireland and establishes a de facto customs border between the two islands. This is a major problem for the anti-EU Protestants in Northern Ireland. Peace-threatening conflicts between certain elements in the Republic of Ireland and Northern Ireland have rekindled, long after such conflicts seemed to have been settled by the Good Friday Agreement in 1998. Brexit has partially aroused feelings of insecurity in Northern Ireland concerning its future. A well-wrought solution to Northern Ireland's special situation is yet to come.
In the Brexit referendum Scotland voted with a significant majority to "remain". Some politicians – and many Scottish people – would now like a second referendum on Scottish independence, i. e. the right to leave the UK in order to eventually rejoin the EU. This is unlikely, however, to be approved of by the present government in London.

In the course of time, Brexit may turn out to be a success story, but the people's will in the referendum vote was strongly influenced by populist politicians as well as their inflated promises and lies. Many British people do not like the new regulations and consequences of Brexit, as they bring changes for the worse, such as visa requirements, export restrictions, reduced research funding or the UK's withdrawal from the Erasmus study programme.

Internationally, Britain has established a strong connection with US foreign policies (for years it had or has been engaged both in Afghanistan and Iraq), which partly results from its alliance with America during the Second World War and the subsequent formation of NATO. However, unlike former American administrations, which often regarded the United Nations as a weak institution, Britain regards the UN as an important framework for promoting international foreign policy. Like the United States, Britain is a permanent member of the UN Security Council.

Glossary of Common Political Terms (Britain)

Act (of Parliament)	(verabschiedetes) Gesetz
administration	Verwaltung (im AE auch: Regierung)
bill	Gesetzesvorlage
chamber	Kammer (z. B. House of Commons)
checks and balances	Gewaltenteilung (in der Politik)
constituency	Wahlkreis
constituent	Wähler/-in
domestic/foreign policy	Innen-/Außenpolitik
election	Wahl
electorate	Wählerschaft
Foreign/Home Secretary	Außen-, Innenminister/-in
in office	im Amt
MP (Member of Parliament)	Abgeordnete/-r
representative	Volksvertreter/-in
(hereditary, life) peer	(erbliches, lebenslanges) Mitglied des Oberhauses
Speaker	Vorsitzende/-r des Unterhauses
to hold office; to take office	amtieren; ein Amt antreten
to stand down	zurücktreten
universal suffrage	allgemeines Wahlrecht

The American Experience

The United States of America came into being as a reaction to a lack of political influence. As colonies of the British Empire, the original thirteen states, which had been settled by British citizens, had to pay taxes to the motherland. Yet their interests were not represented in parliament; hence the famous slogan "No taxation without representation". Instead of granting their overseas citizens a say in their own affairs, the British crown continued to impose taxes, which led to several uprisings that eventually turned into outright war between the colonies and their motherland. The imbalance of power led the American settlers to declare their independence in 1776. The famous document, originally written by Thomas Jefferson and signed by representatives of the American people (today called the "Founding Fathers"), questioned the rights of the British King, George III, and included the following statement, which would later become the basis of democratic thought and popular emancipation from the ruling aristocracy: "We hold these truths to be self-evident, that all men are created equal, that they are endowed by their Creator with certain unalienable Rights, that among these are Life, Liberty and the pursuit of Happiness."
This concept of equality and equal opportunities became the key to America's self-perception and national identity and led the US to emerge from the War of Independence (1771–1776) as the world's first modern democracy. In its time (and long before the French Revolution), the concept of equality, as expressed in these lines, was revolutionary.

The American Constitution

- written in 1787
- new ideas of a democratic state stated in the **preamble** of the constitution: "We the People of the United States, in Order to form a more perfect Union[1], establish Justice, ensure domestic Tranquility, provide for the common defense, promote the general Welfare, and secure the Blessings of Liberty to ourselves and our Posterity, do ordain and establish this Constitution for the United States of America."

The Bill of Rights

- the first ten amendments to the American Constitution
- written because some delegates feared that the new American government would threaten everyone's chance of achieving personal freedom and the pursuit of happiness
- The First Congress of the United States originally proposed twelve amendments in 1789, ten of which were added to the constitution as a preamble.
- guarantee America's citizens certain unalienable rights, e. g. freedom of religion, freedom of speech and the press as well as the right to bear arms

[1] Barack Obama took up the idea of "a more perfect union" in a speech he delivered on 28 May 2008, in which he elaborated on the issues of race and inequality in the USA.

The American Dream / American Nightmare

Keyword
"The American Dream": There is no single definition of what the American Dream actually is, as it varies for each and every American. The term was first used by James Truslow Adams, an American historian, in his book *The Epic of America*, in 1931: "[The] American Dream [is] the dream of a land in which life should be better and richer and fuller for every man, with opportunity for each according to his ability or achievement."

In order to understand how people who had grown up in a monarchy and were used to being subjects of a king or queen could come to the conclusion that they possessed equal rights, one must consider the motives which led the early settlers to leave Britain.

The Puritans, religious values, New Canaan

- The first English settlers to arrive on American soil were religious outcasts, Protestants who had wanted to cleanse the Anglican Church from remaining Roman Catholic influence. These **Puritans**, as they called themselves, were persecuted in England and thus left for the colonies. Other religious sects like the Quakers, Baptists and Methodists followed.
- In September 1620, a group of 102 people left England for America, sailed on a ship called the Mayflower, which arrived 65 days later in a bay they called Plymouth Bay.
- Between 1620 and 1640 thousands of Puritans emigrated to New England and founded the first settlements in Plymouth and Massachusetts Bay. To them, America was God's promised land, a **"New Canaan"**, a reference to the biblical country to which Moses led his people to free them from slavery in Egypt. In America the Puritans hoped they would be able to follow their religious beliefs and live freely.
- Puritan values such as integrity, virtue, the right to education, individual freedom and communitarianism still constitute central aspects of American self-perception.
- At the same time, the Puritans imposed strict moral rules on their communities, and today "Puritan" is a term associated with extreme conservatism and prudishness.

American values and beliefs

The key to the image of the United States as the country of unlimited opportunities, where each and every person can turn "from dishwasher to millionaire, from rags to riches", lies in these early visions of individual freedom, opportunity and self-reliance which led millions to emigrate to the former British colonies. These ideals shape the American Dream, which is not one single concept but a combination of individual goals and general values.

- **Individualism/self-reliance:** The underlying belief is that everyone is responsible for their own fate and has the liberty to determine their way of life.
- **Opportunity:** If a person is given the chance to take matters into his or her own hands, they will prosper. If that person fails, however, they have has not worked hard enough.
- **Freedom:** This has two faces. On the one hand, it allows all individuals to pursue their own vision of happiness without being controlled by a central government. On

the other, this belief also led to a general scepticism towards any kind of federal interference in individual affairs. Even today, Americans still tend to be sceptical of decisions made by the central administration in Washington, D.C., suspecting it of limiting their communal, state or personal rights.
- **Community:** Individual hardships such as unemployment are seen as personal failures, yet the local communities readily offer help to those in need. Because of this communal spirit, federal programmes of social welfare and common health care often meet with opposition as they are seen as an intrusion into personal rights.

The American Dream is still alive, and each year many people come to the United States to pursue it, although the number of people able to obtain a "green card" has always been limited and many immigrants today arrive illegally. After the original settlement period, the main waves of immigration entered the US between the middle of the 19th until the beginning of the 20th century, when the United States was in need of workers and a sufficient number of people to settle new territories in the west. Millions of mostly European immigrants arrived at Ellis Island, New York, were inspected and continued on to the city of New York and later to places across the entire country. German immigrants, for example, settled mostly in the Midwest, as can still be observed when looking at city names on a map.
The first thing many immigrants saw when they came by ship to New York City during the 19th and the first half of the 20th century, was the Statue of Liberty, which is located on Liberty Island.

The American Dream today

- A growing number of people regard the American Dream as an illusion, as not everyone has access to the opportunities usually associated with it.
- Examples of American nightmares include the Vietnam War, 11 September 2001, the financial crisis starting in 2008 and the storming of the Capitol on 6 Janury 2021.

The Frontier Experience

Since its independence in 1776, the country had continually acquired larger territories to the west. Put simply, both the Pacific and the Atlantic coast had been settled and explored, yet the middle of the vast continent was still mostly open territory which remained unknown. The fringe between the settled and unknown territories, more commonly called the "Wild West", not only refers to the geographical border between wilderness and civilisation but also to the social and political aspects which characterised these areas. The **westward movement** of the early settlers was not a federally organised enterprise. Instead, the federal government simply assigned the right to obtain land in the west to people who were willing to take on the challenge of discovering these unknown lands. While the **pioneers** moved westward in covered wagons, law enforcement and legal order were slow to follow. This left the frontier zone, which was already inhabited by the Native American tribes, in a state both of lawlessness and seemingly unlimited opportunity. This sense of entitlement, combined with the idea of Manifest Destiny (see below), led to the brutal treatment of the Native Americans. The Indigenous nations were taken full economic advantage of, often via Christian missionaries and by fostering alcoholism. From the early 19th century onward, Native tribes were forced to relocate from their ancestral homelands reservations (most notably, "Trail of Tears").

The Turner Thesis (1893)

Frederick Jackson Turner defined the "frontier experience" as the key which determined the American belief in freedom and unlimited opportunities. The abundance of land in the west and the experience of unlimited space provided the psychological basis for the American conviction that anything can be achieved. Once the west had been explored, the US sought to overcome new frontiers. Thus, the frontier experience was later also considered an explanation for American endeavours to overcome frontiers in a much broader sense (for example in areas such as technological advancement or space exploration).

Manifest Destiny

The term "Manifest Destiny" was coined by the American journalist John L. O'Sullivan in 1839.

- stands for the belief that America is the one nation ordained by God to expand across the North American continent
- according to John L. O'Sullivan: "[America is] the nation of progress, of individual freedom, of universal enfranchisement"; according to him, the American people had been chosen "to establish on earth the moral dignity and salvation of man – the immutable truth and beneficence of God."[2]
- America = a country that is superior to all other countries
- stresses the virtue of the American people, as they are the ones to establish moral rules and values across the globe; American patriotism is deeply rooted in the concept of "Manifest Destiny"

A picture that illustrates the idea of the "Manifest Destiny" is the allegorical representation of the new west in the painting *The American Progress* by John Gast (1872).

The US as a World Power

The United States of America became the foremost world power after the end of the Cold War with the Soviet Union. Because of once having been a colony ruled by a foreign nation, it chose to stay out of global politics for over a century. Its involvement in two world wars in the first half of the 20th century led to a change in its foreign policy from isolationism to interventionism.

[2] Source: John L. O'Sullivan, "The Great Nation of Futurity," *The United States Democratic Review*, Volume 6, Issue 23, pp. 426–430.

When, after WW II, the US and its allies found themselves in a worldwide struggle for influence and power with the Soviet Union, the American ideal of freedom and democracy turned into an outright ideology opposing the communist system. In 1947, President Truman formulated the so-called **Truman Doctrine,** which would define US foreign policy: Truman stated that it was "the policy of the United States to support free peoples who are resisting attempted subjugation by armed minorities or by outside pressure". The main aim of the US in the years 1947–1989 was to restrict the expansion of the Soviet Union. This period also shaped post-Cold War US policy and led it to apply new concepts of preemptive intervention to protect national interests (as in Nicaragua and Iraq). The key to American foreign policy is its self-image as a nation offering the promise of freedom and democracy; a promise whose roots lay in the concept of Manifest Destiny (see p. 22 f.). US foreign policy has repeatedly been criticised as being hypocritical in the sense that the nations and peoples the US military supposedly sought to set free from oppressors were then in fact subjected to American interests. Indeed, some overt and covert international interventions, especially in Central and South America and the Middle East, can be seen as mainly motivated by commercial interests and matters of national security (by securing natural resources, controlling the influx of drugs into the US, etc.) rather than the altruistic aspiration of bringing peace and democracy.
From a German perspective, however, the role of the US and its allies during the Second World War must be considered as that of a liberator without whom our nation might never have grown to become an internationally accepted democracy.

Glossary of Common Political Terms (USA)

amendment (to the constitution)	Zusatzerklärung zu der Verfassung; die ersten zehn amendments sind in der *Bill of Rights* verfasst
assimilation	Assimilation, Angleichung an Bestehendes
civil rights movement	Bürgerrechtsbewegung
constitution	Verfassung
Declaration of Independence	Unabhängigkeitserklärung
equality, emancipation	Gleichheit, Befreiung/Emanzipation
failure	Misserfolg, Versagen
freedom (of speech, of the press, religious freedom)	(Rede-, Presse-, Religions-) Freiheit
from rags to riches	Redewendung: vom Tellerwäscher zum Millionär
immigrant	Einwandernde/-r
immigration	Einwanderung
Immigration Act	Einwanderungsgesetz
influx of immigrants	Zustrom von Einwandernden
multiculturalism	Multikulturalität

"In God we trust"	offizieller Wahlspruch der USA: „Wir vertrauen auf Gott."
naturalisation	Einbürgerung
pioneer	Pionier
pioneer spirit	Pioniergeist
pursuit of happiness	das Streben nach Glück
religious/political persecution	religiöse/politische Verfolgung
settlement	Siedlung
settler	Siedler
success	Erfolg
the Founding Fathers	die Gründungsväter, die Unterzeichner der Unabhängigkeitserklärung
the Promised Land the land of milk and honey God's own country the New Canaan	das gelobte Land das Land, in dem Milch und Honig fließen Gottes eigenes Land das neue Kanaan alles Bezeichnungen für Nordamerika (später die USA)
to attain self-fulfilment	sich selbst verwirklichen
to be persecuted	verfolgt werden
to immigrate	einwandern
to pledge allegiance to the flag	den Fahneneid leisten Ausdruck des amerikanischen Patriotismus, wird u. a. in Schulen an offiziellen Feiertagen gesprochen: "I pledge allegiance to the flag of the United States of America, and to the Republic for which it stands, one nation under God, indivisible, with liberty and justice for all."
to prosper	Erfolg haben, gedeihen
to settle	(be)siedeln
unalienable/inalienable rights	unveräußerliche Rechte

Postcolonial/Neocolonial Experience

This chapter will outline the main aspects of two issues:
- How did Great Britain influence other nations as an empire? What consequences does its role as a former empire have for the UK?
- What consequences does its role as a former colony have for the US? How does its society deal with its minorities?

Keywords

Postcolonialism: term first used in the middle of the 20th century; refers to the time after the British had left the colonies, i. e. after their formal rule over the colonies had come to an end

The withdrawal of the British often caused fresh complications or laid bare problems they sowed during their rule. Many countries thus faced difficulties in setting up a functioning government. In addition, political independence did not necessarily lead to economic independence.

The Commonwealth: a group of 56 states; many former British colonies joined at the end of the decolonisation process; aims at racial equality and national sovereignty; British monarch is head of the Commonwealth

From Empire to Commonwealth

- At the beginning of the 17th century, Britain started to expand its empire worldwide.
- In most cases, the British colonisers ruled with brutal force, seizing land at will, ending rebellion in bloodshed, causing widespread famine as well as implementing slavery and exterminating whole ethnic groups.
- After the Second World War the British Empire changed rapidly.
- Most British colonies had become independent from Britain by 1970, but a large number of them stayed closely connected with their former coloniser by joining the Commonwealth.
- While the British ruled the colonies, they regarded their culture, values, traditions and language as superior to those of the colonised. Cultural identities and boundaries were thus often disrespected.
- After independence, the former colonies faced the difficult task of recreating their own identity, bridging the gap between their country's native traditions and values and British ones.
- As people from member countries of the Commonwealth were allowed to emigrate to Britain, many people did so in the second half of the 20th century. First they were welcomed, as workers were needed after the Second World War, but in the 1970s, when more and more workers faced unemployment because of the economic crisis, immigration came to be seen more critically.
- Much postcolonial writing – both from the former colonies and Britain – deals with the issue of being caught between two cultures or of trying to find one's identity.

Minorities in the UK

Nationalisation and Immigration Acts
Imperial Act (1914): People from the colonies were given British citizenship.
British Nationality Act (1948): New status of Citizen of the United Kingdom and Colonies (CUKC) came into effect for those living within the Commonwealth. This preserved their existing status as British subjects whilst allowing them national citizenship of their own country of origin. However, this did not apply to countries that had gained independence by that date.
Immigration Act (1962, 1971): These acts, passed to counter increasing immigration, tightened the law on immigration of British subjects from other parts of the Commonwealth. Immigrants had to prove strong links to the UK (partiality) in order to be allowed to live and work in Britain.
British Nationality Act (1981): Today's nationality law differentiates between several forms of citizenship, in particular for those living in the overseas territories. Only those with British citizenship and some Commonwealth citizens are still automatically entitled to reside in the United Kingdom.

- About 13 % of the population in the UK were born abroad (2014). India remains the most common non-UK country of birth, while Polish has been the most common non-British nationality in the UK since 2007.[3]
- Between the 1960s and 1980s, many Indians, Pakistanis and Bangladeshis immigrated to Britain. They now form the largest immigrant communities.
- Many of them settled in the Midlands or in towns in Lancashire, Yorkshire and Strathclyde, where they worked, for example, in the textile industry.
- The highest percentage of ethnic minorities can be found in the London area.
- In recent years, the UK has constantly tightened its laws on immigration.
- The main immigrant groups to Britain – from India, Pakistan, the Caribbean, Africa, Southeast Asia and Eastern Europe – differ widely in culture, religion and language.
- **Ethnic diversity** enriches Britain, not only when it comes to music, fashion and food.
- Many embrace the opportunities and advantages of ethnic diversity (such as the former Foreign Secretary Robin Cook, who said that chicken tikka masala " is now a true British national dish"[4]).
- Others fear that "Britishness" will eventually be lost; they interpret multiculturalism as meaning that various cultures coexist peacefully but without having a common basis of shared values.
- **Second-generation immigrants,** i.e. children born to parents who immigrated to Britain prior to (or shortly after) their children's birth, faced and still face a variety of problems:

[3] Source: https://www.ons.gov.uk/peoplepopulationandcommunity/populationandmigration/internationalmigration/articles/populationbycountryofbirthandnationalityreport/2015-09-27 (accessed on 1 April 2024)

[4] Source: https://www.theguardian.com/world/2001/apr/19/race.britishidentity (published on 19 April 2001, accessed on 1 April 2024)

- They often experience a clash of cultures. Outside their parents' home they adopt a western lifestyle similar to that of their friends and classmates. At home, however, they live according to values, beliefs and traditions typical of their parents' home countries, which many of these children and teenagers have never visited. Quite often they do not speak their parents' language any more either. For some, the transition between these two different lifestyles is not easy.
- They face difficulties when it comes to living up to the expectations of their parents, friends, teachers, etc.
- They often face discrimination and overt racism.
- According to a 2007 poll, about a third of British Asians felt it necessary to "act and think white" in order to fit into British society. About the same number did not feel British but believed they needed to be a "coconut", meaning to be "brown on the outside but white on the inside"[5].
- Therefore, defining one's identity and becoming confident in both cultures has been a central issue for most second-generation immigrants.

Today, the third or fourth generation slowly but surely becomes more integrated into British society and have arrived in British politics and public positions like the mayor of London, Sadiq Khan.
The large number of immigrants from the EU, mostly coming from Eastern Europe after the opening of the borders in 2004 and subsequent years, have had less problems to adapt to British society. However, their existence in Britain remains the subject of public scrutiny and was one reason for the Brexit vote in the 2016 referendum. In 2024, it is still unclear what their status in Britain will be in the future.

In literature, this clash of cultures is portrayed most prominently by British writers such as Hanif Kureishi, Farrukh Dhondy, Zadie Smith and Salman Rushdie.

Keyword
Postcolonial / New English Literature: the literature which deals with the consequences of the British Empire is called postcolonial literature or New English literature. Its authors reflect their nations' history as parts of the former British Empire and the role of the individual in these contexts.
The main issues which are addressed in postcolonial literature are: social and cultural changes/conflicts, exploitation and the misuse of power, cultural alienation and integration of the individual torn between the values of the former colonisers and his or her traditional values and beliefs.

[5] Source: BBC poll, http://news.bbc.co.uk/2/hi/uk_news/6921534.stm (published 30 July 2007, accessed on 1 April 2024)

Examples of Postcolonial Societies: India and Pakistan

At its height, the British Empire encompassed about a quarter of the world's landmass and dominated its crown colonies politically, economically and culturally. One must distinguish two types of colonies:
- those which were mainly colonised by the British and which had a relatively small indigenous population (such as Australia); these are sometimes referred to as the "white" colonies
- those colonies with a large indigenous population (such as India).

The decline of the British Empire resulted from internal demands for more independence from the British crown (the earliest colonies to leave were those in North America, see page 19). In most cases this progression from colonial rule to independence was achieved peacefully. But in those countries with a large indigenous population, the way to independence was often paved with rebellion and violent conflict. In the following, the route to independence of four former colonies of the British Empire will be described briefly.

India

India became independent in 1947 and was the first non-white colony to gain complete independence from Britain.
- British influence in India started as early as the 16th century with the founding of the British East India Company. Because of its spices, cotton and tea, India was mainly a trading colony.
- 1858: The British Crown took over the areas ruled by the British East India Company, and in 1876 Queen Victoria became Empress of India. The time of British rule is also called the "Raj" (Hindu for "reign").
- 15 August 1947: The Indian Empire became independent but was divided into the Union of India and the Dominion of Pakistan.

The case of India is unique in the way it gained complete independence from the British Empire at a rather early date and by non-violent means. In India, the British rulers were by far in the minority, and dissatisfaction with British rule led to a national independence movement headed by Mahatma Gandhi. At first, he demanded equal civil rights for Indians in their own country and accused the British government of mistreatment and oppression of the Indian people. Gandhi's struggle sparked a nationwide independence movement. His key to achieving independence was the revolutionary concept of civil disobedience. Being in the majority, the Indians were able to halt all social and economic life by simply refusing to comply with the British. Gandhi's aim was to achieve independence by non-violent means. After many years of struggle and several years spent in prison, Gandhi achieved his goal. Being unable to rule the country any longer, the British complied with India's demand for independence and thus lost one of their most important colonies.

Gandhi's concept of non-violent resistance became a role model for other leaders of oppressed peoples and minorities. Leaders like Nelson Mandela (in South Africa) and Martin Luther King (in the US) considered him to be their inspiration to fight peacefully for racial equality and civil rights.

Pakistan

Pakistan is a country located in South Asia, with a current population of over 236 million people. The majority of Pakistan's population is Muslim (96,5 %), with Sunni Islam being the dominant. However, there are also significant minority communities of Hindus, Christians, Sikhs and others. The country has two official languages: Urdu and English, but there are also many regional languages spoken throughout the country such as Punjabi (39 %), Pashto (18 %), Sindhi (15 %) and Saraiki (12 %). Pakistan is a parliamentary federal republic, with a president as head of state and a prime minister who is the head of government. The country has faced political instability and military rule throughout its history.
Pakistan was formerly part of the British Indian Empire, ruled over by the East India Company as a sovereign power for the British crown. It gained independence in 1947, following a movement led by Muslim leaders who wanted a separate homeland for Muslims in South Asia. Pakistan abolished its monarchy in 1956 while remaining in the Commonwealth. The separation from India and the creation of Pakistan was a traumatic and violent process, which led to the displacement and migration of millions of people. The country has since faced numerous challenges, including conflicts with neighbouring India, political instability, economic struggles and ongoing security threats from extremist groups. While Pakistan's history as a British colony has influenced its political and cultural development, the country has also retained its own unique identity and traditions. Today, Pakistan remains a complex and diverse country with a rich cultural heritage and a vibrant, dynamic population. Some of the country's most famous cultural exports include music, poetry and cuisine.

Sarfraz Manzoor, *Greetings from Bury Park* (gA)

A note on the author

Sarfraz Manzoor is a British writer, journalist and broadcaster. He is known for his work exploring themes of identity, culture and social justice, particularly in relation to the British Pakistani experience. He has written for a variety of publications and has also worked extensively in television and radio. Sarfraz's memoir *Greetings from Bury Park* was the basis for the 2019 film *Blinded by the Light*.

Synopsis

Sarfraz Manzoor's autobiography *Greetings from Bury Park* explores themes of identity, culture, religion and family. Manzoor was born in Pakistan but raised in the town of Luton, England, where he grew up as a British Pakistani Muslim. The book begins with his childhood, which is marked by Thatcherism and the racial tensions and economic decline of 1980s Britain, e.g. fuelled by E. Powell's "Rivers of Blood" speech, following protests and acts of discrimination. Manzoor struggles with a sense of cultural dislocation as he feels torn between his Pakistani heritage and his British environment. He also deals with the tensions that arise from generational conflicts (especially with his father) and navigates multiple cultural identities. Manzoor finds solace in music and particularly the songs of Bruce Springsteen. Throughout the book, he reflects on the challenges and joys of growing up as a British Pakistani Muslim in a society that often views him as an outsider.

Analysis

In his autobiography, Manzoor functions as author, narrator and protagonist, making the narrative insightful but highly subjective. As the title (*Greetings from Bury Park* alludes to Bruce Springsteen's first album, *Greetings from Asbury Park*) and the quotes at the beginning of each chapter illustrate, Manzoor's love of Springsteen's music serves as a central thread throughout the narrative. After befriending Amolak, his "blood brother", he becomes obsessed, not only because Springsteen shares their experience of an emotionally distant and strict father figure but also because his lyrics speak to the two boys' sense of longing and belonging within the struggles of everyday, blue-collar life. Springsteen's music becomes a way to communicate and connect with others, to bridge cultural divides and to find meaning in life in **multicultural Britain** and beyond. This is especially evident in Manzoor's friendship with Amolak, since they never speak explicitly about their feelings but by talking about Springsteen's songs instead. Consequently, music serves as a catalyst for self-discovery and personal growth, and Manzoor's love of music is a testament to the power of art to inspire and transform.
Another important theme is the tension between **tradition and modernity,** highlighted by the relationships and (first- and second-generation immigrants') conflicts within Manzoor's family, most of whom adhere more closely to traditional Pakistani values. He describes how only the boys have the advantage of an advanced education, while the role of women remains not to be selfish but to work and marry instead, and how his older brother shoulders the entire family's responsibilities after his father's death. Eventually, Manzoor comes to realise that the other family members paid a price for his freedom. **Growing up**, he struggles to reconcile his desire for independence and self-determination with the expectations of his family and community, especially his father. However, over time, they all learn to accept and respect each other's differences, demonstrating the enduring love and resilience of family relationships, especially during times of hardship (e.g. Rasool's stroke, Mohammed's death). Ultimately, Manzoor's decision to marry Bridget, a non-Pakistani, non-Muslim English woman, represents a rejection of tradition and a commitment to forging his own path.
Manzoor grapples with his individual relationship with Islam and his family's expectations around religious practice. He considers himself "comfortably British, occasionally Pakistani, and only technically Muslim" and only abides by some of the most principal religious practices. While is mother regards religion as important, teaching him Arabic and the Qur'an, his father identifies more as a Pakistani than as a Muslim. Thus,

Manzoor's experiences as a British Pakistani Muslim reflect the broader challenges of navigating religious identity in a multicultural society, which intensify after the terrorist acts of 9/11 and the London bombings on 7 July 2005. However, the book also highlights the power of religion to provide a sense of meaning, purpose and community for Manzoor and his family.

Additionally, the autobiography is infused with a sense of longing for America, which Manzoor considers a magical land of freedom and opportunity. From an early age, he immerses himself in books, travel guides, documentaries and TV shows of and from the US. He also follows its politics, witnessing American life shaped by people like John F. Kennedy, Martin Luther King, Malcom X and Rosa Parks as well as by the Black Civil Rights Movement and the Freedom Riders. As there were no British Pakistanis advocating better conditions and less discrimination in the UK, Manzoor adopts King and Malcolm X as role models instead.

Growing up, Manzoor feels unable to identify as wholly British or wholly Pakistani. Although experiences of open and indirect racism shape his entire life and the political realities (e. g. the "Rivers of Blood" speech) make it impossible for him to feel welcome, this feeling of confusion gradually changes with the rise of "Cool Britannia" (a slogan associated with the second half of the 1990s, describing the spread of British pop culture and its icons such as Oasis, the Spice Girls and David Beckham), New Labour (a political philosophy spearheaded by Tony Blair advocating welfare, social justice and equality) and the 1996 UEFA cup. Eventually, he realises that his current life and its opportunities were mostly formed by the UK. This acceptance of his **Britishness** represents a significant turning point in his life, as he takes control of his own destiny and embraces not only his Pakistani roots but also his British **identity**. However, with his father deceased and his mother becoming older, the direct link to Pakistan slowly weakens. To counter this, Manzoor writes his autobiography as a "keeper of memories, the teller of stories", to ensure a sense of origin for his own daughters.

Migration and the World of Work

Human migration means that people move from one place to another. They do this temporarily or permanently. In the history of mankind, migration has been an evolutionary necessity, as in the hunter and gatherer societies, where people were nomadic and were always looking for better places to find food and shelter. Freedom of mind as well as better working opportunities have always been driving factors of migration, as in 19th-century immigration to the US.

Today, in a more or less fixed system of states with state borders, migration is still a huge factor in the development of a society, but in increasingly wide sections of society – especially in right-wing and nationalist political groupings –, it is also seen very critically. In addition to the post-WW II migration to the UK from its former colonies, the past two decades, after Poland and nine other countries joined the EU in 2004, have seen a huge influx of people from Eastern Europe. People from the new EU member states have been more willing to do unskilled and low-paid jobs than their British counterparts. This has caused a political debate in Britain and can be seen as one of the many reasons why

some people voted for Brexit. As this is a world of large economic differences, i.e. the so-called North-South divide, migration will remain one of the problems of our times, with societies that are better off facing huge numbers of refugees from poorer countries until a certain measure of equality is reached.
In the US, migration has been the driving factor of the nation's creation. However, attitudes towards migration differ with regard to countries of origin. The southern border of the US has been the subject of fierce political debate for a long time, as a lot of immigrants from Mexico and other Latin American countries cross this border, many of them illegally. The discussion about the so-called "dreamers" (sons and daughters of illegal immigrants to the US – the term probably originates in the abbreviation of the name of a piece of 2001 legislation) was particularly fuelled by former President Donald Trump.

Individual and Society

The following chapter will focus on the various facets of identity – both ethnic/cultural and personal identity. How does identity affect a person's position in society?
Central issues to be tackled are:
- the different roles an individual might assume and the potential conflicts between those roles;
- the connection between one's biologically determined sex and the largely socially defined gender of a person;
- minorities and outsiders.

Keywords

Individual: The term derives from the Latin "indivisible" and commonly refers to an individual subject, i.e. a person, who can be distinguished from their surroundings. As such, the individual has to position themselves vis-à-vis the society in which they are living. The relationship between the individual and their society can be difficult if the former comes into conflict with the latter's norms and values.

Society: This term refers to a collective of individuals united e.g. by a shared territory, history or ways of living and thinking. In order to be effective and not to fall prey to anarchy, a society is organised according to a set of rules and regulations which can even overrule the interests of the individual for the sake of the community.

Roles and Role Conflicts

- While the individual was traditionally believed to be a unified "whole", the concept of the different roles of a person underlines the fact that one does not just have **one** single identity but actually has to fulfil a number of different roles in different situations and contexts.
- A social role consists of a certain pattern of behaviour, of rights but also of obligations. Social roles are performed in **interaction** with other persons. Roles are mostly to be seen in relation to others (child – parent; teacher – student).
- Whether one's behaviour is in line with one's particular role can be judged by society's **expectations** of that role.
- If an individual shows forms of behaviour that are considered **inappropriate** for the social role in question, they may face various forms of **punishment** (ranging from being made aware of one's improper behaviour to actual punishment); if the behaviour in question is deemed **appropriate**, there will, in return, be **rewards** from society.
- A role (e.g. doctor, teacher, bus driver) can be **achieved** by or **ascribed** to an individual (e.g. child).
- In certain situations, a person can be faced with a **conflict** between contrasting roles which they should take on at the same time. Thus, if a mother happens to be her own child's teacher, she would be expected to be simultaneously strict towards the child in her role as teacher and loving in her role as mother.

Gender Identity and Diversity

A central component of an individual's identities is their[1] **gender**. Unlike the biologically determined **sex** (male/female), **gender** and **gender roles** (such as masculine and feminine) are often perceived as being social constructs. Accordingly, a society holds a set of certain stereotypical ideas about how a "real" woman and a "real" man should behave, what they should look like but also what they are capable of.
Traditionally, men are thought of as masculine, strong, rational and powerful, while women are considered to be feminine, weak, emotional and submissive. These assumed characteristics have also been used as a "justification" for men's dominant role in society. With the advent of the Feminist Movement in the 1960s, the validity of conventional gender roles was called into question.
However, the media in particular still present largely conservative images of "typical" men and women, thereby keeping these concepts alive. If a person does not conform to the gender role assigned by their society to their sex, they may face resentment. Even in the comparatively tolerant western societies, particularly "masculine" women and "feminine" men are not universally accepted.
However, concepts surrounding sexual diversity have been extended. The word „transgender" is generally seen as an umbrella term for people whose gender identity and expression might vary from cultural expectations based on the sex they were assigned at birth. „Non-binary", on the other hand, refers to a person that does not identify exclusively as a man or a woman or identifies completely outside these categories.
The aim of gender diversity is to represent people of different genders in a fair way. This concerns mostly men and women and their ratio in companies, politics or other fields of life. Traditionally, men have dominated many areas of public life such as politics, engineering, science, medicine or computing. Gender diversity has been widely discussed but progress towards having less male and more female company directors – and indeed bosses in many walks of life – has been slow.
However, after the feminist and post-feminist debates of the past decades, discussions about gender have recently become more open, including transgender and non-binary people. This has meant that more people have had the courage to come out with their particular sexuality or their gender identity.

~~*Pride* (gA)~~

Synopsis

Directed by Matthew Warchus, the film *Pride* was released in 2014 as a historical comedy-drama. It tells the true story of Mark Ashton and a group of LGTBQ activists who raised money for miners financially affected by the UK miners' strike in 1984.
Joe Cooper takes the train to London to celebrate his birthday. After his arrival, he runs into Gay Pride where he meets activist Mark Ashton. He and his group are marching in the parade not only on behalf of gay rights, but also on behalf of economic equality and the miners, whose strike is taking place at that time. Mark spontaneously arranges a

1 In English-language texts, the pronouns „he"/"she" and their possessives „his"/"her"/"hers" are often substituted with „they" and „their"/"theirs" in order to avoid attributing a gender.

bucket collection for the miners, to great success. He then founds "Lesbians and Gays Support the Miners (LGSM)" because he believes that the gay movement might benefit from establishing solidarity with the miners. However, the group's first attempt to donate the money to the union is turned down because of their sexual orientation. Mark's friends feel confirmed in their skepticism towards the miners since many of them have been bullied by them back home. But when Mark and his group decide to give their donations directly to the small mining village Onllwyn in Wales, a member of the committee finally accepts the funds. The resulting newspaper story leads the National Union of Miners to decline LGSM's support because they feel that the story humiliated them but also because they want the strike to come to an end. Frustrated, Mark abandons LGSM. Joe comes out to his family, but because of their prejudiced beliefs, they try to keep him away from the group. At the same time, Mark finds out that one of his former lovers is dying of AIDS. In March 1985, the strike ends and the miners of Onllwyn take up their work again. When he sees the news, Joe sneaks out his parents' house to show solidarity in Onllwyn and is immediately confronted by Mark about hiding his sexual orientation from his parents. During the following Gay Pride Parade, Mark apologises in front of the group for abandoning the cause and leads LGSM to the parade. Soon they are joined by miners who came to march in solidarity.

Analysis

The issue of **sexual diversity** is clearly outlined in the movie. While gender roles are defined in a traditional way in the miners' community (men in the pits, women at home), they are not so clearly defined within the gay community. Also, the women of LGSM resist patriarchal structures and form an exclusively lesbian group in order to fight not only for gay but also for feminist rights. With respect to sexuality, LGSM members are also more open, tolerant and equal in contrast to the miner's community, where sexual intercourse is seen as a male right, while women are simply expected to tolerate it.

The exploration of (sexual) identity is also central to the films discussion of **coming of age.** At the beginning of the movie, Joe "Bromley" is shy and simply intends to watch the Gay Pride march since he has not yet publicly come out. He is fascinated by Mark and the LGSM group but joins them secretly and hides the newspaper clippings. His mother finally discovers not only his book but also the fact that he leads a double life. Misunderstood by his mother and somewhat alienated from his father, Joe finally makes his transition to adulthood by taking a stand for himself. He leaves his parents' home, returns to LGSM and proudly marches in front of the parade in London.

Another topic that the film weaves into a moving story is **tolerance.** Beyond each others' reservations and prejudices, both miners and LGSM develop an understanding and learn about each others' community. The **discrimination** aimed at the homosexual community is shown to be deep-rooted due to old conservative and patriarchal attitudes. This is also shown by the police that acts aggressively towards the miners and mocks them for their collaboration with gays. Jokes are made about AIDS, Joe's parents are shocked about his sexual orientation and by turning down LGSM's donations, many miners contribute to an oppressive atmosphere. Historical discrimination and homophobia against minority groups in Britain such as LGBTQ members are clearly shown in the film. However, it also indicates that this intolerance can often be worn down through community action when two minority groups find a common cause.

Background information

Margaret Thatcher	– Conservative prime minister from 1979 to 1990 – championed economic deregulation, social conservatism and privatisation – planned to close inefficient pits and import coal in order to grow economy
UK miners' strikes 1984–1985	– coal miner employment underwent a big decline in the 20th century – by 1984, coal in Britain more expensive to mine than to import – mechanisation replaced many miners – 6th March 1984: announcement to cut output and close pits; loss of 20,000 jobs – 12th March 1984: union of mine workers called national strike against pit closure – frequent violent confrontations with the police – by January 1985: strike began to disintegrate because miners needed their pay
Gay rights in the UK until the 1980s	1533: homosexuality punishable by death 1861: homosexuality punishable by a minimum of 10 years imprisonment 1885: any homosexual act (e.g. love letter) illegal; never explicitly targeted lesbians after 1945: significant rise in prosecution of homosexuality 1951: first UK transgender women undergo surgery 1957: homosexuality no longer regarded as disease 1967: homosexual acts legalised in UK between men over 21 if conducted in private 1970: founding of the UK Gay Liberation Front 1988: prohibition of funding educational materials and projects on LGBTQ rights in schools
HIV and AIDS in the 1980s	1981: first known UK case 1982: term "AIDS" (acquired immune deficiency syndrome) proposed by gay-community leaders and federal bureaucrats to replace "GRID" (gay-related immune deficiency) 1983: development of the PCR technique, a milestone in AIDS research 1984: discovery of probable cause of AIDS: retrovirus 1985: first commercially available test 1986: retrovirus named HIV (human immunodeficiency virus)

	1987: development of first antiretroviral drug 1988: first pamphlet distributed to US households to provide information on AIDS 1989: Florida court rules that AIDS-positive student could share classroom with others using isolation partitions

Boy Erased (Film, eA)

Synopsis

Boy Erased is a 2018 biographical drama based on the memoir by Garrard Conley. The movie follows the story of 18-year-old Jared Eamons, the son of Baptist preacher Marshall and hairdresser Nancy in Arkansas, who reluctantly agrees to attend a conversion therapy programme named "Love in Action" after being outed as gay. The programme is run by a self-appointed therapist Victor Sykes, who purports to "cure" homosexuality. Jared and the other participants of his group are subjected to extreme emotional and physical abuse until he realises the programme's cruel intentions and slowly comes to terms with his sexuality and identity. He eventually confronts the instructors and begs his mother to get him out. Nancy does so with the help of fellow attendee Cameron and finally stands up to her husband by supporting Jared in his decision. Soon after, Jared learns of Cameron's suicide while still in the programme's care. Four years later, he lives in New York with his boyfriend and writes a book about his experiences. After his article about the programme is published, he has a clarifying discussion with his father, who reluctantly agrees to change his attitude. In gifting him the pen he used to write sermons with, "from one writer to another", his father tries to take a first step towards reconciliation.

Analysis

One of the central themes of the film is the tension between **individual and society.** The film depicts how Jared's journey towards self-discovery and acceptance challenges the traditional notions of conformity and emphasises the importance of independence. His struggle to reconcile his sexual orientation with his family's strict Baptist beliefs forces him to confront the expectations and social cohesion of the community around him. Furthermore, the film raises important questions about the harm caused by societal expectations and the pressure to conform to narrow gender and sexual norms. It explores the shame and fear that many LGBTQ+ individuals feel when they are not able to live up to these expectations and the often painful consequences of coming out in an unsupportive environment. Despite the trauma and abuse that he experiences, Jared is able to find strength and support from his fellow attendees and ultimately rejects the harmful messages of conversion therapy.

Another significant theme in the film is **coming of age,** which is portrayed through Jared's journey of self-discovery. The film shows how his experiences in the conversion therapy programme, despite being deeply traumatic, ultimately serve as a catalyst for his growth and development as a young adult. Through his struggles Jared learns to assert his independence, confront his fears and embrace his true self. This is illustrated by his increasingly rebellious behaviour when he decides to stick his hand out of the window to "surf the wind" before, during and after "therapy". They thus serve as leitmotifs to portray his coming-of-age process.

Sexual diversity is also a prominent theme in the film, as it highlights the complexities of exploring one's sexual orientation and the impact of societal pressure on the identity and emotional well-being of individuals who identify as LGBTQ+. However, Jared's relationship with Christianity, especially in the light of his sexuality and rape, remains unexplored. The latter remains the only scene of homosexuality, depicted needlessly explicitly, and Jared's way of coping with its trauma is likewise not addressed. The film therefore misses an opportunity to delve into the context of rape culture and homophobia. The circumstances of the other attendees remain mostly unaddressed as well.

Additionally, the film brings attention to **discrimination,** as it shows the harmful consequences of prejudice and bigotry towards the LGBTQ+ community, embodied by Marshall, Pastor Wilkes as well as Sykes and his staff. Conversion therapy as their chosen method of discrimination highlights the damaging effects of attempting to force individuals to conform to heteronormative standards. On the other hand, Nancy's development from a meek wife to a protecting mother who eventually comes to terms with her son's sexuality as well as the doctor who, despite being religious herself, believes homosexuality to be a natural phenomenon and in no need to be "cured", illustrate the importance of standing up against discrimination and intolerance.

Outsiders

- If an individual deliberately or unintentionally fails to conform to the rules of the society in which they live, they can easily become socially stigmatised **outsiders**.
- When a larger group of people rejects the conventional norms of mainstream culture, this might lead to the formation of a **counterculture** which openly propagates a set of values significantly different from those of the society in which they live.
- Such countercultures are often associated with younger generations that rebel against their parents' way of life.
- Famous countercultural movements include the "Beat Generation" of the 1950s, the "hippies" of the 1960s, the "punks" of the 1970s and 1980s and the "hip-hop" scene, which developed from the 1970s onwards, all of which included such forms of artistic expression as music, graffiti and dance.
- There are numerous ways of expressing one's dissatisfaction with mainstream culture, e.g. through the use of taboo language (as employed by writers of the Beat Generation), through the open violation of generally accepted moral standards (as in the form of "free love", practised by the hippies), through one's appearance (clothing and hairstyle of the punks), or by aligning oneself with strata of society that are far removed from the mainstream (e.g. hip-hop culture).
- Often aspects of countercultures are eventually commercialised and assimilated by mainstream culture, thereby losing their originally rebellious impetus.

Minorities in the US

Since its birth in 1776, the United States of America has been a nation of immigrants. Especially during the 19th and early 20th century, millions of people (at first mostly from Europe, later also from other continents) were allowed to enter the country, since the young nation was in need of settlers and workers. The US has therefore always been an ethnically and culturally mixed nation, which has led to discussions about how this society might deal with its diversity and how it can be defined.

Keywords

Multicultural society: a society where various ethnic groups and their cultural heritage are accepted in their own right

Salad bowl: the various ethnicities living in the United States mixing their traditions, cultural values, etc.; the various cultures do not merge into one but stay distinct ("unity in diversity")

Melting pot: The various ethnic groups do not retain their cultural heritage but amalgamate into one new nation. The term first appeared in an essay by Jean de Crèvecœur, entitled "Letters from an American farmer" in 1782.

The term "salad bowl" is now considered to be more politically correct.

One main group which did not enter the United States voluntarily but was deported to the US is the group of millions of slaves from Africa who were shipped to the British colony and later to the newly founded nation. The descendants of these slaves form the second largest minority in the US (in recent years the number of Hispanic immigrants has exceeded the Black population). Their history is one of discrimination and deprivation, which will be summarised briefly below.

African-American History

- 1619: first documented ship of African slaves bound for Jamestown, Virginia
- 17th–19th century: the **Atlantic slave trade;** by 1860 an estimated 3.5 million enslaved Africans lived in the US; another 500,000 lived freely in the (northern) states or territories
- 1861–65: American Civil War; caused by the separationist movement of eleven slave states which refused to end slavery; the North fought to prevent secession of these states and eventually won
- 1863: **Emancipation Proclamation:** during the Civil War, President Abraham Lincoln declared that all slaves in the secession states (South) were free
- **Jim Crow Era:** after the Civil War, slavery was illegal; however, many former slave states passed laws which discriminated against Black people, prevented them from purchasing land and voting and segregated Black from white people in almost all areas of public life
- racial segregation remained into the 20th century; this system of separation and discrimination was met with increasing resistance and led to the formation of the Civil Rights Movement between 1954 and 1968

The Situation of African-Americans during Reconstruction

The former slaves formally gained freedom after the North won the Civil War, but they were far from having equal rights. Especially in the South, repressive laws and regulations prevented them from purchasing land, participating in elections, etc. (see "Jim Crow Era" above). This led to a number of developments:
- Many former slaves left for the industrialised cities of the North, in which all-Black ghettos developed.
- Freemen who stayed in the South often continued to work as sharecroppers for former slave masters. Unable to buy land, they remained dependent on white landowners and still lived in great poverty.
- Discrimination and racism continued (not only) in the South in an institutionalised form of racial segregation and state legislature. Both in the North and the South, Black people began to put up resistance against all forms of discrimination.

The Civil Rights Movement

- 1909: African-Americans founded the National Association for the Advancement of Colored People (NAACP); the aim was to call attention to discrimination in the South and the cities of the North
- 1954: landmark decision of the Supreme Court in the case of Brown vs. Board of Education, which declared the racial segregation of schools to be unconstitutional
- 1955: Rosa Parks, an NAACP member, refused to give up her seat in a bus for a white person in Montgomery, Alabama and was consequently arrested; led by Martin Luther King, thousands of Black people in Montgomery boycotted public transportation (Montgomery Bus Boycott); in 1956, the Supreme Court declared racial segregation on buses to be unconstitutional
- 1950s and 60s: protests continued on various issues, many of them led by the Southern Christian Leadership Conference (SCLC), formed by Martin Luther King; following the example of Mahatma Gandhi, they organised peaceful protests and acts of civil disobedience to stop segregation in other areas of public life
- 1963: March on Washington; an estimated 250,000–300,000 people (about 80 % Black) marched to the Capitol in Washington, D.C. to demonstrate peacefully for jobs, freedom and an end to racial discrimination
- During this march Martin Luther King gave his famous speech "I have a dream", which moved millions of people and brought widespread attention to the the Civil Rights Movement. King later received the Nobel Peace Prize in 1964 and was assassinated in 1968.
- Forced by the public to take action, the government passed laws to stop racial discrimination and segregation: the Civil Rights Act of 1964 and the Voting Act of 1965.
- Racial discrimination did not end and exists covertly and overtly to this day; African-Americans still have a higher risk of unemployment, poverty and imprisonment in comparison with the white majority population.
- Systemic racism towards Black people today has motivated new campaigns against violence like the "Black Lives Matter" movement in June 2013 (cf. below).

- Shortly before and after former President Trump's inauguration in 2017, a lot of new movements were started, including huge demonstrations for human rights and other issues such as women's rights, immigration reform, healthcare reform, racial equality and freedom of religion. Thousands of women wore pink woollen hats in their march on Washington to accuse Trump, among other things, of using sexist and racist language.

Black Lives Matter

Black Lives Matter (BLM) is a socially motivated movement internationally known for its spectacular "die-in" actions and street demonstrations. It is a decentralised network of activists without a formal hierarchy, which started its actions and protest marches in order to take a stand against racially motivated police brutality towards Black people.
BLM appeared on the scene in 2013 and entered public awareness in 2016 when the movement became more active in protest against Donald Trump's racist utterances. In May 2020, it gained global attention in denouncing George Floyd's death in Minneapolis (Minnesota) during a police arrest. According to BLM, Floyd died from suffocation. The acting officer was found guilty of murder in court in April 2021; the three other policemen were found to have been violating Floyd's civil rights.
The protest marches related to Floyd's death led to lootings and rampage, resulting in curfews and deployment of the National Guard. The police violence shown there brought Amnesty International into the arena, criticising violations of human rights.
Sometimes, BLM is criticised from within its own ranks as supporting racial bias and deepening the divide between Black and white people, as well as sidelining Black women's experiences. So, "Say Her Name" has been created to focus attention on female victims of police violence.

Ethnic identity

- "Ethnicity" refers to shared cultural characteristics such as language, ancestry, practices, feelings, values and beliefs, while "race" is a social construct that is not universal; race is not always a defining factor even though it is often connected to ethnic identity.
- An ethnic group can, but does not have to be based on geographic origin.
- Ethnic identity is a personal, highly individual construct which an individual uses to categorise themselves.
- Ethnic identity can be a rarely overtly acknowledged fact of someone's life, while others are deeply influenced by their ethnic identity with respect to their choice of clothing, food, relationships, education or neighbourhood.
- Ethnic identity is not static but can change over time.
- There are four major components of ethnic identity:
  - ethnic awareness – the way we understand our own and other ethnic groups;
  - ethnic self-identification – the label(s) we use for our own ethnic groups;
  - ethnic attitudes – the feelings we have about or own and other ethnic groups;
  - ethnic behaviours – the behavioural patterns specific to an ethnic group.[2]

[2] Source: Jean S. Phinney, "The Multigroup Ethnic Identity Measure: A New Scale for Use with Diverse Groups", *Journal of Adolescent Research* 7 (2), 1992, 156–176.

- A strong sense of ethnic identity can influence a person's self-esteem, both in a positive or negative way, such as the idea of the "superiority" of one particular ethnicity, thus putting too much emphasis on ethnicity as a defining factor.

Tolerance and Discrimination

- discrimination in general: treating some people differently from others in comparable situations
- Intolerance refers to a lack of respect for someone's practices or beliefs if they differ from one's own and can be expressed in actions ranging from avoidance to physical harm.
- Discrimination is one of the most frequent forms of human rights violations and abuses.
- Discrimination and intolerance are closely related.
- Factors that discrimination can be based on include age, weight, ethnicity, race, culture, disability, political or religious beliefs, sex, gender, sexual orientation and language.
- Discrimination not only affects individuals but also society as a whole.
- The principles of equality and non-discrimination are laid down in the Universal Declaration of Human Rights (UDHR): "All human beings are born free and equal in dignity and rights" (Article 1). This concept of equality in dignity and rights is embedded in contemporary democracy, so states are obliged to protect various minorities and vulnerable groups from unequal treatment. Article 2 enshrines freedom from discrimination: "Everyone is entitled to all the rights and freedoms set forth in this Declaration, without distinction of any kind".[3]
- Discrimination can be practiced in a direct or indirect way: Direct discrimination occurs when a person is openly treated unfavourably; indirect discrimination refers to a requirement that appears to be neutral but in fact is disadvantageous to certain groups.
- Structural/systemic discrimination occurs on a macro level in the way a society is organised. Disadvantages to certain groups appear in the form of norms, attitudes, prejudices and behaviour.
- Discrimination is usually carried out by majorities, but discrimination from minorities also exists.
- Examples of discrimination and intolerance are anti-Semitism, xenophobia, racism and sexism.

[3] Source: https://www.ohchr.org/en/human-rights/universal-declaration/translations/english (accessed on 1 April 2024)

Critical Race Theory (CRT)

CRT is an academic civil rights movement that began forming in the US in the 1970s. It examines social, cultural and legal issues with regards to race and racism. It argues that racism is institutionalised and favours the interests of white people. Laws, for instance, may seem to be colourblind but still have racially discriminatory effects. Since early 2021, several US states have introduced laws that ban or restrict the teaching of CRT in schools.

~~Camille Acker, “Cicada” (gA)~~

A note on the author and the text

Camille Acker spent her childhood in Washington, D.C. Upon completing her education in English and Creative Writing, she taught at various universities and writing organisations, while additionally bringing stories of young Black girls, women and people of colour to life. Currently, she works as a writer, researcher and editor in Philadelphia. Her debut collection of short stories centres around characters who also call Washington, D.C. their home. Throughout the collection, all of them are confronted with their definition of identity and belonging while struggling to attain both respectability and freedom.

Synopsis

Camille Acker's short story “Cicada” is about Ellery Cook, a young Black girl from Washington, D.C. who wins her first piano competition, although her joy is short-lived as she realises the extent of unyielding differences between her situation in life and the ones of her all-white competitors.
The story starts by highlighting Ellery's family's low income and social standing. Despite their struggles to make ends meet, however, her parents spare no effort to support Ellery's talent. Ellery‘s piano lessons eventually lead to a competition, which her parents likewise attend. There, Ellery is fascinated by the affluent neighbourhood and the magnificent synagogue, functioning as the recital hall. After entering, her piano teacher, Mrs Hamilton, introduces Ellery to Cara and Lori, two competitors, both of whom are white. While Cara is friendly, Lori makes racist remarks about Ellery's hair and displays a disdainful demeanour. However, Ellery emerges victorious. This feeling immediately turns to exasperation once she realises that her prize is a savings bond instead of a cheque she intended to use to support her family, and they have to return home without having their lives altered for the better, while Lori gets to keep her wealth and privileges despite coming in second. Frustrated and furious, Ellery runs behind Lori's car and throws cicada shells at it.

Analysis

“Cicada” is told by a third-person selective narrator with a limited point of view. This offers insights into Ellery's thoughts and feelings but also leads to a biased interpretation of events. The story is traditionally structured into exposition (setting scene and introducing characters), rising action (competition starts, Ellery and Lori meet), climax

(Ellery plays and winners are announced), falling action (prize is explained, everyone leaves) and denouement/resolution (venting her frustration on the car of Lori's family). Its themes focus on rivalry, growing up, social class, racial differences and discrimination. Throughout the story, Ellery is acutely aware of her **ethnic identity** as the only black participant in an affluent neighbourhood she is not accustomed to. She feels isolated and out of place among the other participants, who are all white and show behaviour that is alien to her.

Lori, the antagonist of the story, is another participant in the piano competition for 9- to 12-year-olds. She is white, has an impeccable appearance (jewellery and clothing, straight teeth, flouncy ponytail), lady-like behaviour (as long as people watch) and leads a life of privilege. She wins second place not because of her talent but mainly as a nod to her becoming a "true lady".

As soon as the two girls meet, the atmosphere changes. Ellery is fixated on Lori's apparent wealth and beauty. Lori on the other hand immediately stresses her feeling of superiority by not introducing herself, making racist remarks about Ellery's hair as well as trying to make Ellery feel as if she was acting inappropriately and unworthy. Even Ellery's triumphant win is only commented on with "Anything can make noise", objectifying her. Although Ellery feels awkward and uncomfortable around Lori, she is generally fearless, confident, knows how to stand her ground and does not pretend to be friendly afterwards, the way Lori does when their families are present. Because Ellery is left with a prize that is worthless to her while Lori continues to enjoy all the privileges that come with being white and rich, the Black girl throws cicada shells at Lori's car to vent her frustration, powerlessness and anger. After doing so, she finally "breathed out and smiled" as she is pleased to have found a way to express herself, elementary to **growing up**.

The story uses cicadas at different times to illustrate the situation that the young protagonist finds herself in: Like the discarded and littered shells, Ellery feels constantly **discriminated against** because of the colour of her skin; the cicadas waiting under ground until they're ready mirror Ellery patiently waiting for her moment to shine; and the tree full of loud cicadas reflects her experience of winning into one buzzing with life. Eventually, the sound of the cicadas becomes a crescendo that leads up to the story's resolution of Ellery throwing cicada shells, which are as empty as she feels, and while throwing them at the car is as ineffective as her win is worthless, the act itself solidifies her transformation. The cicadas thus function as a symbol for personal change, growth, renewal and rebirth.

Nafissa Thompson-Spires, "Fatima, the Biloquist: A Transformation Story" (gA)

A note on the author

Nafissa Thompson-Spires was born in San Diego, California in 1983. After earning a Master in Creative Writing and a doctorate in English, she worked on her first publication, *Heads of the Colored People,* which then won numerous prizes. Its title is a nod to James McCune Smith's ten sketches of mundane, Black middle-class life around antebellum New York. Throughout her texts, she concentrates on Black identity, flawed communication and (the deterioration of) mental health, especially in "white spaces". She is currently teaching as an Assistant Professor at Cornell University.

Synopsis

Nafissa Thompson-Spires' short story "Fatima, the Biloquist: A Transformation Story" follows the life of Fatima, an African-American high school student, who struggles to find her identity. Being torn between fitting in at her predominantly white school and feeling like she is not Black enough, Fatima eventually befriends Violet, a Black teenager with albinism. Violet teaches Fatima different facets of Black (pop) culture, lifestyle and language, which lets Fatima be more assertive. As a result, people like her classmates begin treating her differently. Initially, the friendship between Violet and Fatima benefits both. However, Fatima's desire to separate her Black and white identity leads her to betray her friend. She keeps her white boyfriend Rolf from her for months, albeit introducing him to everyone else, and even shares Violet's most personal insecurities with him. When all of them eventually meet by chance, Rolf immediately references the nickname people used to mock Violet with. Fatima's behaviour, born from vacillation and self-doubt, and Rolf's cruel and tactless comments most likely lead to an irreparable rift in Violet's and Fatima's relationship.

Analysis

Nafissa Thompson-Spires' short story is told by an omniscient third-person narrator and explores the theme of **ethnic identity** as well as the struggles that come with trying to be true to it.

Protagonist Fatima is a shy, nerdy, Black teenage girl who attends a predominantly white private school. Her surroundings have led her to repress her Blackness, causing her to feel detached and invisible and making her insecure about her identity. The title of the story indicates that Fatima is able to speak with two voices – her darker top and pink lower lip – codeswitching between them depending on who she is with. The urge to do so results from the need to influence people's perception of her and consequently their immediate impressions and assumptions they make about her. This can affect tone, intonation, vocabulary, appearance and behaviour. Fatima describes her two lives as "two souls trying merge into a better self", but she remains stuck between them, struggling to pick one or find a way to embrace, combine and reconcile both worlds.

Fatima's frustration is highlighted when she interacts with Wally, a white classmate who seems to have no qualms about appropriating Black culture as his own. His popularity is due to his wannabe-Black behaviour, while Fatima, as an actual Black girl, remains ignored at best. This **discrimination** makes her feel even more invisible and unimportant. Meeting Violet, however, Fatima is confronted with her own adapted behavioural patterns and her transformation begins.

Even though she faces discrimination, mockery and her own insecurities because of her albinism, Fatima's new acquaintance is that of an outwardly confident African-American woman and thus helps Fatima deepen her sociocultural knowledge on how to be Black.

Consequently, Fatima gradually becomes more self-aware and thus empowered and liberated, beginning to embrace this part of her identity. Their friendship intensifies, both sharing a unique understanding of one another. However, when Fatima begins a relationship with a white boy named Rolf, she is unable to balance her two lives and falls back into her adapted patterns of whiteness to fit in. Eventually, "she wasn't sure which lip she was supposed to use", and her fear of Violet perceiving Fatima's new relationship as a betrayal of Blackness, her teachings and their friendship leads to the ruin of their bond and Fatima returns to a worse version of feeling lifeless again.

Camille Acker: "Mambo Sauce" (eA)

Summary

Constance, a Black woman, meets Brian, a white man, in a bar with mainly white guests. Although she really likes him and agrees on a second date, she feels out of place. Yet, they start dating seriously and move in together when Brian accepts a job in Washington, D.C. The neighbourhood they move into is mostly Black, and Constance worries about being the only interracial couple.

When strolling through the neighbourhood, Constance comes across a chicken joint called *Winging It!*. She orders food and jokes with the staff, trying and liking their mambo sauce. The encounter invigorates her and connects her to her Black identity.

Shortly after, Brian and Constance are invited to dinner at Brian's college friends, Alissa and Mark. Again, Constance feels out of place being the only Black person. Brian tells their hosts about *Winging It!* and the sauce, which he – in contrast to Constance – did not like. Alissa and Mark not only laugh about this but also call it "ghetto sauce", joking about the neighbourhood Brian and Constance live in. Constance is angry about their behaviour, calling them ignorant and snobbish. On their way home, Brian defends his friends and both start fighting.

Sometime later, Constance returns to *Winging It!* and has a little chat with the women serving her. She tells them about herself but does not mention that she is dating a white man. During that conversation, she learns that the store will be closing at the end of the month because the building will be sold to developers.

Back home Constance decides to do something to prevent the shop from closing and to stop gentrification. After calling several newspapers, a live TV interview takes place at the restaurant. After the interview, the owner – who Constance calls "Gina" since she does not know her real name – argues with her because no one asked Constance to talk to the press and that her behaviour was encroaching. "Gina" is scared that the sale will be ruined by Constance's interview because she really wants to sell the shop and help the neighbourhood develop. Also, she confronts Constance for hiding her relationship with Brian and accuses her of acting superior like a white person.

On her way home Constance is consumed with shame. Brian is hurt that she never mentioned him and leaves. Constance feels misunderstood and fears her relationship with a white man is changing her.

Analysis

One main theme of "Mambo Sauce" is **ethnic identity.** Constance struggles with her interracial relationship with Brian because she does not feel comfortable in white-dominated situations, which makes her struggle with her own identity as a Black woman. She frequently thinks about her past and the environment she grew up in and the one she moved to while in New York or D.C. She liked New York because it was multicultural and diverse and she could be herself and feel at home. This changed when she and Brian moved to Washington, D.C. She has lost herself in the new environment and does not fully know who she is anymore. Like her new neighbourhood, she is afraid that her identity is becoming gentrified, that she is betraying her Black self. She starts hiding her relationship with Brian and separating her identity into someone she is around white people and someone she is around Black people. Constance sees her own identity affected by her love for a white man who does not seem to fully understand the complexity of these racial issues.

Likewise, the dinner at Brian's white friends points out that **discrimination** lurks everywhere in Constance's life. Mocking mambo sauce and their largely Black neighbourhood, Brian and his friends show that they consider themselves fundamentally superior. Constance feels uncomfortable in the face of this racism. Brian, on the other hand, is incapable of recognising this behaviour for what it is and understanding the identity crisis his girlfriend is struggling with.

Symbols

Mambo Sauce

- title of the short story
- symbolises how Constance reconnects with her Black identity through food
- being sweet and spicy = symbol of interracial relationships
- underlines cultural differences between the couple because Brian neither appreciates it nor understands why Constance is upset when it is referred to as "ghetto sauce"

Winging It!

- symbol of her connection to the Black community in Constance's new neighbourhood
- acts as cornerstone to community but also symbolically to Constance's identity; impending closure feels to Constance like she is losing part of her African-American identity

Nafissa Thompson-Spires: "Heads of the Colored People: Four Fancy Sketches, Two Chalk Outlines, and No Apology" (eA)

Summary

The short story "Heads of the Colored People: Four Fancy Sketches, Two Chalk Outlines, and No Apology" introduces the reader to four characters whose individual stories intersect on a day that two of them are shot by the police. It starts off by introducing one of the protagonists, African-American Riley, a cosplay fan who is on his way to a convention. He is stopped by another Black man, Richard Simmons, who calls himself

"Brother Man" and wants to sell him his dystopian comic series. Riley pushes him aside, which makes Brother Man angry, and the two start fighting.
In the next section, Kevan, a painter, is on his way to a meeting together with his daughter Penny. He finds it difficult to follow their discussion about superheroes because he is preoccupied with his plans for an exhibition portraying African Americans and their struggles.
Next, the reader is introduced to Paris Larkin, who is Riley's girlfriend. After her shift as a tour guide, she is supposed to meet Riley at the convention. When she gets there, she sees that Riley has been shot by police trying to break up the fight between Riley and Brother Man.
The story ends with a news report saying that Riley and Brother Man were shot by the police, however admitting that there might have been shortcomings in the telling of the story. Since the narrator is emotionally involved, she/he says this was the only way the story could have been told.

Analysis

The most eye-catching aspect about the short story "Heads of the Colored People" is its plot, which follows a non-linear structure while weaving together the stories of several people. Hence, Kevan sees the news story of the police shooting in the middle of the narrative, and Paris contributes sketches of Riley to his exhibition quite some time after the shooting. Also, the climax of the story, the death of Riley and Brother Man, is not explicitly narrated but frequently foreshadowed instead. Furthermore, the narrative style is also unusual since the story is told in the third person for the most part, but towards the end a first-person narrator comments on the events and addresses the reader directly.
The question of **(ethnic) identity** is crucial for the story because it is explored through each of the characters and their struggles with who they are. Riley's striking appearance with blue contact lenses and bleached hair, the narrator insists, is not an attempt to appear more "white" but a product of his self-confidence. Interested in cosplay, both Riley and Paris enjoy taking on the identities of fictional characters, making them feel seen and confident. Although people react with hostility when they see Paris dressed up as a non-Black character, her identity is acknowledged. Brother Man on the other hand, uses many aliases. His whole appearance triggers people's racial prejudices, causing them to see him as violent even though he regards himself as an intellectual as well as talented and skilled.
In the end, the press also ignores the victims' real identities and only offers a biased portrayal of Riley and Brother Man, based on outdated snapshots: the former is depicted as a thug and the latter is characterised as a criminal peddling indoctrinating material. Kevan, on the other hand, is interested in the individual stories of African Americans and wants to give them a voice in his exhibition.
Discrimination is also a crucial aspect of the short story and the author tries to raise awareness about the Black victims of racist police violence. Although the shooting of Brother Man and Riley is not explicitly described by the narrator and the reader is left in the dark as to what really happened when the police arrived, the narrator's agitation

and commentary at the end exposes the officers' action as racially motivated and voices pent-up anger at the frequency and ubiquity of such occurrences in the US.

Innocence and Guilt

- The term innocence can refer to two different concepts: the fact that a person is not guilty of a crime or the fact that a person doesn't have much experience of life.
- Guilt on the other hand is defined as a moral emotion that occurs when a person realises that they have violated universal moral standards of a society. It is closely related to other psychological concepts such as regret, remorse, shame and atonement.
- In law, "guilt" refers to the fact that a person can be held legally responsible for actions (or inaction) that caused harm to others or their property. "Not guilty" does not equal "innocent". A person who did not commit a crime is innocent, while "not guilty" means that the prosecution was not able to prove that a person committed a crime. When charged with a crime, a person is assumed to be innocent until proven otherwise. At the end of a trial, someone is declared "guilty" or "not guilty" instead of "innocent" because an acquittal does not require actual innocence.
- The philosopher Karl Jaspers (1883–1969) defined four dimensions of guilt and responsibility:
  - criminal guilt,
  - political guilt,
  - moral guilt,
  - metaphysical guilt (meaning responsibility that is universally shared across a society).[4]
- The definition of guilt is culture-specific and may vary over time.
- The term "collective guilt" refers to a group of individuals and their emotional reaction to illegitimately harming members of another group and requires a shared social identity.

Perceptions of Reality

- Perception and reality have very different meanings:
  - Perception refers to the way that something is regarded, viewed or understood. It varies from person to person.
  - Reality is the actual existence of something and an absolute truth and does not depend on individual perception.
- While someone's perception occurs mentally, reality in contrast exists outside the mind.
- Other than perception, reality cannot be easily manipulated. Perception is not reality, yet someone's perception can become a person's reality.
- The common misconception is that how we perceive reality is an accurate representation of it. What people believe to be reality is highly subjective. A person's perception is shaped by their past experiences, knowledge, their emotions, attitudes, motiva-

[4] Source: Karl Jaspers, *The Question of German Guilt,* Translated by E. B. Ashton, New York: Fordham University Press, 1965.

tions, self-interest and cognitive distortions but also their genetic predispositions, so it is highly complex.
- Severe mental illnesses show a substantial disconnect between perception and reality.
- Controlling the perception of reality has frequently been an important aim in human existence, from suppressing scientific thought to finding spurious justifications for military aggression. Perceptions of reality can thus be powerful and dangerous.

Ian McEwan, *Atonement* (eA)

A note on the author and the text
Ian McEwan (born in 1948 in England) is a British novelist, short-story writer and screenwriter. After spending much of his childhood in the Far East, Germany and North Africa, he studied English literature at the University of Sussex. His central themes include childhood, politics, crisis and transformation. Multiple viewpoints are created in most of his novels, which develop more rounded characters and different interpretations of events. This is also a key feature of *Atonement* (2001), which was a *New York Times* bestseller and shortlisted for the Booker Prize in 2001. In 2007, Atonement was made into an award-winning film, starring Keira Knightley and James McAvoy.

Synopsis

Atonement is a novel written in three major parts and time periods: 1935 England, Second World War England and France, and present-day England, with a final denouement.

The first part of the story, set in the summer of 1935, focuses on the protagonist Briony Tallis, a 13-year-old girl whose wealthy family lives on a country estate in England. Being the youngest of three, Briony has an older sister, Cecilia, and an older brother, Leon, and dreams of becoming a writer. Cecilia has recently graduated from Cambridge University with her friend Robbie, who is the son of the Tallis family's housekeeper. The family is joined by Briony's cousins – 15-year-old Lola and her nine-year old twin brothers. When her cousins arrive, Briony decides to stage a play called "The Trials of Arabella", which she wrote herself, to be performed at dinner for Leon's homecoming from Oxford. The play, however, fails as it cannot be rehearsed properly. The same day Briony witnesses a scene between Cecilia and Robbie as they argue in front of a fountain. During their fight a vase breaks and falls into the water. Cecilia undresses herself to her underwear in order to dive in to retrieve the pieces. Watching this from a window, Briony is highly confused by what she sees and believes that Robbie is threatening her sister. The whole situation is worsened when Robbie asks Briony to deliver a letter to Cecilia. He accidently hands Briony an early draft, written in vulgar language. Being worried for her sister's safety, Briony reads the letter and is disgusted. She hands it over to Cecilia, who confronts Robbie, prompting him to confess his feelings to her, and the two end up having passionate sex. Briony witnesses the scene and again, being too young to understand the whole situation, is confirmed in her belief that Robbie is hurting Cecilia.

During a dinner with Leon's friend Paul Marshall, a well-off manufacturer, the twins go missing. The party breaks into teams to search for them. In the dark, Briony finds Lola as she is being raped by a man that neither of the girls can see clearly. Still, Briony accuses Robbie of raping Lola and even announces her suspicions to the police, resulting in Robbie's arrest. Shortly after, Cecilia is so distraught that she abandons her family.

The second part of the novel moves to the beginning of the Second World War. Robbie has served several years in prison and is released on the condition that he enlists in the British Army. He and Cecilia have stayed in touch through letters, while the latter has still cut off any contact with her family and has become a nurse. During one of her lunch breaks, she briefly meets Robbie before he has to leave for France. After they kiss, Robbie promises to return after the war but is soon badly injured. During this time, he concludes that Briony was too immature to be blamed for what she has done to him. In a letter, he advises Cecilia to reconnect with her family. His condition deteriorates and he finally becomes delirious as the German army advances.

In the third part of the novel, Briony is 18 years old and training to be a nurse but also still dedicating herself to her writing. Her past and what she has done to Robbie are haunting her. Now she is convinced that Paul Marshall must have raped Lola. When she learns that Lola is engaged to him, she decides to let the past rest and attends their wedding. Afterwards, she decides to visit Cecilia in London, where she is also surprised to encounter Robbie. Both Robbie and Cecilia refuse to forgive Briony for her mistake, even though the younger sister promises to put things right. After leaving Cecilia, Briony is convinced that she can atone for her mistake.

The epilogue is set in London in 1999. Briony is 77 years old and has finally become a successful writer but has recently been diagnosed with dementia. The text is Briony's diary entry in which she reveals that most of the second part of the novel was actually an invention because Robbie and Cecilia died in the war. While she did attend Lola and Paul's wedding, she failed to visit her sister because she was aware of the pain she had caused her. The reader now learns that Briony is the author of all the preceding sections of the novel. Her writing serves as a lifelong attempt to atone for her mistakes and the fact that Robbie and Cecilia were never reunited.

Analysis

Atonement is a multi-level narrative using a story within the story as its essential technique. The first three parts of the novel are told by an omniscient, seemingly reliable narrator, while the postscript changes to a first-person narrator, the 77-year-old Briony, who is rather unreliable and biased.
Briony admits to having written the previous parts as an act of atonement for the tragic mistake she made in her childhood. **Perceptions of reality** are therefore a central theme: Briony's individual reality is a product of her own assumptions and bias but also of her naive and limited knowledge that leads to her tragic misperception of what happened between Robbie and Cecilia.

Atonement thus raises the question of the relationship between reality and fiction. The story answers this question towards the end when Briony attempts to use her writing skills to correct the mistakes that her imagination made her commit in the past.
Likewise, the theme of atonement is essential as the title indicates. Briony spends the rest of her adult life trying to make amends for what she has done to Robbie and Cecilia in her childhood. By constructing a whole new reality, she apologises in a way she was never able to in real life.
Another questions that can be raised is the one of **innocence and guilt.** Because of her age and limited view, Briony's false testimony against Robbie is innocent. She cannot be considered guilty because, as a thirteen-year-old, she neither knows enough about adult relationships nor is she capable of fully comprehending the harm her testimony might cause to everyone involved.
Finally, **Britishness** is an important aspect in *Atonement*. British society used to be rigidly divided into working class, middle class and upper class, while there was hardly any upward social mobility. In the 20th century an upper-middle class evolved that often aspired to live a lifestyle similar to the upper class, whose wealth usually stems from their own businesses or careers in the field of banking. The Tallis family and Paul Marshall represent this typical upper-middle class. However, the Tallis' country house is depicted as a rather poor and shallow imitation of an upper-class residence. Its somewhat derelict state parallels the dysfunctional family that inhabits it.

Symbols and motifs

Uncle Clem's Vase

- family heirloom that was given to uncle Clem as a reward for his part in World War I
- damaged vase forms the basis for Briony holding Robbie responsible for Lola's rape
- destruction of the vase symbolises the rupture in the family itself

"The Trials of Arabella"

- Briony's play performed at her 70th birthday by a new generation of the family
- reappearance within the story symbolises that Briony's role is beyond her control
- plot of the play mimics the story of *Atonement*: love story between a heroine and her doctor resembles love story of Cecilia and Robbie; Briony wants to tell story with a happy ending in both cases

Glossary – Individual and Society

alienation	Entfremdung (z. B. von der Ursprungskultur)
assimilation	Anpassung (Aufgabe der urspr. Kultur)
boycott	Ablehnung etwas zu kaufen oder zu benutzen, um z. B. eine Institution zu schwächen
citizenship	Nationalität, Staatsangehörigkeit
civil disobedience	ziviler Ungehorsam

civil rights	Bürgerrechte
colonialism, coloniser, colonised	Kolonialismus, die/der Besiedelnde, kolonisiert
covert/overt discrimination	versteckte/offene Diskriminierung
cultural clash	kultureller Zusammenprall (Konflikt)
deprivation	Aberkennung, Entzug (z. B. von Rechten), Benachteiligung
ethnic minority, ethnicity	ethnische Minderheit, Volkszugehörigkeit
gentrification	Gentrifizierung (Strukturwandel, durch den ein ärmliches Stadtviertel auch für wohlhabendere Bevölkerungsteile attraktiv gemacht wird, die oftmals die ursprünglichen Bewohner/-innen verdrängen)
immigrant, to immigrate, immigration	Einwanderer/-in, einwandern, Einwanderung
imperialism, imperialistic	Imperialismus, imperialistisch
indigenous	einheimisch
integration	Integration
loss of identity	Verlust der Identität
melting pot vs. salad bowl	„Schmelztiegel" vs. „Salatschüssel" (unterschiedliche Konzepte, die die Vielfalt der Kulturen in den USA beschreiben sollen)
mutual understanding	gegenseitiges/beiderseitiges Verständnis
naturalisation	Einbürgerung
open-minded vs. narrow-minded	aufgeschlossen vs. engstirnig
oppression, to be oppressed by s. o.	Unterdrückung, von jmd. unterdrückt werden
pluralistic society	pluralistische (vielseitige) Gesellschaft
Pride	öffentlicher Event, oftmals verbunden mit einem Umzug; zelebriert LGBTQ-Kultur und -Identität
racial equality	Gleichwertigkeit verschiedener Rassen
(racial) segregation	Rassentrennung
refugee, asylum seeker	Flüchtling, Asylsuchende/-r
to adapt to sth.	sich an etwas anpassen
to blend in	sich einfügen, integrieren
to integrate	integrieren
to receive / to be granted citizenship	die Staatsbürgerschaft erhalten
union	Organisation von Arbeitnehmerinnen und -nehmern, die deren Rechte und Interessen vertritt

Globalisation

Effects on the World of Work and on Personal Lives

Keyword
Globalisation: a worldwide development involving the integration of financial, economic and communications systems; often seen as an unstoppable process, affecting people all around the globe, no matter whether they live in industrialised or developing countries, in big cities or rural villages; transfer of goods, capital and services as well as communications make life easier, but not everyone profits from the development; smaller economies may suffer
The world is said to be getting smaller, i. e. it has become a **"global village"**. The term was coined by Marshall McLuhan, a Canadian philosopher and media specialist.

Economic Challenges

As today's customers wish to buy products at the best cost-performance ratio, the global market has become very **competitive**, with the following (and related) consequences:
- More and more jobs are outsourced or offshored to cut down production costs, thereby severely damaging local labour markets.
- When jobs are outsourced to low-wage countries, the workers often work in so-called "sweatshops" for long hours at a stretch, earning only minimum wages and under working conditions that are often inhumane.
- While "global players" consider efficiency, speed, flexibility and profit most important, employees are increasingly unable to defend their rights.
- Critics like the Canadian journalist Naomi Klein accuse multinational companies of exploiting the poor and indirectly supporting child labour by only having their own profits in mind.
- People in developing countries often live in poor conditions, without a decent education or access to new means of communication. Therefore they cannot reap the benefits of globalisation.
- In order to reduce the number of sweatshops, fair trade is becoming increasingly important. Its aim is to ensure that workers and small-scale producers in poor countries are paid a fair price for their work and products.
- Despite these attempts, the gap between the rich and the poor is widening.

Aspects of the "global village"

- The development of aeroplanes, fast ships and trains has made fast transportation of goods and people from one part of the world to another possible.
- New means of communication, especially the internet, have made collaboration between business partners and private individuals easier.

- Multinational companies have branches all over the world, and cost-effectiveness is a decisive factor when new production sites are set up.

Effects on the way of life

Anyone can experience the effects of globalisation, e.g. when
- travelling (and meeting people from one's own town halfway round the globe);
- keeping in touch with friends or business partners in distant countries with the help of new means of communication, which are faster than ever before;
- buying new goods that come from or were processed very far away; or
- calling a service "hotline" of a company that uses a call-center in India.

Globalisation is not always regarded as a positive process:
- Some people fear that individual cultures will finally blend into a single global culture, thereby losing their identity and the benefits of diversity.
- Despite or because of a globalised world, millions of people in developing countries still suffer from malnutrition or die of incurable diseases.
- Others work under cruel working conditions, producing goods that will be shipped to and sold in industrialised countries at a low price.
- One of the latest financial crises, starting in the USA in 2008, has shown that such catastrophes will ultimately affect other nations as well, as businesses are linked and global trade is now the rule.
- Due to increased mobility, diseases like H1N1 ("swine flu") or the coronavirus (cf. p. 56 f.) can easily spread all around the globe, developing into a pandemic.
- The refugee crisis in Europe can partly be seen as connected to globalisation: People from all over the world want to participate in growing economic wealth. Many people from poor countries want to find a better future and leave their homes – just like people have always done over the centuries (e.g. emigration to America in the last two centuries). At the same time, civil and other wars as well as climate change force people to emigrate. As more and more countries close their borders, problems in many regions are growing. Among these problems are huge refugee camps, pushback policies denying migrants their right to apply for asylum and people drowning and starving during dangerous journeys.
- Terrorism has become an ongoing global threat, which has led to a growing feeling of insecurity in many societies. In some countries (e.g. Israel), terrorist attacks have been a permanent aspect of everyday life for six or seven decades. In most Western as well as Middle Eastern countries, what we know as Islamist terrorism (Al-Qaeda, the "Islamic State") began with the "9/11" attacks on the World Trade Center in New York and the Pentagon in Washington on 11 September 2001. This led to the controversial "War on Terror" on the part of the USA and its allies, most notably in Afghanistan from 2001 to 2021. Since then, the world has seen a large number of terrorist attacks connected with Islamist ideology (e.g. in France, England, Nigeria, Germany) or with the ideology of white supremacy (e.g. in Christchurch in New Zealand or Utøya in Norway).

INFO Anti-globalisation movements

Many ecological and political movements around the world criticise the levelling and disadvantageous effects of globalisation. This has led to the formation of NGOs and alliances opposing the rule of capitalism over the economy of this increasingly smaller world. In opposition to the G8 summit, these organisations formed the **World Social Forum**.

Global competition

The increasingly globalised working world demands new skills and abilities of each individual. Since not only multinational companies but also smaller firms are outsourcing parts of their production, making use of cheap and well-educated workforces abroad, people in industrialised countries will experience more competition when looking for work as well as on the job. This requires both white-collar and blue-collar workers in the West to:

- acquire skills and competencies that are either very specialised or carried out with special qualities no one else can offer;
- become more flexible; one must be able to adapt to changes on the job and learn new ways of working quickly;
- continue learning throughout one's whole life; it is no longer sufficient to learn a job and expect to stay in it for the remainder of one's career;
- be familiar and keep up with new forms of (computer) technology and communications, since these are constantly changing and improving; and to
- be able to compete with workers from all around the world who can offer the same or similar skills and abilities for lower wages.

Globalisation and the COVID-19 Pandemic

At the beginning of 2020, a highly-infectious and often lethal pandemic caused by the coronavirus started to spread rapidly across the world. Governments worldwide faced a situation threatening health and lives as never before. Harsh measures, including travel bans and stay-at-home orders which sometimes stretched over several weeks, were imposed to keep the disease at bay, temporarily infringing fundamental rights like freedom of assembly and movement. All kinds of public services and shops were put under lockdown; night-time curfews were decreed to prevent people from leaving their homes. As there was initially no vaccine to cope with the virus, the pandemic had the world under control until the first vaccines were developed and administered a year after the original outbreak. The vaccination programme unfortunately developed into a problem in its own right, with manufacture, distribution and administration obstacles arising at international as well as national and local levels.
The spread of the pandemic can be seen as a negative effect of globalisation: it has definitely been fostered by long-distance travelling from one continent to another.
In economic terms, the epidemic severely damaged global trade and caused heavy financial losses. Even famous, financially strong brands suffered because customers have had to stay at home. Online orders flourished but could hardly cushion the drastic

losses to local businesses. Moreover, distortions in global supply and demand – as for FFP2 masks – demonstrated the vulnerability of global trade to unscrupulous business practices.
The various lockdowns hit social and cultural life in particular very hard, closing entire entertainment branches like theatres, cinemas and concerts, along with museums and art galleries as well as restaurants, hotels and bars. The restrictions on even informal group and family meetings made people very lonely. Elderly people and people living on their own who were not allowed to receive visits or to visit other people suffered greatly from this situation.
School – and with it family – life was also massively affected. Teachers and students had to adjust to digital schooling without any personal presence, and families had to get used to the new discipline of home schooling. Similar conditions were imposed on university staff and students. Children from underprivileged backgrounds were hit particularly hard as they often lacked the necessary hardware and internet connection as well as their own study space. The natural needs of children and young people to grow up together were disrupted, and the changing requirements imposed by governments, sometimes relaxing and then reinstating lockdowns, did nothing to alleviate matters.
As governments and institutions struggled to deal with the COVID-19 health crisis, our globalised world proved shockingly vulnerable to the virus, its economic effects and the spread of misinformation. How we prepare ourselves for future pandemics, with vaccines distributed fairly to all nations, will be a real test of globalisation.

Global Responsibilities

Migration – A Global Challenge[1]

- Migration has been a worldwide phenomenon since the beginning of human history.
- People have a number of reasons for leaving their places of origin: poverty and the dream of a better life elsewhere, climatic reasons, wars and civil wars or religious persecution, to name only the most important.
- One has to distinguish between migrants and refugees:
- **Migrants** leave their countries of origin for a limited period of time or permanently, usually for economic reasons. They might have job offers in a different country or they might have heard of good opportunities. Examples of this are emigration from European countries to the USA in the 19th century, immigrants from Poland to the Ruhr district also during the 19th century, migrant workers inside Europe today, for example to help on farms, as carers for elderly people or to work in hospitals, and people from Africa trying to find better living conditions in Europe.
- **Refugees** usually flee their homes in order to get away from immediate threats to their survival, such as persecution, wars or climate change. Examples of this at present are the Muslim Rohingya from Ukrainians to Poland, Germany and other European

[1] Source for all figures: https://www.unhcr.org/figures-at-a-glance.html and https://publications.iom.int/books/world-migration-report-2022 (both accessed on 1 April 2024)

countries, or Syrian and Afghan people to Europe. An important example from the past are the Jews from Germany and other countries who had to flee from the Nazis.

- The International Migration Report of the UN from 2022 states that most migrants worldwide go to countries in Asia, followed by Europe and North America. The countries with the most migrants are the USA, followed by Germany and Saudi Arabia. These migrants for the most part seek – and find – employment in their countries of destination. They are not refugees, but quite a large number of them are illegal immigrants. According to the UN, there were 281 million migrants in 2020.
- The UNHCR (United Nations refugee agency) states in its statistical report for 2022 that the world is now witnessing the highest levels of displacement on record. 108.4 million people around the world have been forced to leave their homes. Among them are over 35 million refugees. 63 million are internal refugees, i.e. they flee from one part of the country to another (Nigeria is one example). There are 5.4 million asylum seekers worldwide. However, 70 % of refugees stay in neighbouring countries: Syrian refugees mainly flee to Türkiye, Jordan and other countries close by. Nearly half the refugees worldwide at present come from Syria, Afghanistan and Ukraine.
- In 2023, Iran hosted the largest refugee population worldwide, with 3.4 million refugees and asylum seekers, followed by Türkiye (3.4 million), Germany (2.5 million) and Colombia (2.5 million). Most refugees come from Syria (6.5 million), Afghanistan (6.1 million) and Ukraine (5.9 million).
- There are also millions of stateless people, who have been denied nationality and access to basic rights such as education, healthcare, employment and freedom of movement.
- More than 1 percent of the world's population have fled their homes.
- Nearly 1 person is forcibly displaced every two seconds as a result of conflict or persecution.
- The fact that most refugees seek help in neighbouring, not always wealthy countries can cause major problems there: The population of these countries has to share access to education, healthcare and jobs with the refugees. Compared to rich countries like Germany, countries like Jordan or the Lebanon find it far more difficult to cope with the situation. Colombia is another example of these conflicts: it is a country which is only just beginning to overcome the effects of a civil war. Recently it has also been the destination of over 1 million refugees from Venezuela.
- On the other hand, migration always also means enrichment: The destination country will, with time, integrate the new arrivals. Their culture, beliefs and customs will become part of the country, thus leading to a more diverse culture in general.
- Many migrants and refugees want to return to their home countries if the situation allows them to. Seasonal migrants, for example, usually leave their families behind and return when their work has finished for the year. Many refugees want to return to their old home after the end of a war, others would like to build a new life elsewhere.

Global Warming and its Consequences

Environmental pollution has been growing rapidly and globally. The following factors in particular create global problems:
- Especially in developed nations, rampant consumerism is still increasing **energy consumption and waste gases** from factories.
- Over the last decades the number of **vehicles** on the roads has steadily increased. Cars are no longer found only in industrialised countries.
- The number of people travelling by plane is also greater than ever, due to the fact that plane tickets have become affordable for a larger number of people. Short-haul **flights** have become particularly popular.
- **food miles:** Whereas some years ago many people bought fruit and vegetables locally and ate seasonal products, they now want to eat strawberries and cherries in December. Hence more goods are transported by plane. Ecologically conscious customers ask themselves whether it is better to buy local product than food (even fair trade) that has been flown across continents. The non-sustainable production of meat and dairy foods is another critical factor in global warming.
- Everyone leaves a **carbon footprint** (emission of greenhouse gases from factories, transportation, food, etc), either directly or indirectly.
- **Greenhouse gases** such as carbon dioxide (CO_2) and methane cause chemical damage to the atmosphere (e.g. holes in the ozone layer) as well as global warming.
- World-wide, pupils have joined the movement *Fridays for Future* started by the Swedish teenager Greta Thunberg in a protest against climate change (see page 61).

After years of heated discussion among scientists and (especially) politicians worldwide, it is now considered common knowledge in most nations around the globe that the world's climate is changing and that these changes are, to a large degree, man-made. This change manifests itself most dramatically in the fact that the global average temperature is rising, and this has many side effects.
The documentary *An Inconvenient Truth* and its follow-up *An Inconvenient Sequel: Truth to Power* lay out the scientific facts on global warming in detail.

Causes of global warming

- Fossil fuel emissions, so-called greenhouse gases, form a layer in the earth's atmosphere which traps the sun's heat and thereby causes the temperature on the ground to rise; this is called "global warming".
- The quantity of greenhouse gases produced worldwide is rising because:
  - more cars, planes and industrial complexes are being built and used;
  - forests are burnt to make way for agriculture, people, roads, etc.;
  - the growing number of cattle is increasing the emission of methane.
- The global rise in temperature is causing the polar ice caps to melt, diminishing their efficiency as a cooling device and mirror to reflect sunbeams and thus speeding up the heating process in the atmosphere.

Effects and consequences

There are many consequences of climate change. Some may seem rather insignificant at first but turn out to be disastrous in the long run. Although these effects are often spoken of as taking place in the future, many of them are already happening.

- Rising global temperatures are causing more water to evaporate both on land and in the oceans, changing historical patterns of rainfall and drought; many people are unable to adapt to these irregular weather phenomena.
- Oceanic warming is causing hurricanes to become more frequent and violent, as the warm water enhances evaporation and (indirectly) wind speed.
- Changes in temperature also cause natural habitats to change. Plants and animals have to adapt, and if they cannot do so, die out. Biodiversity is therefore endangered, limiting the natural resources on which we subsist.
- Diseases are spreading more quickly because parasites like mosquitoes and their animal hosts are affecting populations in previously safe areas.
- As polar ice caps melt, more and more of the earth's landmass is flooded, leaving people homeless.
- If enough polar ice melts, the North Atlantic current (Gulf Stream), which guarantees Europe's warm climate, might stop. In a worst-case scenario, Europe might experience another ice age.
- In other areas, desertification will continue to increase, a phenomenon which is already taking place.
- All these developments will dramatically reduce the area of land on which human existence is possible and will therefore lead to worldwide migration that we will be unable to deal with.

The effects are threatening the entire planet and the way we live today. Because of this, scientists, politicians and citizens worldwide have a duty to seek ways of reducing greenhouse gases in order to slow down climate change. Each individual can participate in reducing greenhouse gas emissions by using better insulation in houses, saving electricity, recycling waste, using public transportation instead of a private car, flying only when absolutely necessary, etc.

Political efforts to reduce greenhouse gas emissions are still faced with various difficulties and conflicts of interest. An appropriate response to these issues is often thwarted by capitalist interests, as is made obvious, for instance, when a climate conference is chaired by the head of one of the world's largest oil companies. Each climate summit therefore only achieves small steps towards stopping or slowing down climate change. Scientists and independent organisations alike argue that these small steps are not enough to prevent the catastrophic consequences of global warming. The main goal remains to cut greenhouse gas emissions, especially those caused by the burning of fossil fuels.

INFO The Paris Agreement and the UN Climate Change Conferences

A global rise in air temperature led to the first World Climate Conference in Geneva in 1979, where the impact of humankind on global climate was discussed. Eventually, the UN Climate Convention came into effect in 1994, trying to prevent further human-induced damages. Since then, annual **Conferences of the Parties** (COP) have been held. The so-called **Kyoto Protocol** of 1997 aimed to reduce the emission of greenhouse gases by an annual 5.2 % by 2012. The **Paris Agreement** of 2005 aims for a global temperature rise of no more than 1.5 degrees Celsius above pre-industrial levels and was ratified in 2016 by 196 countries. A notable point of contention, the financial compensation developed nations need to offer developing countries for their copious contributions to climate change was addressed at **COP 27** via a Loss and Damage Fund. In 2023, **COP 28** faced controversies, particularly involving its president, Sultan Ahmed Al Jaber, who was reported to have planned oil and gas deals during the conference. The summit officially recognised fossil fuels as the primary cause of climate change but stopped short of calling for a total phaseout, opting instead for a push to increase investments in renewables. Major emitters like the USA and China did not join the declaration or did not even attend the summit.

Fridays for Future

- In August 2018, Greta Thunberg, a then 16-year-old Swedish climate change activist, started protesting outside the Swedish parliament in Stockholm in order to raise awareness of the dangers of climate change and calling for government action. Thunberg's solitary school strikes soon caught the attention of the media in countries all over the world.
- Up to May 2019, an estimated 1.4 million teenagers and young adults worldwide had followed her example by going on strike from school every Friday and protesting against climate change. This movement is known as "Fridays for Future", a global movement that engages in political discussions without centralised leadership.
- Thunberg has delivered several high-profile speeches such as at a UN Climate Conferences and the EU parliament, in which she put pressure on politicians and world leaders to combat climate change more swiftly and resolutely.

Alternatives to Using Fossil Fuels

Recent discussions on fossil fuels and their effect on the atmosphere have supported the development of technology to make use of renewable sources of energy such as wind, water and solar power. In many European countries, national programmes to subsidise these technologies have been established. The US is also aiming to support these alternative energies more substantially, but this has not been achieved by recent administrations. The Fukushima disaster in spring 2011 led the German government to withdraw from using nuclear energy in future. Other parties urge that nuclear power should be used instead of fossil fuels (which are still the most common source of energy). However, the use of nuclear energy has always been controversial.

Natural alternative energy sources

In general, the use of wind, water and solar power seems far less risky and also less expensive in the long run. The challenge engineers face is to make these technologies more efficient and find ways to store the energy produced. One main hindrance is posed by companies investing more money in fossil fuel exploration and exploitation and in expanding nuclear power facilities. Since these technologies are well established, their exploitation yields enormous profits, whereas investment in new, ecologically-friendly sources of energy is costly, but could create many jobs.

Non-renewable and/versus renewable energy

- Since the Industrial Revolution, Western societies have been in constantly growing need of energy resources to power industrial production and satisfy communal and household requirements for fuel and electricity.
- This increasing demand for energy has led to various developments:
  - The exploitation of natural resources such as oil, gas and coal has led to the destruction of natural habitats on land and in the oceans.
  - The use of nuclear power plants has created a seemingly safe, cheap and climate-friendly source of power. This view is, however, disproven by accidents like those in Chernobyl and Fukushima as well as the ongoing problem of where to store nuclear waste.
  - New inventions have succeeded in making use of renewable energies such as wind, water and solar power.
- The most immediate drawback of the use of fossil fuels since the Industrial Revolution is the amount of carbon dioxide and other pollutants emitted into the atmosphere.

Environmental sustainability

It will prove difficult to sustain usable natural resources. Industrialisation and capitalism, together with a continuously growing world population, have led to a massive exploitation of limited resources. Thus, finding ways to make our societies and lifestyles sustainable is one of the most important global challenges.

Global goals

In 2015, United Nations member states formulated 17 objectives - or „Sustainable Development Goals" - for a fairer and better world to be achieved by 2030. These included issues such as gender equality, clean water, physical and mental well-being, international peace and justice.
For example, they aim to end global poverty by ensuring that economic resources and fundamental services such as healthcare are available to everyone and by making sure that even the poor are protected from potential environmental disaster. They also seek to implement policies aimed at promoting equality with respect to income, political inclusion and opportunities, but that also allow developing nations in particular a fairer economical share. With respect to climate change, the 17 global goals point to raising awareness for this issue, protecting against disasters related to climate change and integrating measures on a national level. They also posit a need to reduce waste, in particular

food waste, manage resources more sustainably and to combat market distortions such as tax reductions and subsidies that reward wasteful consumption.[2]
The signatory states have shown variable speed at implementing these goals in their policies. Germany was one of the first to begin this process in the shape of the „Deutsche Nachhaltigkeitsstrategie“ in 2017. Whether, however, these 17 aims can be converted from words on paper to real action is yet to be seen. A first stock-taking in 2020 saw positive developments on a communal level and well as in grassroots movements such as Fridays for Future. On the other hand, the report also notes that povery is still growing, basic needs are still nowhere near being met on a global scale and natural resources and habitats continue to be recklessly destroyed. Clearly, more public pressure and political daring will be required in the coming years.

English as a Global Language

The general importance of English in the globalised world of international trade and politics, science, popular culture and travel is still unrivalled. No matter where you are in the world, a command of English will always help.
Worldwide, 1.456[3] million people speak English as a native speaker or as a second language, followed by Mandarin, the main language in China (1.120 million), Hindi (600 million) and Spanish (543 million).[4]
Especially in the countries of the former British Empire, English is not just a language universally understood and spoken, it is very often still an official language. In India, for example, more than 3,000 newspapers are published in English, but English is spoken by only about 12 % of the population. There are 1,652 languages and dialects in India, which makes English as a working *lingua franca* even more important. All in all, English is the official language in 58 countries today.
It has been estimated that about a billion people worldwide speak English as a second language. According to the EU statistical service, 98 % of all students at lower secondary level in Europe study English as a second language.[5] International organisations like NATO or OECD use English exclusively, as do many internationally operating enterprises like Airbus Industries and even Volkswagen in their Shanghai branch.

[2] Source: https://www.globalgoals.org/ (accessed on 1 April 2024)

[3] Source: https://www.statista.com/statistics/266808/the-most-spoken-languages-worldwide/ (published on 16 June 2014, accessed on 1 April 2024)

[4] Source: https://www.statista.com/statistics/266808/the-most-spoken-languages-worldwide/ (published 16 June 2023, accessed on 1 April 2024)

[5] Source: https://www.eurydice.si/publikacije/Key-Data-on-Teaching-Languages-at-School-in-Europe-2023.pdf, accessed on 1 April 2024)

According to Bill Bryson[6], English differs from other languages in three outstanding respects that make it attractive even to speakers of other mother tongues. First, its rich vocabulary is wider than that of other languages. The latest edition of the *Oxford English Dictionary* lists 600,000 words; 200,000 words are commonly used in English, compared to 184,000 in German and just 100,000 in French. What adds to the wide range of words is the large number of synonyms. The best known collection of synonyms and antonyms, *Roget's Thesaurus*, has over 443,000 words. Thirdly, there is an almost endless list of words that can be used both as noun and verb.

English as a *Lingua Franca*

A *lingua franca* is a language that can be used by speakers who do not have any knowledge of each other's mother tongue. It is therefore also referred to as a "contact" or "link" language. English used in this context bridges the linguistic gap for non-native speakers of English who do not share a common first language and thus serves as a means of intercultural communication. Since this happens worldwide, English has been called a "global *lingua franca*". The result of this extensive use of English is that it is shaped not only by its native speakers but also by those who use it as a foreign language. Researchers[7] have found that although speakers of English as a *lingua franca* do not always adhere to the rules of grammar and pronunciation, communication is not necessarily inhibited by this. What seems more important in this respect is language awareness, along with a command of communication strategies. Nevertheless, the more closely a person's grammar approximates to Standard English, the more readily they will be understood.

Varieties of English[8]

American English

- American English is relatively homogeneous compared to British English. About 80 % of the population speak with the same accent.
- The USA contains four speech groups:
  Northern, Midland, Southern and New England. Midland is subdivided into North and South Midland.
- Regional variation due to geographical and historical factors: colonists on the East Coast were in touch with people from England via trade; therefore similarities with British English (e.g. the pronunciation of "Tuesday", "news"; the absence of [r] in "horse", "car").
- Social prestige is linked to pronunciation, e.g. the sound of [r] is carefully produced by upper-middle-class speakers when they want to indicate their social standing.

[6] Source: Bill Bryson, *Mother Tongue. The Story of the English Language*, London: Penguin, 1990, S. 3 f.

[7] Source: Barbara Seidlhofer, "English as a lingua franca", in: *ELT Journal* 59/4 (October 2005), p. 339 f.

[8] You can find lots of additional information as well as sound examples of these and other varieties of English on video platforms online.

- There has been some rivalry between England and America as to the question whose language is more correct. On becoming independent, Americans emphasised the differences between British and American English, thus creating a sort of linguistic nationalism.
- Immigrants often try to conceal their origins by overemphasising vowel sounds, e.g. in "coffee". This is called hypercorrection.
- The phenomenon of t-dropping is widely practised. That means that [t] is not pronounced in the middle of a word, e.g. in "winter" or "internet".
- [o] in "clock" is realised like the [a] in British English "car". A British native speaker could therefore mistake the American "clock" for the word "clerk".
- The way Americans speak is often referred to as "the American twang". This most commonly refers to "General American", which is a generalised Midwestern accent used by many TV and radio hosts. (cf. p. 67 for AAVE / Black Vernacular).

British English

- In the Middle English period, Oxford, Cambridge and London shared the same kind of English. Because of the prestige attached to it, London English became the basis for Standard English as early as the time of Chaucer's Middle English and in turn formed the national language.
- One variety of English spoken in London is called Cockney. In the sixteenth century this was not associated with the language of the East End working-class, as it is today, but it was the language spoken by all Londoners outside the court. It was only in the eighteenth century that Cockney became regarded as coarse or low English. One of the reasons for this development was that the City became the centre of commerce and trade, thereby making the old inhabitants move east to Wapping, Shoreditch and Bermondsey.
  Characteristics of Cockney include h-dropping, which means that the [h] at the beginning of a word is not pronounced, and the "glottal stop", which is the result of not pronouncing the [t] in words like "butter" or "bottle". Furthermore, the [g] in word endings is often omitted, for example in "eatin'".
- Standard English as spoken by a mere 2–5 % of the British population has also been labelled "Received Pronunciation" or simply "RP". It was, until recently, spoken by British middle-class people, especially in the South, and it was used by most TV and radio news presenters.

Australian English

- Like American English, Australian English is fairly uniform in pronunciation.
- Three different social accents can be distinguished: "Cultivated" (similar to British English; 10 % of speakers), "Broad" (working-class accent; 10 %) and "General" (80 %). On the whole, there is not much regional variety in dialects.
- Girls and women tend to speak General or Cultivated Australian, whereas boys and men prefer General or Broad Australian.
- Using a rising tone at the end of a statement, which has become popular with girls and women (not only in Australia), is called "rising inflection".

- Australian English contains various words from the Aboriginals, for instance "billabong", "didgeridoo", "boomerang", "koala" and "kangaroo".
- Usage is also influenced by vocabulary from American English, for example: "cookies", "station wagon", "teller", "mail", "labor" and "dollar".
- Australian English has been influenced by large numbers of immigrants, so-called "New Australians" from Türkiye, Greece, Italy, Sri Lanka, etc.

New Zealand English

- It is very similar to Australian English, although New Zealanders regard their way of speaking as more sophisticated and try to be as close to British English as possible.

Canadian English

- In the wake of the American Revolution, Loyalists (supporters of the English) fled to Ontario, providing the basis for "General Canadian" as an urban, middle-class variety.
- Along the Atlantic coast there were many English-speaking settlements.

English in India

- Approximately 130 million people, or 10 % of the population, use English in India, thus making it an important language of official life.
- English is spoken mainly by the educated ruling classes.
- Many national daily papers are in English (e.g. *The Times of India*).
- All-India Radio broadcasts in English all over India.
- English was used in the fields of government, education and imperial rule.
- In 1857, English-speaking universities were established in Bombay, Calcutta and Chennai (formerly: Madras).
- English has become the language of prestige and of nationalist opposition.
- A large number of Indian words have been integrated into English, e.g. "curry", "bungalow" or "veranda", especially by English administrators in the nineteenth century.

Pidgin

A pidgin is an artificial, auxiliary language without any native speakers. It is used by people with different mother tongues who need a common means of communication. Pidgin English was the traders' and slaves' *lingua franca*. The word "pidgin" is derived from the way the Chinese pronounced the word "business".

Creole

- If a pidgin is used as a first language, it is called a creole. This process happens gradually and it takes several generations.
- When slaves from many different African tribes with different languages were transported to America by slave ships, they needed a common language. Therefore, they spoke pidgin English, which was accessible to all of them.
- Examples are the Caribbean creole of Barbados, which is based on English, or Haitian creole, which is based on French. The creole of Papua New Guinea (Tok Pisin) has a written as well as a spoken form.

African American Vernacular English (AAVE)

- Formerly called Black English, AAVE has absorbed aspects of African pidgin and Caribbean creole and has a long and distinctive tradition. It has a distinct set of rules, although it is still often misjudged as inferior because certain grammatical structures of English are simplified or do not occur. Nowadays, however, it is considered to be simply another variety of English. It is also called "Black Vernacular".
- The verb "to be" is left out under certain circumstances („She at home.“) and habitual "be" is used in place of simple present („He be watching TV every night.“).
- On the one hand, AAVE is representative of a disadvantaged past, on the other hand, it is also a means of self-expression.
- Contributions from the African world to everyday English are words and expressions like "voodoo", "banana" or "high five".
- Black Vernacular probably originated even before the slave trade began.
- Due to music and popular films and series, it has achieved wide public attention. Some features of AAVE are apparently unique to this variety, but the structure is often similar to other English varieties spoken in the US and Caribbean. The number of speakers of AAVE is extremely difficult to establish.

South African English (SAE)

English was first brought to the Cape area by British settlers, fortune seekers and missionaries in the late 18th and early 19th century. The minority of about 3 million first-language SAE speakers is outnumbered by second- and third-language speakers because English is seen both as the language of communication and aspiration as well as a 'colonist' language. For many Black parents English is an instrument for their children's advancement. SAE is dominant in public life for reasons of practicality, even though official documents are also translated into the other ten official languages.
In the Soweto uprising in 1976, the question of a teaching language in Black schools was crucial: the students opted for English, as they did not want to study in Afrikaans, the language of their white oppressors. So English has always been seen in opposition to Afrikaans, with the Black population preferring to use English and the language of their own cultural origin, whereas many white people have kept to Afrikaans.
Strong influences on SAE vocabulary and pronunciation mainly come from the surrounding African languages as well as from Afrikaans or unclear sources. Due to SAE having different native tongues, the pronunciation tends to vary a lot. In general, pronunciation is closest to NZE (New Zealand English), tending to become more levelled through teaching in urban schools and through modern media.

Glossary – Globalisation

anti-globalist	Globalisierungsgegner/-kritiker
backwardness	Rückständigkeit
company philosophy	Geschäfts-/Firmenphilosophie

competition; to be competitive	Konkurrenz(kampf)/Wettbewerb; konkurrenzfähig sein
corporate identity	Firmenimage
crop diseases	Krankheiten von Pflanzen/Saatgut
debt relief	Schuldenerlass, Entschuldung
desertification	die Wüstenbildung, das Vordringen der Wüste
developing countries	Entwicklungsländer
development aid	Entwicklungshilfe
driving forces of globalisation	die Antriebskräfte der Globalisierung
drought	Dürren, Dürreperioden
earth's atmosphere	die Erdatmosphäre
economic growth	Wirtschaftswachstum
economic prosperity	ökonomischer Wohlstand
emerging markets	Schwellenländer
environmental commitment	Umwelteinsatz
environmental damage	Umweltzerstörung
environmentally friendly	umweltfreundlich
expansion of capitalism	Ausbreitung des Kapitalismus
fair trade	fairer Handel
floods	Hochwasser, Überschwemmungen
global interconnection	globale Querverbindungen
global marketplace	globaler Marktplatz
global player	Weltfirma
global superpower	globale Supermacht
global warming	Erderwärmung
going global	*umgangssprachlicher Ausdruck, der ursprünglich für die globale Expansion von Firmen verwendet wurde*
greenhouse gases	Treibhausgase
human rights	Menschenrechte
increase profit margins	die Gewinnspanne erhöhen
Industrial Age	das Industriezeitalter
industrial nations	Industrieländer/-nationen
international stock markets	internationale Börsenmärkte
labour laws/market	Arbeitsgesetze/ Arbeitsmarkt
lingua franca	eine Sprache, die von Personen mit unterschiedlichen Muttersprachen benutzt wird

low-wage countries	Niedriglohnländer
mass tourism	Massentourismus
microcredits	Kleinkredite
NGO (non-governmental organisation)	Nichtregierungsorganisation
outsourcing	Produktionsverlagerung
political turmoil	politischer Aufruhr, politische Turbulen-zen
pollution	Verschmutzung
population overshoot, overpopulation, excess of population	Überbevölkerung
poverty	Armut
greenhouse gas emissions	Ausstoß von Treibhausgasen
cost of production	Produktionskosten
rise in global temperature	ein weltweiter Temperaturanstieg
robotised production	computergesteuerte Produktion/Ferti-gung
shareholder	Aktionär
supremacy	Vormachtsstellung, Überlegenheit
sustainability	Nachhaltigkeit, Zukunftsfähigkeit
sweatshop	ausbeuterischer Betrieb
trade	Handel
trademark policy	Markenpolitik
undernutrition, malnutrition	Unterernährung; Mangelernährung
unemployment	Arbeitslosigkeit
workforce	Arbeiterschaft
working conditions	Arbeitsbedingungen

Science and Technology

The dawn of science in the modern sense of drawing factual conclusions from empirical, experimental or statistical data can be dated back to ancient Greece, when scholars aimed to explain the world on the basis of observation and elaboration. During the Renaissance, science experienced a rebirth, and in the wake of the Industrial Revolution it evolved to become what it is today: the basis of our modern way of life.

Gaining background knowledge
The emergence of today's technology-oriented societies can only be understood by studying the Industrial Revolution. The full extent of these changes cannot be presented in this context. Various informative sites can be found online, e. g.:
- https://www.bbc.co.uk/history/scottishhistory/enlightenment/features_enlightenment_industry.shtml (accessed on 1 April 2024)
- https://www.history.com/topics/industrial-revolution/industrial-revolution (published on 29 October 2009, accessed on 1 April 2024)

Chances and Risks

Scientific research aims to explore and explain the world around us and improve the means by which we cope with it. Technology, in turn, is the practical outcome of this research, resulting in the tools and machines we use to make our lives (seemingly) easier. Every new technology, however, harbours risks as well as opportunities and creates new kinds of dependencies unknown before. One simple example will suffice to prove this point: At the end of the 19th century, the first automobiles were produced; eventually they would replace horse-drawn vehicles and other means of individual transport. In contrast to older technologies, cars need fossil fuel. Demand for cars increased during the 20th century, production became cheaper, and today almost every household in Western societies owns at least one car.
The increasing use of cars has had various consequences:
- more demand for fossil fuels: increased drilling for oil on land and at sea,
- demand for larger roads: expansion of highways, parking lots, etc.,
- consequences: growing destruction of natural habitats and resources,
- increasing mobility: the former luxury of owning a car has become a must; some jobs cannot be done without a car, one is expected to own a car; public transport systems aim to meet general mobility needs,
- cars produce exhaust fumes, dramatically increasing the amount of carbon dioxide and other climate-changing fumes released into the atmosphere.

Once limited to the so-called developed countries, cars are now in increasing demand in developing countries such as India and China. This development will further increase the amount of atmospheric pollution and have an effect on the global climate. Recently a lot of research has been done in the field of hybrid and electric mobility.

Of course, the invention of the car has improved our lives in numerous ways by making transport and mobility easier and cheaper. The example of the car represents a simple model of how you should view technological developments: always consider their positive as well as negative potential. One such ambivalent area of current scientific research is genetic engineering.

Visions of the Future

Humankind has always dreamed about the future and keeps seeking to create the world it wants to live in. People have always aimed at new challenges and tried out new ideas. In literature, these attempts have been formulated in utopias and dystopias, positive and negative visions of the future. Technological innovation has fuelled the creation of dystopian visions of societies, often in the form of a science fiction novel. Prominent examples are Huxley's *Brave New World*, Orwell's *Nineteen Eighty-Four* and Ishiguro's *Never Let Me Go*. However, broadly dystopian ideas are also present in popular fiction like *The Hunger Games* by the American novelist Suzanne Collins.
Meanwhile, some social movements are still actively seeking new and positive ways of living with each other, sharing space, goods and skills in community projects and living. In the aging societies of the West, this is proving very important. Increasingly, ideas like urban gardening might also change the city space to create a more liveable environment.

Artificial Intelligence (AI)

Definition

- Alan Turing (1950): "Can machines think?"
  → **Turing Test** ("imitation game"): a human interrogator tries to distinguish between a computer text and a human text
- "It is the science and engineering of making intelligent machines, especially intelligent computer programs. It is related to the similar task of using computers to understand human intelligence, but AI does not have to confine itself to methods that are biologically observable." (John McCarthy, 2004)
- More differentiated approach (cf. Stuart Russel & Peter Norvig, 2016):
  Human approach:
  - systems that think like humans
  - systems that act like humans

  Ideal approach:
  - systems that think rationally
  - systems that act rationally

  Turing's definition would have fallen under the category of "systems that act like humans".
- In its most basic shape, artificial intelligence is a field which employs computer science and datasets to solve problems.

Milestones

- 1950: Alan Turing proposes the answer to the question "Can machines think?" and introduces the Turing Test to determine if a computer can demonstrate the same intelligence as a human.
- 1956: John McCarthy coins the term "artificial intelligence".
- 1956: Logic Theorist, the first-ever running AI software program
- 1967: first computer based on a neural network that "learned" though trial and error
- 1980s: Neural networks training themselves by means of a backpropagation algorithm become widely used.
- 1997: IBM's "Deep Blue" beats world chess champion Garry Kasparov in a chess match (and a rematch).
- 2015: Supercomputer can identify and categorise images with a higher rate of accuracy than the average human.
- 2023: Large language models (LLMs) such as ChatGPT create an enormous change in the world of communication.

Types of artificial intelligence—weak AI vs. strong AI

- **Weak AI** (also: Narrow AI) is AI that is trained and aimed at performing precisely delineated tasks. Current every-day applications are virtual assistants such as Siri and Alexa, and autonomous vehicles.
- **Strong AI** (also: General AI) is a theoretical form of AI where a machine would have an intelligence equal to or even surpassing humans. It would have consciousness, the ability to solve problems, learn and plan for the future. Strong AI is still entirely theoretical with no practical examples in use today, but research is being done on it. Fictional examples: 3-CPO and R2-D2 in the *Star Wars* franchise, HAL in *2001: A Space Odyssey*, Ava in *Ex Machina* and Samantha in *Her*.

Deep learning vs machine learning

- Deep learning and machine learning are sub-fields of AI.
  Deep learning is a sub-field of machine learning.
- Classic machine learning needs human intervention to process data and "learn", whereas deep learning does not.
- **Generative AI:** Deep-learning models that can take data and "learn" to generate statistically probable outputs. Generative models have been used for years in statistics to analyse numerical data. Their use has recently been extended to images, speech and other complex data types (e.g. ChatGPT, DALL·E).

Applications

- There are numerous, real-world applications of AI systems today. Below are some of the most common uses:
  - **speech recognition:** speech to text, voice search; known from many mobile devices and texting
  - **customer service:** virtual online agents answer frequently asked questions (FAQs); examples: messaging apps, virtual assistants and voice assistants

  - **computer vision:** enables computers and systems to gather relevant information from visual input such as videos and images and perform specific functions based on these inputs; more than just image recognition; examples: photo tagging in social media, radiology imaging in healthcare and self-driving cars
  - **recommendation engines:** based on their consumption behaviour, AI can make relevant recommendations to customers that buy online

Ethical Issues

benefits

- "solve intelligence, and then use that to solve everything else" (Demis Hassabis, Google)
- numerous applications (see above)

risks

- large collection of data
  - concerns about privacy
  - concerns about copyright
  - concerns about misinformation (fake news; images, audio, video and text that are indistinguishable from real photographs, recordings, films or human writing), conspiracy theories and extreme partisan content
  - concerns about "artificial stupidity" (AI mistakes)
  - lack of transparency (AI application may be so complex that nobody knows how it works anymore)
- technological unemployment
- algorithmic bias (see below)
- military AI (e. g. used by US and Israeli military to identify human targets)
- decision making (purely statistical, may be unethical, e. g. in autonomous driving: who to hit in an accident)
- existential risk, irreversible loss of control

Biases in AI systems

- AI systems will be biased if they learn from biased data. Developers may not be aware that the bias exists.
- **Language bias:** Current LLMs are mostly trained on English-language data, thus they may present western views as true.
- **Gender bias:** LLMs may reinforce gender stereotypes, assigning roles and characteristics based on traditional gender norms.
- **Racial bias:** There is often a racial bias with regard to e. g. violence. AI systems may also have a higher fail rate in identifying key factors in minority groups, e. g. AI diagnostic systems in healthcare have a lower accuracy for Black patients than for white patients.
- **Stereotyping:** Apart from gender and race, AI can reinforce stereotypes, including those based on age, nationality, religion or occupation. This can lead to unfair generalisation or caricature of groups of people, which may even be harmful or derogatory.

- Bias and discrimination may remain undetected because developers are mainly white and male: among AI engineers, about 4 % are Black and 20 % are women.

The Media

Keyword
The Media: a collective term that denotes means of mass communication, particularly referring to newspapers, radio, TV and the internet. Communication through these media is characterised by the fact that it is public, reaches a broad audience, is not bound to a particular place and time and that it is largely unilateral, i. e. the audience does not normally interact with the sender of the messages it has received.

In the following chapter diverse aspects of the media will be presented. The central issues are:
- various forms of the the media and their prime functions
- the concept of "media literacy"
- the role of the media in contemporary society
- advertising as an example of a text that makes an appeal to the reader.

Types of Media

Newspapers

- printed publications that appear regularly (most commonly daily or weekly) and that are issued in an inexpensive form, affordable for a broad audience
- normally cover a wide range of up-to-date topics from politics, economics and sport to culture and entertainment, also featuring a certain amount of advertising
- The first newspapers were published in the early 17th century.
- Due to the growing availability of information on the internet, however, the number of printed newspapers has been steadily decreasing.
- One can distinguish between the so-called **quality press**, i. e. newspapers in which well-researched information is offered at a high level of credibility (e. g. *The Times*, *The Guardian*) and the **tabloids** (Am. **yellow press**), in which sensational stories are combined with eye-catching headlines and images (e. g. *The Sun*, *The Daily Mirror*).

Radio

- invented in the late 19th century, originally referred to as "the wireless"
- from the 1920s onwards, more and more radio stations started broadcasting and radios became affordable for an ever growing audience
- "Golden Age" of radio: between the 1930s and the mid-1950s, when radio programmes included not only music, news and advertisements but also shows and radio plays
- with the advent of television, the popularity of the radio declined

TV

- first introduced to the general public in the late 1930s
- did not become widely available and popular until after World War II
- originally based on a limited number of state-owned broadcasting stations
- the number of private channels, funded either by advertising or by subscriptions, has increased in the last few decades
- most recently, streaming television has enjoyed a growing audience

Advertising

- Advertising is a vital financial aspect of all forms of the media.
- It is a form of communication that makes an appeal to the reader, viewer or listener and as such tries to persuade them to carry out an action (to buy the advertised product or to use the advertised service).
- With the advent of the "new media" (primarily the internet), new advertising opportunities opened up for companies. Nowadays, online advertising – e.g. in the form of pop-ups, banners and influencers – is a growing market, whereas the rate of advertising in the traditional media has been steadily declined.
- One way of describing the effects which a particular ad might have on the receiver is the **"AIDA"** principle: the ad should first catch **A**ttention, then arouse **I**nterest, create a **D**esire for the advertised product or service and finally lead to **A**ction, i.e. the purchase of that particular product.
- Advertising is often criticised for promoting ideal images of people, thereby putting consumers under psychological pressure by making them feel inadequate.

The internet

- term derives from the longer "interconnected networks"
- system of computer networks which enables users to publicise and access information on a global scale
- originally developed to allow some American universities to exchange data quickly
- was made accessible to a broad public and commercialised in the 1990s
- by 2022, the number of internet users worldwide had risen to 5.3 billion, i.e. 65 % of the global population[1]
- in many areas, the internet is mostly accessed via mobile phone
- **advantages**, e.g.
  - makes it possible to communicate with people over long distances in real time, thereby turning the world into a **"global village"**
  - easy access to almost every kind of information imaginable
- **disadvantages**, e.g.
  - misinformation ("fake news") is equally easy to distribute**r**
  - the rate of **criminal activities** via the internet (from the violation of privacy to internet fraud) has been steadily rising

[1] Source: https://www.statista.com/statistics/273018/number-of-internet-users-worldwide (accessed on 1 April 2024)

- some countries try to suppress information that collides with their own ideologies, employing **censorship** (e.g. China)

The mass media fulfil a number of **functions**. Originally, its primary use was the transmission of **information** to the broadest possible audience, which made the media a vital means of **education**. Public **entertainment** soon came to be seen as equally **important**. With the advent and ever-growing popularity of online social networks such as Facebook, Instagram and X (formerly „Twitter“), forging and maintaining **social relations** independently of time and place has also become a crucial function.

Keyword
Media literacy: This term refers to the ability of a recipient to analyse and evaluate the messages they receive through the media. Thus, one is expected to question the information one is given, e.g. by asking who is the actual creator/sender of the message, what is their aim in sending this message, how does the message try to catch my attention, what is the point of view presented in the message? Ultimately, media literacy is also vital in producing one's own messages.

The Influence of the Media on Society and Personal Life

- Being **the prime source of information**, the media can influence a whole society's opinion about certain topics.
- With the help of more or less open forms of **censorship**, public opinion can be controlled; this was most famously fictionalised by George Orwell in his novel *Nineteen Eighty-Four*, in which a totalitarian regime represses its people by – amongst other means – **controlling** and **manipulating** the **information** communicated through the media.
- It is still being debated whether **images of violence** presented on **TV** and in **computer games** facilitate adolescent violence.
- In consumer societies, **advertisements** determine to a high degree what is considered to be a desirable lifestyle. This can be seen as a form of **indoctrination** and **social control**.

INFO "Fake news"

"Fake news" refers to false stories appearing as genuine news items on the internet or other media. It is usually created to influence political opinion or as a joke or provocation. Recently, fake news has been used to manipulate public opinion and to affect election results.

Keyword

Social Networking Services (SNS): Social networking services such as Facebook, Instagram and X are online platforms that enable users to build or maintain social and business relationships via a wide variety of communication tools. Users usually create individual profiles and share experiences and opinions by posting texts, photos and videos. These virtual communities allow them to be connected regardless of where they live and across boundaries such as social status, profession, age and gender. Among the benefits of these platforms can be listed the strengthening of interpersonal relationships, increased freedom of self-expression and sense of belonging as well as simplifying grassroots organisation.
In the past few years, however, social networks, in particular Facebook, have come under increased scrutiny. Firstly, the business models of the companies are often based not only on selling advertising space but also their users' data for marketing purposes. In 2018, an investigation uncovered that the British firm Cambridge Analytica had illegally harvested the personal data of millions of Facebook users and resold it for political advertising, potentially even the Brexit vote and Donald Trump's 2016 presidential campaign. Facebook has also become the battleground for systematically disseminating misinformation, often used by lobbying groups and intelligence agencies to try and manipulate elections abroad. In September 2021, leaked documents revealed that Facebook Inc. (now Meta Platforms) was fully aware of the negative impact that its platforms had on the health of its teenage users as well as their product's propensity to help spread misinformation.

Keyword

X: X, formerly known as "Twitter", is a social media platform that allows users to post and interact with short messages. Users can follow other accounts to see their posts in their feed and can also use hashtags to categorise their own posts and make them more discoverable to other users. X's popularity is based on allowing users to share their thoughts in real-time and provides a platform for celebrities, politicians and other public figures to connect with their fans and followers. Additionally, X has been used extensively for political activism and social movements, particularly through the use of hashtags to organise and mobilise supporters around specific causes. One of the most notable examples of political hashtag activism on X is the #BlackLivesMatter movement. The hashtag was used to draw attention to issues of police brutality and systemic racism and helped spark a broader conversation around race and social justice. X has also had a significant impact on language, with its 280-character limit and emphasis on brevity and conciseness encouraging users to develop new forms of expression and linguistic shortcuts. However, the platform has also been criticised for contributing to the spread of misinformation and hate speech as well as for its role in amplifying and normalising extremist views and ideologies.

NOTE: The play as well as its analysis here refer to X by its previous name, "Twitter", as well as to its posts as "tweets".

Jasmine Lee-Jones, *seven methods of killing kylie jenner* (gA, eA)

A note on the author

Jasmine Lee-Jones (born 1998 in North London) is a writer and actor of Jamaican heritage whose drama "seven methods of killing kylie jenner" (2019) has been honoured with various prizes, among them the "Evening Standard Award for Most Promising Playwright". She has kept any personal information private, and despite incorporating the power of social media strongly into her works, she deleted her own accounts at the end of 2020, claiming that – while being a powerful tool to finally enable marginalised people to being heard – these media also distorted her image, portraying somebody she did not consider herself to be in real life.

Synopsis

The play's plot is initiated when Forbes magazine declares Kylie Jenner the world's first self-made billionaire. This tweet infuriates @INCOGNEGRO, a Twitter user who argues that Kylie's success is not her own doing since she was born into a wealthy family. As a result, @INCOGNEGRO tweets a series of messages suggesting seven ways to kill Jenner. Each of these tweets is connected to an explanation that contrasts Jenner's privilege with the disadvantages of Black people, particularly Black women. The tweets trigger a Twitter storm that ranges from fascination to outrage and ultimately calls for violence, abuse and doxing. After the identity of Cleo – the person behind @INCOGNEGRO – has been revealed, she uses the medium for a long monologue in which she unfolds her feelings, thereby causing the Twittersphere to explode. In the "IRL" passages, her friend Kara tries to persuade Cleo to stop tweeting. The dialogue between the two women focuses on the discrimination against Black women in combination with the dynamics of misogyny, abuse, colourism, gender, sexual orientation and the hurt inflicted by the two women upon one another in the past.

Analysis

The play explores themes of racism, colourism, appropriation, queerness and social media culture through the characters of Cleo and Kara, two Black women. It uses a variety of techniques, including flashbacks and multiple timelines, to tell its story.

The play initially introduces the setting, focusing on the most important headlines of the past two years, as the audience needs to understand the topicality of what is about to come. It then opens with Kara and Cleo dragging and burying something that looks like a body. This scene is a teaser to the post-mortem of the play, creating a sense of dread, mystery and suspense.

The play then flashes a couple of hours backwards in time and immediately introduces its central conflict. Cleo's catalyst is a Forbes tweet that triggers her anger as Kylie Jenner comes from a rich family and has made more by appropriating Black features and turning them into beauty standards for white women, while Black women continue to be considered ugly and are discriminated against because of them. Cleo considers this a form of theft and vents her frustration.

Cleo's anger is complex and multifaceted. She is angry at Jenner but also at the system that not only allows the influencer to profit while Black women are still discriminated against but inherently also perpetuates systematic racism and discrimination. Therefore, Cleo seems to suggest, Jenner should suffer the same negative experiences as Black people have since she already cashes in on their appropriation. Cleo then explores seven methods to kill Jenner, each one being a commentary on the ways in which Black bodies are used, abused and appropriated by white people.

The **1st method** involves Jenner dying from her own lip fillers' poison. Cleo sees this as a form of poetic justice, as full lips are considered beautiful in white women and hideous in Black women. The **2nd method** is a play on "shooting". Instead of Jenner's photo shoots, Cleo alludes to police brutality and the shooting of predominantly Black victims. The **3rd method** involves having Jenner drown in the sea, like thousands of refugees do, instead of in her wealth and images of herself. The **4th method** is perhaps the most provocative. Cleo proposes skinning Jenner's body so she can adorn herself with it, just like white people do with Black features. The **5th method** involves sacrificing Jenner, as if burnt by the flames pinned underneath Jenner's instagram posts declaring her appropriated Black features hot and attractive. In the **6th method,** Cleo wants Kylie Jenner shamed to death the same way Black people have been throughout history, e.g. in minstrel and "freak" shows but also through constant discrimination, slurs, harassment and violence. The **7th** and final **method**, death by displacement, does not reference Kylie Jenner any more but instead tells Saartje Baartman's story and the suffering she had to endure – urging the audience to remember her story as an epitome of colonial exploitation and racism.

The Twittersphere's reactions evolve from initial amusement to racist behaviour and ultimately calls for violence. Cleo explains that said Forbes tweet not only promotes capitalism, cultural appropriation and exploitation but also the ongoing dehumanisation of Black women, while elevating and idolising white women within oppressive white structures. As Cleo points out, these harmful beliefs have been present for centuries and continue to perpetuate inequality and harm towards marginalised groups, especially Black people.

Additionally, the play touches on the issue of colourism ("shadeism"), e.g. when Cleo claims that her abuse was greater than Kara's due to her darker skin tone or when the two women speak about being fetishised. She also challenges the image of Martin Luther King Jr., stating that he was just as problematic as every other man she has known. On top of this, the play explores trials of friendship, relationships between homo- and heterosexuals, how social media can amplify hate speech and how Black women are often the target of online harassment.

The play's language draws heavily on internet culture, including acronyms and Jamaican patois, suggesting the characters' cultural background. Its form is defined by an increasing blend of virtual and real spaces, ultimately even breaking the fourth wall. Most importantly, it highlights the complexity of being a Black woman in a world that appropriates and profits from their culture while also fetishising, marginalising and dehumanising them.

Topics:

- (ethnic) identity
- discrimination
- sexual diversity
- influence of social media
- role(s) of women

The Digital Revolution

While the Industrial Revolution changed the way people worked and lived together, the so-called Digital Revolution has done the same by digitalising large aspects of the formerly analogue world. This process started soon after WW II and increasingly accelerated from the moment when data storage facilities became smaller and smaller and when wireless technologies were introduced.

The year 2002 is generally seen as a turning point because since then more data has been stored in a digital than in an analogue way. It was the invention and worldwide accessibility of the internet that made this process possible. Today, more than half the world's population is continuously online, thanks to the usage of computers and smartphones. This interconnectivity means that everyone who is connected to the internet has the world's information at their fingertips and can communicate worldwide.

The notion of privacy will have to be closely monitored, as more and more people give personal data to a few big companies such as Apple, Google or Amazon. Physically tracking or locating a person has become easy, as smartphones continuously show their position through GPS and wireless technologies.

Digitisation has entered all areas of life: communication, homes, banking, work and industry. The Internet of Things (IoT) – as found in a smart home – means that objects and machines are online and have hardware with sensors that interconnect them and communicate autonomously – i. e. without human interference. The IoT is not without hazards, so far as privacy, data storage and security are concerned. In fact, cybersecurity is an increasingly important issue. People have made themselves dependent on the exchange and storage of data, and hacking into data systems, whether personal, corporate or governmental, has become a real threat to modern society.

Glossary – Science and Technology

biodegradable	biologisch abbaubar
carbon dioxide (CO2)	Kohlendioxid
climate change	Klimawandel
deforestation	Waldrodung

drought	Dürreperiode
energy-efficient	Energie sparend
flooding	Überflutung
fossil fuels	fossile (endliche) Brennstoffe (z. B. Öl)
fuel rod	Brennstab (im Kernkraftwerk)
genetic engineering	Gentechnik, -manipulation
(exhaust) fumes	Abgase
global warming	globale Erwärmung
greenhouse effect	Treibhauseffekt
half-life	Halbwertzeit (die Zeit, die es dauert, bis ein radioaktives Material die Hälfte seiner Strahlkraft einbüßt; bis zu mehreren Mio. Jahren)
incineration	Verbrennung
landfill	Mülldeponie
methane	Methan
non-renewable energy	nicht erneuerbare Energien (Öl, Kohle, Gas)
oil spillage/spill/pollution	Ölverschmutzung/-pest
power station, power plant	Kraftwerk
precipitation	Niederschlag
raw materials, natural resources	Rohstoffe, natürliche Rohstoffe
renewable energy	regenerative (erneuerbare) Energien
soil	Boden, Erde
subsidies	Subventionen
to contaminate	etw. vergiften, verseuchen
to emit, emission	ausstoßen/emittieren, Ausstoß/Abstrahlung
to evaporate, evaporation	verdunsten, Verdunstung
to have an adverse effect	eine nachteilige Wirkung auf etwas haben
to reprocess something	etwas wiederaufbereiten
water supply	Wasserversorgung
(radioactive, chemical, ...) waste	(radioaktiver, chemischer, ...) Abfall

Glossary – Artificial Intelligence

algorithm	Algorithmus
artificial intelligence (AI)	künstliche Intelligenz (KI)
autonomous driving	autonomes Fahren, Selbstfahren
bias	Verzerrung; unproportionale Gewichtung eines Faktors zu (Un-)Gunsten einer Person, Sache oder Idee

big data	große Datenmengen bzw. Firmen/Technologien, die damit arbeiten
computer vision	Computer Vision (Wissenschaft, wie von Kameras erfasste Bilder analysiert und weiterverarbeitet werden können)
data mining	Data-Mining (statistische Auswertung großer Datenmengen hinsichtlich möglicher Trends und Muster)
deep learning	mehrschichtiges/tiefes Lernen (Form des maschinellen Lernens neuronaler Netzwerke)
deepfake	Deepfake (Medieninhalte wie Fotos, Videos und Tonaufnahmen, die auf kaum feststellbare Weise digital erstellt oder manipuliert wurden)
facial recognition	Gesichtserkennung
generate	generieren
LLM, large language model	großes Sprachmodel (künstliches neuronales Netzwerk, das Sprache generieren kann und durch (halb-)autonom überwachtes Training lernt
machine learning	maschinelles Lernen
Natural Language Processing	natürliche Sprachverarbeitung
neural networks	neuronale Netzwerke
optimisation	Optimierung
prediction	Vorhersage
robotics	Robotik
test data	Testdaten
training data	Trainingsdaten

Glossary – The Media

access	Zugang/Zugriff
censorship	(politische) Zensur
credibility	Glaubwürdigkeit
indoctrination	Indoktrination / ideologische Beeinflussung
internet fraud	Internetbetrug
literacy	Lese- und Schreibfähigkeit
primary function	Hauptfunktion
public	öffentlich/Öffentlichkeit
spread	Ausbreitung
unilateral	einseitig

William Shakespeare (erhöhtes Anforderungsniveau)

The World that Made Him: The Elizabethan Age

Keyword
The Elizabethan Age: named after Queen Elizabeth I, born 1533, crowned 1558, died 1603 (reign of 45 years)

Politics and Economics

- England emerged as a world power; exploration of New World (Drake, Raleigh)
- international trade → the rise of capitalism
- strongest naval force (defeat of the Spanish Armada in 1588)
- internal problems: constant clash between Catholics and Protestants
- establishment of a Protestant Church with Elizabeth as head of the Church of England

Culture

Keyword
The Golden Age: term used for the Renaissance in Britain at the time of Elizabeth I
- freedom of spirit → imagination
- Greek and Roman thought
- domestic study of the Bible, widely read and heard
- opened new worlds of history and poetry, stimulated English culture
- cultural flowering: theatre, music, poetry, art, architecture
- writers: William Shakespeare, Christopher Marlowe, Edmund Spenser
- architect: Inigo Jones (introduced Italianate architecture to England)
- composers: Thomas Tallis, William Byrd

The era was dominated by contrast: life for ordinary people could be hard, but economic growth also meant better conditions for many.
negative aspects:
- harsh criminal laws (e.g. whipping and hanging for minor offences)
- illiteracy
- short life-expectancy
- no rights for women

positive aspects:
- public provision for the poor (possible because of economic growth)
- few beggars

The Elizabethan World Picture

Elizabethans still saw the Earth as the centre of the universe (geocentric world view) and therefore as the nucleus around which everything else revolved.
The guiding principle of this world view was universal order, which formed two ideas that crucially shaped Elizabethan society and thought: the **Great Chain of Being** and the **correspondence of microcosm and macrocosm**. Their world view was this a fixed and highly constructed one, deeply rooted in Christianity and concepts such as divine providence.

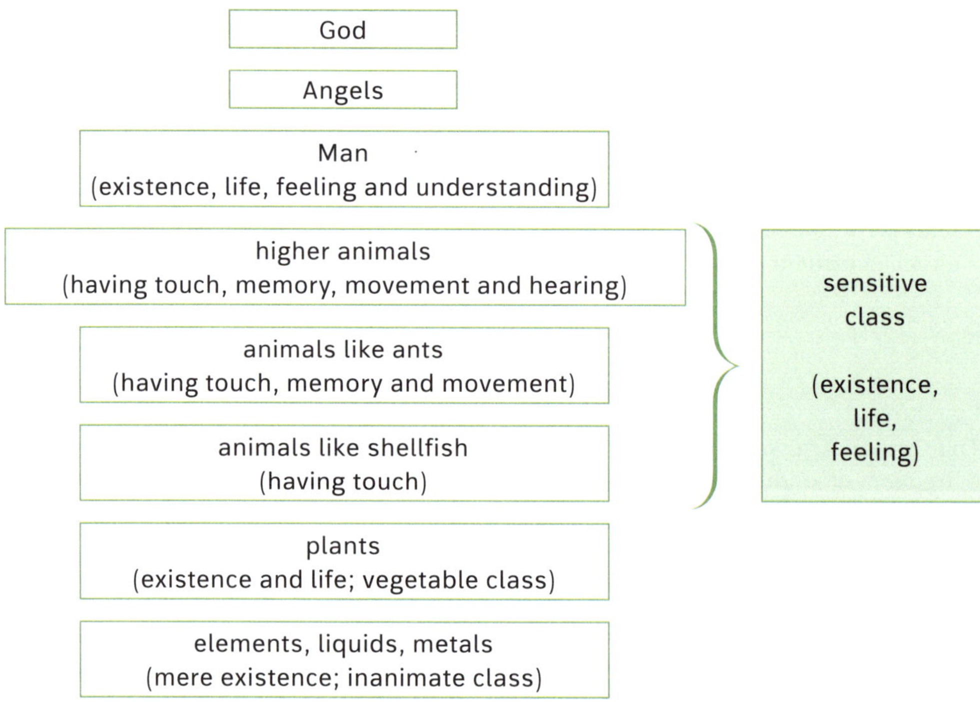

The Great Chain of Being

To Elizabethans, everything that existed was organised in a cosmic order. In this system, everything and everyone has a designated place, as if on a very large ladder: the Great Chain of Being. This hierarchy was based on importance, which in turn was determined by the relative proportion of spirit and matter: the more spirit something or someone had, the higher was its/their place in the chain. At the top of this system sat God, followed by angels, humans, animals, plants and minerals. Each part of the chain was in turn hierarchically structured from most to least important. Each link also had a 'primate' - in the human chain, for instance, this was the king. Being higher in the chain meant natural or God-given authority to rule over those beneath one's position.
As long as all the elements stay in their designated place, the hierarchy and therefore the order of being remain intact. However, if this order is disturbed, the chain is broken

and chaos reigns. The attempt to changing one's place on the chain is therefore doomed. Romeo and Juliet, the "pair of star-cross'd lovers" (Prologue), are such a case. The couple falls in love across social boundaries and is bound to fail. Therefore, any attack on the balance has to be rectified - as in a disease of the body - to restore the original balance of the universe.

The corresponding planes

Different segments of the chain are reflected in other segments. This means there is universal interdependence, i. e. there are correspondences.

Corresponding planes

- divine and angelic
- universe (macrocosm)
- commonwealth / body politic
- man (microcosm)
- lower creation (animals, plants, ...)

The planes were connected by an immense network of correspondences.

> **Keyword**
>
> **Correspondences:** Since the planes were interconnected with each other, order and disorder in one plane had the same repercussions in the other planes as well. For instance, the sun governs the other planets as the father rules his children. Elizabethan literature abounds with examples of this idea: for example, King Lear's madness is mirrored in the thunderstorm he walks in, and on the night Macbeth murders the king, horses are seen eating one another. In the same sense, debates between king and council in the body politic are mirrored in the microcosm as commotions in a person's mind.

Elements and humours

Since the human being was seen as a microcosm (literally, a "little world"; cf. John Donne: "I am a little world made cunningly / Of elements"), it reflected the structure of the world as a whole, the macrocosm. The world was composed of four "elements" (earth, water, air, fire), the qualities of which were based on the notions of hot and cold, dry and moist.

Correspondingly, the human body was composed of four substances called "humours", with characteristics corresponding to the four elements. Imbalance among the humours, i. e. when they did not exist in proper proportion to each other, caused illness.

element	humour	common quality
earth	melancholy	cold and dry
water	phlegm	cold and moist
air	blood	hot and moist
fire	choler	hot and dry

Elizabethan Theatre

Theatres in Elizabethan London were venues of mass entertainment.

Performing Shakespeare

Like most companies, Shakespeare and his men performed in theatres situated outside the City of London, on the Southern banks of the River Thames. The quarter was known for its many pubs and brothels. Theatres also acted as venues for bear-baiting, a brutal entertainment popular with Elizabethan in which a bear is tied to a stake and killed by dogs.

Because audiences, who were allowed to smoke, drink and eat in the theatre, were often rowdy, this entertainment was frowned upon by religious people as well as those in power. Common complaints included the accusation that
- the theatre was disorderly,
- the immoral characters on stage corrupted the audience, particularly young people,
- the stories told were depraved and primitive instead of religiously inspiring,
- it kept people away from work and prayer,
- it attracted criminals, for example pickpockets.

After touring through different locations like the Rose Theatre, Shakespeare had his own playhouse built in 1599, the *Globe Theatre*. It is a round, wooden structure with the stage protruding into the audience. Performances were held in the middle of the day, as the Globe had no artificial lighting. Elizabethan theatre also used very few props; instead, actors created the setting by describing it ("word scenery"). They did, however, wear highly elaborate costumes to embellish the characters they were portraying. Women were not allowed on stage, as it was deemed inappropriate for them by the fiercely religious government. Instead, their roles were acted by young men. This fact was frequently exploited by Shakespeare in comedies such as *Twelfth Night,* in which a man played a woman disguising herself as a man.
The Elizabethan theatre was attended by people from all social ranks: Poorer people stood in the space right in front of the stage ("pit"), while those who could afford it took a seat in the circle around the stage. The distance between the actors and the audience was minimal and spectators often interacted with the actors on stage. This had a strong influence on how Shakespeare wrote his plays as there are comic scenes that are purely written to entertain the masses as well as monologues by the protagonists explaining their thoughts and decisions.

Elizabethan Poetry

Sonnets

Keyword

Sonnet form: originally from Italy, 14th century
Sonnets were made popular by Francesco Petrarca (in English: Petrarch).
The fashion of sonnet writing spread to France and England.

Important Elizabethan sonnet writers:
- Thomas Wyatt (introduced sonnets to England, translations from Petrarch)
- Sir Philipp Sidney
- Edmund Spenser
- John Donne
- William Shakespeare

The Italian (Petrarchan) sonnet

octave/octet		turn	sestet	
a b b a	a b b a		c d e	c d e
quatrain	quatrain	turn	tercet	tercet

Characteristics of the sonnet
- addressed to a beloved
- 14 lines
- clearly defined rhyme scheme (the most common is given above)
- divided into an octet and a sestet
- turn after the octave

The turn after the octave is a shift in thought or feeling, often indicated by "but" or "yet". Variations in the rhyme scheme within the conventional structure are justified by the function they serve.

The English (Shakespearean) sonnet

octave/octet		turn	sestet		
a b b a	c d c d		e f e f		g g
quatrain	quatrain	turn	quatrain	turn	couplet

The turn in the English sonnet occurs after the third quatrain. Ideally there should be "three turns of the screw" in the three quatrains, before the point is driven home in the couplet. The couplet therefore offers a conclusion or a summary. However, one should still be aware that there can be the traditional turn after the octave.

Shakespeare's sonnets

- Shakespeare wrote 154 sonnets.
- Sonnets 1 to 126 are addressed to a young man.
- Sonnets 127 to 154 are addressed to a "dark lady".

Main themes: love, beauty, transience, old age, death

The **basic metre** is iambic pentameter, but Shakespeare does not use it slavishly. Metre is used functionally, e. g.
- regular metre: harmony, peace, tranquillity, balance, stability, etc.
- irregular metre: disharmony, confusion, parody

Shakespeare's Plays

The universal appeal

By 1592 William Shakespeare had managed to establish his reputation as a playwright in London. Due to his success, other writers envied him enormously.
A remarkable feature of Shakespeare's time is the complete lack of what we know today as copyright regulations. Authors could not protect their work from being adapted freely or even copied as a whole. Shakespeare himself was engaged in this process of "play-doctoring", modifying existing plays for his acting company. As a consequence, his authorship of a number of plays has been questioned.
From about 1595, however, Shakespeare no longer cooperated with other authors and became the respected playwright with the reputation he has had until today.
The fascination of his plays has not been lost over the more than four centuries since their first appearance. It can at least partly be attributed to the universal appeal of the topics he deals with. Love, happiness, envy, jealousy, treachery, humour – all of these profoundly human emotions and forms of behaviour enter easily into every spectator's heart.
Unfortunately, the dating of the plays, and therefore the order in which they were written, is difficult to determine. Shakespeare did not issue a printed collection of his dramatic works since no copyright existed. *Richard II*, however, appeared in six printed editions from 1597 to 1623, and *Romeo and Juliet* had five printed editions in the same time span. If all the plays had been printed and published in Shakespeare's lifetime, they would have been used by countless actors and authors. As a result, only an approximate order can be suggested. Shakespeare's opus can thus be broadly divided into four periods:

Timeline

Period 1 (1590–1595): The first period is clearly the one that least shows Shakespeare's literary genius. The style and imagery of the plays are rather simple. Although he does use rhyme, there is also a lot of prose. It is a time of experimentation with the genre.
Period 2 (1595–1600): During this period, which is marked by improved characterisation and style, Shakespeare wrote some of his best comedies and history plays, among which are *Henry IV* and *Henry V*. He also wrote his sonnets during this period.

Period 3 (1600–1608): Many scholars consider this to be the most important period. Shakespeare wrote great tragedies like *Hamlet* and the so-called "problem plays".
Period 4 (1608–1613): In this period Shakespeare wrote his romances, which deal with the topic of losing and regaining happiness. The plots are rather melodramatic, but they also display an idyllic atmosphere. Shakespeare's last play was *The Tempest*.

Period	Comedies	Tragedies	History plays
1590–1595	*The Comedy of Errors* *The Taming of the Shrew* *Two Gentlemen of Verona* *Love's Labour's Lost*	*Titus Andronicus*	*Henry VI*
1595–1600	*A Midsummer Night's Dream* *The Merchant of Venice* *The Merry Wives of Windsor* *Much Ado About Nothing* *As You Like It* *Twelfth Night*	*Romeo and Juliet*	*King John* *Richard II* *Henry IV* *Henry V*
1600–1608	*Troilus and Cressida* *Measure for Measure* *All's Well That Ends Well*	*Julius Caesar* *Hamlet* *Othello* *Timon of Athens* *King Lear* *Macbeth* *Antony and Cleopatra* *Coriolanus*	
1608–1613	*Pericles* *Cymbeline* *A Winter's Tale* *The Tempest*		*Henry VIII*

Source: Wilhelm Rotter and Hermann Bendl, *Your Companion to English Literary Texts.* München: Manz, 1991. S. 182 ff. (gekürzt)

Shakespeare's language

The language Shakespeare used is not easy to understand because it differs from the English spoken today. Some words have changed their meaning since the Elizabethan Age, others have been dropped altogether and certain grammatical peculiarities need to be explained. We must also keep in mind that the lines Shakespeare makes his characters speak were intended to be performed on stage. In order to achieve a combined dramatic and artistic effect, he frequently employed blank verse, which is a fixed rhythmical pattern of iambic pentameters, as in this example from *Macbeth:*
Tomorrow and tomorrow and tomorrow

Especially for the less serious or comic characters, however, Shakespeare used prose, whereas verse is spoken by the noble ones.
Shakespeare's impact on the English language has been immense. He coined more than 500 neologisms (new words), and his works are still appreciated worldwide as examples of true linguistic genius. It should be kept in mind, though, that Shakespeare never intended his plays to be read as books; they were to be performed on stage. This is where the beauty of their language is most evident.
The following table lists some examples of characteristic vocabulary and grammar used in Shakespeare's plays:

Shakespeare	**Modern English**
thou	you (used for children, subordinates, ordinary people and friends; Juliet in *Romeo and Juliet*, however, addresses Romeo as "you".)
ye, you	you (plural); form showing respect
thee	you (object form)
thy/thine	your (determiner) / your (determiner before vowels)
mine	my (determiner) before vowels
doth	does
hath	has
thou canst	you can
thou wilt	you will
I have writ	I have written
I would	I wish
Why call you ...?	Why do you call ...?
The guests are come.	The guests have come.

A Midsummer Night's Dream (eA)

William Shakespeare's *A Midsummer Night's Dream* is believed to have been written in about 1595 or 1596. Although the comedy is neither an adaptation of ancient literature nor mythology, many scholars believe that Shakespeare used various sources such as the Roman poet Ovid and his works as an inspiration for the play's plot. The comedy has been one of Shakespeare's most popular plays until today.

Synopsis

In the palace of ancient Athens, Theseus, the Duke of Athens, and Hippolyta, Queen of the Amazons, are preparing for their upcoming wedding when Egeus, an Athenian nobleman, enters with his daughter, Hermia, and her two admirers, Lysander and Demetrius. Egeus seeks Theseus' intervention because Hermia does not accept her father's choice of Demetrius as her husband as she is in love with Lysander. Egeus is outraged and declares that if Hermia disobeys him, she will die. Theseus agrees with Egeus but

offers Hermia another option: spending a celibate life in a nunnery. Hermia must decide until Theseus and Hippolyta's wedding.
Content with neither choice, Lysander and Hermia plan to elope to Lysander's widowed aunt's house. They share their secret with Helena, Hermia's friend who is secretly in love with Demetrius. Helena tells Demetrius of Lysander and Helena's plan to leave Athens, hoping to win his affection. However, Demetrius decides to hurry ahead of the runaway couple and is followed by Helena, who still trusts that he will choose her over Hermia. When Lysander and Hermia run away from Athens, they get lost in the woods.
Meanwhile, Peter Quince, a carpenter, and his group of amateur actors are preparing the play "Pyramus and Thisbe" to perform on Theseus' and Hippolyta's wedding day. Nick Bottom, the weaver, is given the role of Pyramus, while Francis Flute, the bellows-mender, reluctantly agrees to play the female lead, Thisbe.
Elsewhere in the forest, Oberon, King of the Fairies, and his queen, Titania, argue over a young Indian prince given to Titania by the prince's mother. Titania refuses to hand him over to Oberon, who wishes to make him a knight. Seeking revenge on Titania's disobedience, Oberon sends his servant Puck to find a magic plant with juice that makes people fall in love with the first creature they see.
Later, Oberon overhears Helena and Demetrius fighting in the forest, so he tells Puck to use the magic plant to make Demetrius fall in love with Helena. However, Puck mistakes Lysander for Demetrius and uses the juice on him instead. When he is woken up by Helena, Lysander promptly falls in love with her. Hermia then furiously attacks her friend because both Lysander and Demetrius end up being in love with Helena.
The craftsmen's rehearsal in the forest is observed by Puck, who plays a trick on them by transforming Bottom's head into that of a donkey. Puck lures Bottom towards the sleeping Titania, so when Titania wakes, the first creature she sees is Bottom, whom she instantly falls in love with.
In the meantime, Puck and Oberon watch the chaos Puck has created with the four lovers. Eventually, Oberon puts the humans to sleep so that Puck can spread the love juice on Lysander's eyes who wakes up being in love with Hermia. All lovers agree that the night's events must have all been a dream.
Being horrified that she has been in love with an ass, Titania reconciles with Oberon while Bottom's head has been removed so he can return to the city in order to prepare "Pyramus and Thisbe".
Hermia, Helena, Lysander and Demetrius agree to share the wedding of Theseus and Hippolyta, so it becomes a triple celebration. The craftsmen perform their play before the wedding guests, and at the end of the festivities, the fairies appear to bless the sleeping palace. Puck is the only one remaining on stage and suggests that what the audience saw might just have been a dream.

Themes

Dream and Reality

- blurring of reality and dreams consistently throughout the play
- reality is linked to the world of humans, while dreams are represented by the world of fairies
- play starts right away with Hippolyta saying: "Four days will quickly steep themselves in night, / Four nights will quickly dream away the time", which means Shakespeare introduces the pervasiveness of dreams as a major theme
- crossing from Athens into the forest means confusing the lines between dream and reality
- Puck uses magic throughout the play to create a new reality
- having a play withing the play ("Pyramus and Thisbe") contributes to blurring the lines of dream and reality
- mirrored worlds of fairy and human (e.g. ending with a triple marriage) references the corresponding planes
- Puck's epilogue at the end serves as a reminder to the audience to ponder if what they saw was real or imaginary

Love and Marriage

- love and marriage are central themes used by Shakespeare
- four types of love within the play: parental love, forced love, complicated love, romantic love
- play ends with a marriage ceremony for three couples (Theseus – Hippolyta, Hermia – Lysander and Helena – Demetrius)
- marriage is either portrayed as the true fulfilment of romantic love (Hermia and Lysander) or as a pragmatic social institution (Theseus and Hippolyta)
- marriage as an institution represents patriarchal control (Theseus)
- the lovers' marriages only occur due to magical intervention (Puck)
- Titania and Oberon's marriage appears to be unsteady and quarrelsome

Gender Roles

- the plot is set in a patriarchal society in which men decide for women (Egeus controls Hermia and tries to force her to marry Demetrius, even on pain of death)
- male dominance is also displayed in the relationships (e.g. Theseus winning Hippolyta as a prize in battle)
- woman are expected to submit themselves to men; if they don't, they may be humiliated and put in their place again (Oberon makes Titania fall in love with a donkey-headed fool and steals her changeling child)
- the play thus reflects the power dynamic of gender in Elizabethan England
- the women are almost purely defined and define themselves based on their outward appearance (e.g. Helena says to Hermia that Demetrius is in love with her beauty)

Modern Adaptations

Shakespeare's works have often reached the cinema or TV screen. One must differentiate here between straight versions and modern adaptations. Concerning storyline, characters and setting, a straight version keeps close to the original by adopting the text as well as usually retaining historical costumes and stage sets. Moreover, the characters keep their original names.

An adaptation – generally also in some way a modernisation of the play – is typically based on the original but may present storyline, characters and settings in a different manner. It may be put in a contemporary setting or an historical setting later than Shakespeare's time – e.g. Richard Loncraine's 1995 version of *Richard III* od Julie Taymor's 1999 film Titus, with their references to recent European fascism. Likewise, the characters can be transplanted into different social or ethnic groups (as in the 1948 musical *Kiss Me, Kate* or in Baz Luhrmann's 1996 Californian *Romeo and Juliet).* Such modernisations often also aim at developing a market for a potential audience that might be attracted by the lightness of a musical version or an animated cartoon such as *The Lion King* (1994/2019), a loose adaptation of the Hamlet story. In such modern presentations the original poetic language, with its distinct metric scheme, is either not adopted at all or strongly abridged.

Michael Hoffman's 1999 adaptation of *A Midsummer Night's Dream* transplants the drama's action from ancient Athens to Monte Athena, an imaginary Italian village at the turn of the nineteenth century. The original text is kept, but major changes are made to the presentation of the characters: Hippolyta is turned into a Victorian feminist, while Theseus appears as a drained bureaucrat. Also, Bottom is represented more troubled and has less working-class character, as he is wearing a suit instead of working clothes. Hoffman also adds Bottom's wife to the play, who shrewishly watches her husband perform and is disgusted by what she sees. Instead of laughing at Bottom, the audience feels sorry for him. Puck too has undergone major changes in Hoffman's version. He has become a middle-aged socialite with an alcohol problem. Putting emphasis on the nineteenth century, Puck rides through the woods on a stolen bike.

Likewise, Hoffman emphasises Titania's selfishness by insinuating that she wants to keep the Indian boy to offend Oberon rather than because she cares for her dead friend's son. Hermia and Helena are depicted as more hostile than in Shakespeare's original conception: Hoffman even adds a scene in which Hermia and Helena end up wrestling in the mud.

Many critics regard the film as inconsistent, not just because of the different acting styles but also because it loses Shakespeare's rich mythological quality and the magic of Shakespeare's original text becomes a pedestrian version of the original comedy.

Methoden der Textarbeit

Anforderungen von Aufgaben mit Textbezug

Alle im Abitur gestellten Aufgaben sind textbasiert. Sie können auch Bildmaterialien sowie audio-visuelle Materialien umfassen, auf die sprachlich reagiert werden muss. Zu den typischen Aufgabenformaten, die bei fiktionalen sowie nicht-fiktionalen Textvorlagen im freischriftlichen Teil gestellt werden, zählen die Zusammenfassung, die Analyse und der Kommentar bzw. kreative Aufgaben, die unterschiedlich ausgeprägt sein können (vgl. Hinweise zu den Operatoren, S. 95 f.). Neben diesen freischriftlichen Aufgaben werden auch neue Aufgabentypen zur Mediation vorkommen, die im Einleitungskapitel bereits thematisiert wurden. An dieser Stelle erhalten Sie Hinweise zu den üblichen schriftlichen Aufgaben, die weiterhin Teil der Abiturprüfung sind.

Aufgabenarten und Anforderungsbereiche

Aufgabenart	**Anforderungsbereich**
u. a. *summary* Operatoren: *describe, outline, state, summarise*	**I – comprehension, orientation, context** – Wiedergabe der zentralen Aussagen eines Textes – ggf. auch Einordnung des Textes in einen bekannten Kontext, aber üblicherweise ist die Aufgabe rein auf Basis des Ausgangstextes zu beantworten
u. a. *analysis* Operatoren: *analyse, examine, compare, explain, contrast*	**II – analysis** – Anwendung von Fachmethoden: textanalytische Verfahren, exakte Arbeit am sprachlichen Detail, Belegen und Zitieren, problemlösende Argumentation – gezielte Anwendung von Kenntnissen und Wissen – z. B. soziokulturelles Wissen oder Wissen über Sprache
u. a. *comment* Operatoren: *comment, discuss, justify, evaluate* ――――― u. a. *write* Operatoren: *write, imagine, continue, find*	**III – comment, evaluation, re-creation of text, creativity** für die analytisch-interpretierende Aufgabenstellung: – Bewertung der Textvorlage auf Basis der vorher gewonnenen Erkenntnisse, Einordnung des Textes in einen größeren Zusammenhang – persönliche Stellungnahme, eigene Meinung für die produktionsorientierte/kreative Aufgabenstellung: – Umsetzung, Bewertung, Reflexion der Problematik des Ausgangstextes bzw. der Analyse in einem kreativen Kontext: z. B. Perspektivwechsel (Sicht einer Figur) – Füllen von Leerstellen (Weitererzählen, neues Ende) – Textsortenwechsel (Brief an Protagonisten, Leserbrief, Brief an *agony aunt*, Tagebucheintrag, Dialog usw.)

Die Bedeutung der Operatoren[1]

Für die Formulierung der Aufgaben gibt es klare Vorgaben. Verben für die Arbeitsanweisungen (= Operatoren) müssen in ihrer exakten Bedeutung verstanden werden. Eine ungefähre Ahnung, was gefordert ist, reicht keinesfalls aus. Die folgende Operatorenübersicht ist der Website des Ministeriums entnommen. Die mittlere Spalte definiert die genaue Wortbedeutung der Anweisung, die dritte Spalte gibt jeweils Beispiele für eine mögliche Aufgabenstellung.

Operatoren	Definitionen	Beispiele
	(schwerpunktmäßig) Anforderungsbereich I	
describe	give a detailed account of (no line references, no quotes)	Describe the situation presented in the excerpt
outline	give the main features, structure or general principles of sth. (no line references, no quotes)	Outline the writer's views on love and marriage.
state	present the main aspects of sth. briefly and clearly (no line references, no quotes)	State the main developments in the family presented in the text.
summarise, sum up	give a concise account of the main points or ideas of a text, issue or topic (no line references, no quotes)	Summarise the text. Sum up the information given about green energy.
	(schwerpunktmäßig) Anforderungsbereich II	
analyse, examine	describe and explain in detail	Analyse the way(s) in which the atmosphere is created in ... Examine the opposing views on social class held by the two protagonists. Examine how the author characterises ...
compare	show similarities and differences	Compare the opinions on education held by the experts presented in the text.
contrast	emphasise the differences between two or more things	Contrast the authors' ideas of globalisation.
explain	make something clear show causes and effects in a given context	Explain the protagonist's obsession with money.
illustrate	use examples to explain or make sth. clear	Illustrate the way in which school life in Britain differs from that in Germany.

[1] Quelle: Niedersächsisches Kultusministerium, Hamburg, 01.02.2024, https://bildungsportal-niedersachsen.de/fileadmin/4_Allgemeinbildung/Zentrale_Arbeiten/ZA_Allgemein/EN_2024Abi_Operatoren.pdf (abgerufen: 01.04.2024)

(schwerpunktmäßig) Anforderungsbereich III		
assess, evaluate	express a well-founded opinion on the nature or quality of sb./sth.	Assess the appropriateness of the central image of the story. Evaluate the effectiveness of the measures proposed by the author
comment (on)	give your opinion and support your view with evidence or reasons	Comment on the writer's view on gender roles.
discuss	give arguments or reasons for and against, especially to come to a well-founded conclusion	Discuss whether social status determines somebody's future options. Discuss the author's assumption that modern media shape an individual's identity.
justify	present reasons for decisions, positions or conclusions	Justify whether the excerpt should be included in the text collection.
write (+ text type)	produce a text with specific features	Write the ending of the story. Write an interior monologue which reflects the character's view of the situation and his/her feelings. Write your letter to the editor in which you discuss Packer's statement that "the American dream quietly dies".

TIPP zum Punktesammeln

Denken Sie daran, die Zusammenfassung mit einem Einleitungssatz zu beginnen. Er muss den Titel des Textes, den Namen der Autorin / des Autors, das Jahr der Veröffentlichung sowie seine Kernaussage enthalten.

Kreative Aufgaben

Der **Anforderungsbereich III umfasst auch kreative Aufgaben**, für die jedoch keine allgemein verbindlichen Operatoren formuliert werden können. Folgende Aufgabenstellungen sind möglich:

- Write a letter, email to a friend / to the the editor / of complaint / of enquiry … .
- Write a dialogue / the dialogue between X and Y / a script (film, play …) based on / XYZ's diary entry … .
- Write an article (for …) / a report (for …).
- Continue the story … / Find a suitable ending … / Imagine you are XYZ. Continue/Tell the story … from her/his point of view … .

TIPP zum Punktesammeln

Befassen Sie sich intensiv mit den Operatoren. Nur wenn Sie genau wissen, was in der Aufgabenstellung gefordert ist, können Sie eine gute Lösung schreiben.

Grundlegende Hinweise zu den Aufgaben: *summary, analysis, evaluation*

Summary

- Hier soll gezeigt werden, dass der **Textinhalt** verstanden wurde.
- Aus diesem Grund ist es entscheidend, sich von der Textvorlage zu lösen und in eigenen Worten die Hauptinhalte wiederzugeben; das heißt auch, dass weder Passagen übernommen noch Zitate integriert werden dürfen.
- Sprachlich ist Folgendes zu beachten: Bei Zusammenfassungen von **fiktionalen Texten** ist durchgehend das **Präsens** zu verwenden (bei Vorzeitigkeit kann vereinzelt das *present perfect*, bei Nachzeitigkeit das *will future* eingesetzt werden, auf keinen Fall aber eine Vergangenheitsform).
- Bei **nicht-fiktionalen Texten** (z. B. Zeitungsartikel) sind die Hauptaussagen des Autors ebenfalls im Präsens wiederzugeben; nur in Einzelfällen ist es zulässig, für Ereignisse, die in der Vergangenheit tatsächlich stattgefunden haben, das *past tense* zu verwenden.
- **Autorenbezug herstellen:** Besonders bei **nicht-fiktionalen Texten** ist es wichtig, immer klarzustellen, wer welche Aussagen trifft (vor allem bei Zeitungsartikeln, in denen verschiedene Meinungen wiedergegeben werden).
- Je nach Operator kann eine pointierte oder umfassende Zusammenfassung verlangt werden (vgl. Operatoren, S. 95 f.).

Analysis

- Inhaltlich soll hier gezeigt werden, inwiefern die **Form des Textes** dessen Inhalt, Aussageabsicht oder die Haltung des Autors beeinflusst.
- Hier wird verlangt, dass die sprachliche Form des Textes genauer untersucht wird (z. B. im Hinblick auf Sprachebenen, stilistische Mittel, Erzählhaltung etc.) und dass daraus Rückschlüsse auf den Textinhalt bzw. dessen Wirkung gezogen werden; auch hier wird der Text im Präsens verfasst.
- Für eine sprachliche Analyse genügt es nicht, lediglich Stilmittel zu identifizieren und aufzulisten; es kommt vor allem darauf an, deren Wirkungsabsicht zu erkennen.
- Typische Analyseaspekte sind bei **fiktionalen Texten**: *point of view, character analysis, analysis of atmosphere/setting, analysis of tone,* usw.
- Typische Analyseaspekte bei **nicht-fiktionalen Texten** sind: *the use of language/structure, the intention or attitude of the author, the intended effect on the audience (i. e. in speeches), the use of language to achieve the text's aim (e. g. to convince, to provoke, to educate, etc.),* usw.

- **Autorenbezug herstellen:** Es ist sinnvoll klarzustellen, welche Aussageabsicht dem Autor oder dem Erzähler oder einer der Figuren zuzuordnen ist und welche Wirkungsabsicht damit verfolgt wird.

Evaluation

- Inhaltlich soll hier gezeigt werden, dass der Textinhalt reflektiert werden kann.
- Diese kritische Auseinandersetzung mit dem Text kann in unterschiedlicher Form gefordert werden:
  - persönliche *evaluation:* Hier wird eine persönliche Stellungnahme zum Material verlangt, die fachlich-argumentativ begründet sein muss und in der Regel auch Hintergrundwissen erfordert; das reine Feststellen der eigenen Meinung reicht nicht; sie muss erläutert werden und fundiert sein.
  - argumentative *discussion:* Hier wird in der Regel eine sachlich-distanzierte Gegenüberstellung von Vor- und Nachteilen bzw. Pro- und Kontra-Argumenten verlangt, die in einem abwägenden und schlüssigen Fazit enden muss.
  - *evaluation* aus der Sicht einer anderen Person: Unter Umständen ist gefordert, dass Sie sich in die Situation einer Figur des Textes oder einer anderen Person versetzen, um aus deren Vorstellung heraus den Inhalt zu kommentieren; hier kann es sinnvoll sein, auch die Sprache / den Ausdruck dieser Figur zu übernehmen, um den Kommentar authentischer wirken zu lassen (insbesondere bei kreativen Aufgaben wird diese Form häufig verlangt).

Hinweise zu kreativen Aufgaben

Typische Formen

- formeller oder persönlicher Brief, E-Mail
- Tagebucheintrag, *blog entry, interior monologue*
- eine Geschichte erzählen (ein Ende für einen Text verfassen, eine Geschichte zu einem Bild erfinden, die Erzählperspektive wechseln etc.)
- einen Artikel schreiben, einen Leserbrief verfassen
- einen Dialog zwischen zwei Figuren eines fiktionalen Textes entwickeln etc.

Wichtige Aspekte für die Bearbeitung

- Zentral ist, dass Sie auf das Material eingehen und dieses einbeziehen. Unabhängig davon, welche Art von kreativer Produktion verlangt wird, sollte der Ausgangstext oder das Ausgangsbild nie aus den Augen verloren werden.
- Der selbst produzierte Text muss den formalen Anforderungen entsprechen (z. B.: Adresszeile, Anrede, ggf. Betreff, Datum, Abschlussformel bei Briefen) und muss als Brief, E-Mail, Zeitungsartikel o. Ä. klar erkennbar sein.
- Sprachlich sollte der Text den Ton der Vorlage bzw. der Figur treffen: Ein Brief aus der Sicht eines Kindes kann nicht in stilistisch gehobenem Englisch verfasst werden, ein Brief an einen Redakteur nicht mit Umgangssprache durchsetzt sein.
- Hier ist es also entscheidend, dass man das eigene Sprachrepertoire durch ein anderes ersetzen bzw. ergänzen kann, damit der Text glaubwürdig wird.

- Auch hier ist es wichtig, dass der Inhalt nicht zu oberflächlich bleibt (auch ein Tagebucheintrag eines Jugendlichen sollte emotionale Tiefe zeigen und nicht lediglich beschreibend sein).
- Insgesamt sollte der Text so verfasst werden, dass er die Lesenden überzeugt und authentisch wirkt.

Literarische Texte

Narration

Keyword
Narrative texts: Narrative texts can have many forms, among them short story, novel, fairy tale, satire, parable, legend, etc.
The ones that are most relevant for your final exam are the short story and the novel.

When asked to analyse a narrative text, you will have to focus on particular elements that are characteristic of short stories or novels.

Elements of narration

Plot

INFO Elements of a complete plot

exposition → rising action → climax / turning point → falling action → ending

A **plot** need not necessarily be complete (there may be an open ending).
The **sequence** need not necessarily be chronological.
There may be foreshadowing or flashbacks or there may be reverse narration (*umgestelltes Erzählen*).
In particular, an excerpt from a longer text, which is the most common sort of text in the final exam, may not contain all the elements of the plot.
Certain **key events** within the action of a story will increase the tension; they will create suspense, rising to a climax or turning point. After that there will be falling tension or relief.

INFO Tension curve

rising tension → climax or turning point → falling tension or relief

Theme

The **theme** of a story is always abstract. Themes can be love, poverty, racism, childhood, etc. The **subject matter** of a story is the concrete realisation of a theme.

Example:
Two stories may have the same theme: racism. The subject matter of one may be the murder of an African American, of the other the bullying of a Black schoolgirl.

Characters

When asked to characterise a figure from a narrative text, you must be aware of different aspects. There are key questions that can guide you.

Direct characterisation
- What does the narrator say about the character?
- What do other characters say about the character?
- What does the character say about himself/herself?
- How objective is what they say? Be aware of words with negative or positive connotations.

Indirect characterisation
- How does the character act?
- What does the character say?
- What kind of language does he/she use?

It might help to fill in a table with the following headings:

Character's outward appearance	Character's language	Character's actions	What the character says	Other characters' statements (or actions)
...	...	...	...	...

Narrator / Point of view

INFO Narrator

The narrator is either a first-person or a third-person narrator.
The first-person narrator is NOT the author!

limited point of view	**unlimited/omniscient point of view**
first-person narrator	third-person narrator (neutral omniscience, God-like knowledge of all the facts)
third-person narrator (one character's point of view, "selective omniscience")	third-person narrator (several characters' points of view)

Modes of presentation

Narratives can be presented in two ways: the panoramic and the scenic mode. **Panoramic** presentation is used to pay great attention to detail, immersing the reader in the events, while **scenic** presentation condenses the action and can summarise the events of several years into a few lines.

Interior monologue is a particular kind of scenic presentation in which the thoughts and feelings passing through a character's mind are depicted. In **reported thought**, thoughts are presented as reported speech.
This is closely connected with the concepts of **narrated time** and **narrating (or acting) time**:

narrated time longer than narrating time	usually summary of events
narrated time identical with narrating time	e. g. direct speech
narrated time shorter than narrating time	e. g. stream of consciousness, interior monologue, detailed description of a scene, comparable to slow motion in a film

INFO Function of mode of presentation and point of view

A neutral, omniscient narrator, who observes the action and the characters from above and who uses a panoramic mode of presentation, is more detached and thus creates a distance between the reader and the action. On the other hand, a narrator who takes a character's point of view creates immediacy and directly involves the reader in what happens.

Setting

The place and time where the action is set is called the setting. It is especially important for *atmosphere* and *symbolism.*

Atmosphere

Atmosphere is created by means of setting, objects, colours, light and darkness but also by reference to a character's mood or the use of language.

Symbolism

Symbols are part of the setting of the narrative. They are objects, characters or even actions that suggest something beyond their mere meaning. For example, the colour white often symbolises purity.

INFO Established symbols

These are conventional symbols which have long been used and have a certain, traditional significance that everybody knows. Examples of established symbols: a rose, a cross, the colour white.

INFO Created symbols

Something becomes symbolic within a certain context because it is closely connected to an event, a situation or a character.

INFO Symbols

Symbols are NOT metaphors!
Symbols are a factual physical part of the story. Metaphors or similes are figures of speech without an actual representation in the narrated world.

Examples:
She was a rose, so beautiful. → metaphor
She was like a rose, so beautiful. → simile/comparison
They fell in love when they first met in her father's rose garden. → symbol

Language and style

In order to determine the style of a text, it is necessary to examine aspects such as register, diction (choice of words), tone and also sentence structure.

Register is the level of language used in a particular situation. It may be formal, neutral, informal, or vulgar. There may be a lot of slang words, even taboo words as well as technical terms or jargon.

The **tone** may be ironic, sarcastic, sad, humorous, serious, playful, angry, etc., depending on the emotional attitude it expresses. This depends on the choice of words, level of speech, rhythm, sentence length, etc.

Stylistic devices will be considered at length in the chapters on drama and non-fictional texts (p. 108 f. and 113 f.).

Poetry

Poetry focuses on the **aesthetic function** of language; it appeals to the senses. It is to be enjoyed for its beauty, its cleverness, its wit, its impact.
This is achieved by
- the sound of words,
- the rhythm of the words and phrases,
- the choice of words,
- the structure of the sentences,
- the composition of the poem,
- the visual arrangement of words and lines,
- and, above all, by means of imagery.

In your final exams, however, you will be asked not so much to enjoy the poem but to examine its meaning and the effect of the language the speaker uses.

How to proceed

Questions to be asked
- Who is the speaker of the poem?
- Where is the speaker?
- Does the speaker address somebody?
- Does the speaker contemplate something?
- Does the speaker describe something or somebody?
- Does the speaker tell a story?
- Does the speaker explain something?
- Does the speaker argue against or in favour of something?
- What is the speaker's attitude? What is he/she saying?
- How is the poem composed? Is it structured by a rhyme scheme, by the division into stanzas or by some other device?
- Is there a correspondence between the structure of the poem and the structure of the speaker's thoughts?
- What is the significance of the title?
- What words does the speaker use? What do they mean?
- What is the structure of the sentences? Simple? Complex?
- What poetic devices does the speaker use?
- And what is the effect of all this? What is the experience of reading the poem?

In order to understand and describe poetry, you need to be familiar with its most important elements.

Elements of poetry

INFO Speaker and author

The speaker of the poem is NOT the author. Poems may be autobiographical, but you must still refer to the "speaker in the poem".

Poems are composed of **stanzas** and **lines**.
Stanzas may have a certain **rhyme scheme.**

Rhyme

Rhyme schemes

pair rhyme	a a b b
alternate rhyme	a b a b
embracing rhyme	a b b a

Types of rhyme

masculine rhyme (one syllable)	kiss/this
feminine rhyme (two syllables)	dreary/weary
true rhyme	kiss/this, dreary/weary
slant rhyme assonance (same vowel) consonance (same consonant)	 comb/coat hope/heap

Lines and rhythm

Lines may have a certain rhythm. The smallest unit that determines rhythm is the foot, consisting of at least one stressed and one or two unstressed syllables. The pattern of stressed and unstressed syllables is called **metre.**
A sequence of stressed and unstressed syllables is not something artificial. It is the natural rhythm of the English language. It is the poet's skill to choose words in such a way that this pattern constitutes a regular metre.Types of foot:

foot	**stresses**	**example**
iamb/iambic	–/ (da-**dum)**	compare
trochee/trochaic	/ – (**dum**-da)	lovely
spondee/spondaic	// **(dum dum)**	drop dead

anapest/anapestic	– –/ (da-da-**dum**)	lemonade
dactyl/dactylic	/ – – (**dum**-da-da)	whispering

The number of feet or stressed syllables in a line determines its metre. The most common types are shown here:

number of feet	metre	example
1	monometer	"And **find** / What **wind**" (John Donne, "Song", ll. 7 – 8)
2	dimeter	"Why **dost** thou **thus**" (John Donne, "The Sun Rising", l. 2)
3	trimeter	"**Go**, Soul, the **bo**dy's **guest** / U**pon** a **thank**less **er**rant" (Sir Walter Raleigh, "The Lie", l. 1 f.)
4	tetrameter	"**Bu**sy old **fool**, un**ru**ly **sun**" (John Donne, "The Sun Rising", l. 1)
5	pentameter	"If **mu**sic **be** the **food** of **love**, play **on**" (William Shakespeare, *Twelfth Night,* l. i)
6	hexameter	"And **in** your **dread**ful **verse** in**grav'd** the **pro**phe**cies**" (Michael Drayton, „Poly-Olbion", l. 33)

INFO Most important metre in English poetry

Iambic pentameter:
"But **thy** e**ter**nal **sum**mer **shall** not **fade**" (Shakespeare, Sonnet 18).

Types of lines

end-stop lines	The meaning requires a pause at the end of the line.	"Shall I compare thee to a summer's day**?**" (Shakespeare, Sonnet 18)
run-on lines (enjambement)	The meaning requires no pause between the lines.	"When yellow leaves, or none, or few, do **hang** **Upon** those boughs which shake against the cold" (Shakespeare, Sonnet 73)
caesura	The meaning requires a pause in mid-line.	"Let me not to the marriage of true minds Admit **impediments**; **love** is not love" (Shakespeare, Sonnet 116)

TIPP Watch out!

The word *imagery* is an abstract noun. There is no plural. You can only talk about single *images*.

Imagery

A writer or speaker using language beyond its dictionary meaning makes use of **imagery.** All figurative use of language is imagery. Imagery appeals to all the senses; it is meant to stimulate the reader's or listener's imagination.

Important types of imagery are: metaphor, simile/comparison, personification and symbol (cf. p. 108 f.).

Drama

When asked to analyse a dramatic text, you will have to focus on particular elements that are characteristic of plays.

Elements of drama

Plot

INFO Elements of a dramatic plot

exposition → rising action → climax or crisis → falling action → dénouement or catastrophe

The action is presented to the audience on stage or on a screen directly. There is no narrator. Yet one can identify the same elements of plot as are found in narration.
In tragedy, the opponents of the hero gain the upper hand in the falling action, which ends in the catastrophe. Comedy has a happy ending, in which conflicts are resolved (dénouement).

Stage directions

The dramatic text consists of **two kinds of text:** the more important kind of text is spoken by the characters (i. e. dialogue, monologue, soliloquy and asides).
The **stage directions** are the second kind of text. They give instructions concerning the stage design, about sounds to be heard, visual effects, the characters' outer appearance and actions and also the way some of the dialogue has to be spoken.
The following visual and acoustic elements will have to be considered in your analysis of stage directions. They will help to characterise the dramatis personae, to create a specific atmosphere or they will function as symbols (cf. p. 108 f.).

concerning the actors		concerning the stage	
visual	**acoustic**	**visual**	**acoustic**
size facial expressions gestures costumes	voice intonation language of the play non-verbal noises	scenery stage design lighting props	music background noise sounds

Characters

The characters are not mediated via a narrator but present themselves through action, interaction and dialogue and, of course, their outward appearance on stage (see above). There are **flat** characters, types that act in a predictable way and do not develop over the course of the action, and **round** characters that appear and act lifelike and non-stereotypical and often undergo some form of inner development during the play.

Language/Dialogue/Communication

When analysing the language of a play, you have to keep in mind that it works on two levels:

1. the inner system of communication, i. e. the communication among the characters
2. the outer system of communication between the playwright and the audience

outer system of communication

playwright

inner system of communication

characters

audience

Dramatic irony

Dramatic irony is an important effect that is created by these two levels of communication. It arises when there is a sharp contrast between what the audience knows and what a character knows or utters. Dramatic irony often serves to great comic effect as well. Shakespeare, for example, puts it to great effect in his comedies when he introduces cases of mistaken identity.

<u>Example:</u>

In Shakespeare's Macbeth, King Duncan praises the peaceful atmosphere at Macbeth's castle, whereas the audience knows that Duncan is going to be murdered.

Aside
In an aside, an actor speaks to the audience in order to provide information on his thoughts and feelings or intentions. The other characters on stage supposedly do not hear what she/he says.

TIPP

As many of Shakespeare's plays are written in verse, you may approach their language in the same way as poetry.

Language and style

Important stylistic devices

device	definition	example
alliteration	repetition of a sound (usually a consonant) at the beginning of neighbouring words	"From forth the fatal loins of these two foes" (Shakespeare, *Romeo and Juliet,* Prologue)
allusion	direct or implied reference	Poetry is great. Just think of the most famous writer of sonnets in English.
analogy	establishing a resemblance between two things that are basically unlike	The heart is simply a pump propelling the blood round the body.
anaphora	neighbouring sentences starting with the same word(s)	"We shall not flag or fail. We shall go on to the end. We shall fight in France" (W. Churchill)
antithesis	contrasting ideas using a parallel syntactic structure	"It's a story that hasn't made me the most conventional candidate. But it is a story that has seared into my genetic make-up the idea that [...]" (B. Obama)
assonance	repetition of internal vowel sounds in neighbouring words	How now, brown cow?
blank verse	poetry without rhyme but with a regular metre: iambic pentameter	"The king has happily received, Macbeth, / The news of thy success, and when he reads" (Shakespeare, *Macbeth*)
chiasmus	the reversal of word order in two parts of a sentence	"Fair is foul, and foul is fair" (Shakespeare, *Macbeth*)
climax	an enumeration of arguments that become stronger	Friendship, affection, love.
ellipsis	incomplete sentence	A good choice!

enumeration	list of arguments	Macbeth is disloyal, greedy and obedient to his wife.
euphemism	replacing an unpleasant expression with a more agreeable one	"Civilising" Australian Aboriginals meant forcibly removing the children from their families.
hyperbole	exaggeration	I've told you a thousand times.
inversion	reversal of word order	Not only did he like chocolate, he also ate a lot of it.
metaphor	indirect comparison without "like" or "as"	Love is a red, red rose.
metonymy	name of a thing or concept is replaced by a part of it or by s.th. associated with it	"wheels" for "car" / "turf" for "horse-racing"
onomatopoeia	word that imitates the sound that it stands for	Bang! Swoosh! Ding-dong.
paradox	an apparent contradiction	This statement is true and false at the same time.
parallelism	same syntactic structure of two or more sentences	"One small step for man, one giant leap for mankind." (Neil Armstrong)
personification	inanimate objects / abstract ideas presented as if human beings	The flowers are begging for water.
rhetorical question	a question that does not require an answer	Do you think I'm stupid?
simile	comparison using the words "like" or "as"	Your love is like a red, red rose.
telling name	a name that represents character traits	"Doolittle": she is too little, or: she does too little (Shaw, Pygmalion)

Glossary – Analysing Literary Texts

the narrator tells of / shows / relates / reveals
the narrator takes xy's point of view
the narrator is omniscient
the story is told in the first-person/third-person form
the narrator uses / employs / makes use of metaphors/similes/comparisons
this metaphor shows / stands for / suggests
the narrator speaks in an ironic/satirical/detached/matter-of-fact/serious tone
the story deals with / treats of / concentrates on / focuses on ...
atmosphere is created

tension/suspense is created/built up
the poem is written/composed
the poem is read/spoken/recited
the recital of a poem
the poem is by Shakespeare / it is a song by Genesis
the speaker of the poem / the poetic I / the poetic persona
the poem consists of / is composed of / is arranged in stanzas
the comedy ridicules/mocks/satirises
the exposition sets the action in motion
the action moves towards and culminates in a turning point
the play has a simple/complex/tight plot
it has a happy/unhappy ending
the main/major/minor character(s) is/are
the protagonist is in conflict with an opponent
the antagonist fights the protagonist
the spectator/audience follows the play
the play is performed/produced/staged
the scenery is shifted
actors perform/play/enact
an actor enters / makes an entrance / exits / makes her/his exit

Sach- und Gebrauchstexte

Argumentative Texts: How to Deal with (Political) Speeches

Keyword
(Political) speeches: aim at convincing *(überzeugen)* the audience of the speaker's position, winning them over to his/her side. Very often, the speaker tries to persuade *(überreden)* the listener by appealing to his/her feelings. In some cases, the orator may even attempt to manipulate *(manipulieren)* his/her audience.
You should always keep in mind that the speaker wants to present his/her opinion / conviction / point of view as positively as possible.

When asked to analyse a political speech, you will have to focus on the topic as well as characteristic features.

How to proceed

Reading the text

1. Read the speech (or, more likely, an extract from it) as a whole, trying to identify the main topic (reading for gist).
2. Re-read the speech/extract several times, paying close attention to certain characteristic features of such speeches. Mark words or phrases in the text and take notes (intensive reading).

Pay close attention to

- key words and phrases
- references to historical events
- the use of symbols, key words, slogans
- references to famous people
- references to works of literature
- stylistic devices (see below)

Questions to be asked

When it comes to analysing a speech, you should always ask yourself the following questions:

- What is the main topic of the speech?
- What is its political, historical and social context?
- What do I know about the speaker (biography, political orientation)?

Elements of a (political) speech

Structure

Speeches can usually be divided into an **introduction**, a **main part** and a **conclusion**. These parts serve different purposes:

INFO Introduction to a speech

In the introduction the orator announces the topic/purpose of the speech and explains its importance. He/She also wants to attract the audience's attention so that they will follow the speech closely and accept his/her opinion.

There are several ways to make listeners interested:

- The speaker can open by telling the audience **something about their personal history / recent experience**, thereby underlining the fact that the topic of the speech is of personal importance to them. By relating a **little story** to the audience, the speaker will also appear more human and less remote.
- Another common way of starting a speech is to **open it with a question** that refers to the main topic and which will be answered later in the speech. By asking the audience a question, the speaker actively involves them, indirectly asking them to think more deeply about an issue.
- A speaker may **present visual material to the audience,** e. g. pictures, concrete objects or a short extract from a film. This also helps to attract the audience's attention: listeners will become curious about how the object or visual material is related to the content of the speech.

INFO Main part of a speech

In the main part of the speech the orator needs to keep the audience interested and to make sure that they can follow the train of thought.

Again, there are several ways to do this. The following techniques are particularly effective:

- **using short and simple sentences**, developing the argumentation step by step and ensuring that the audience can follow,
- quoting reliable sources/experts, referring to statistics and **providing the audience with facts and necessary background information**, which shows that the speaker is well-informed and has researched the subject,
- **pointing out problems** but also providing solutions to them, thus showing that the speaker is competent, and
- **including personal experiences** and vivid, specific events, again aiming for a personal relationship with the audience, often using personal pronouns like “we”, “us”, “our”.

Towards the end of a speech the speaker might
- take up a question posed at the beginning of the speech,
- appeal once more to both the audience's heads and hearts,
- ask for support, giving the listeners the feeling that their support is of major importance, and
- develop a vision for the future.

Language and style

There are certain stylistic devices which are often used in speeches. They aim at making the speech more lively and interesting.

Important stylistic devices

analogy	A resemblance is established between things which are dissimilar.
simile	This is a direct comparison using the words "like" or "as", e.g. *He fought like a lion in the battle.*
metaphor	This is an indirect comparison without using the words "like" or "as", e.g. *He was a lion in the battle.*
alliteration	A consonantal sound is repeated in two or more adjacent words, e.g. *We will win; "We must understand that ties of trade bind nations in closest intimacy"* (Warren G. Harding: Inaugural address, 4 March 1921).
repetition	Repeating certain words or phrases puts emphasis on their meaning, e.g. *"The answer to the slavery question was already embedded within our Constitution – a Constitution that had at its very core the ideal of equal citizenship under the law; a Constitution that promised its people liberty, and justice"* (Barack Obama: *A More Perfect Union)*
parallelism	Two or more parts of a sentence (or two or more sentences) have the same (or similar) syntactic structure. Like repetition, parallelism serves to emphasise the parts of the sentence in question, intensifying the force of the statement and encouraging the audience to think about its meaning, e.g. *"Let us be our sister's keeper. Let us find that common stake we all have in one another, and let our politics reflect that spirit as well."* (Barack Obama: *A More Perfect Union)*
antithesis	Two ideas are opposed to one another, using a parallel syntactic structure to achieve the desired effect, i.e. establishing a contrast, e.g. *"It's a story that hasn't made me the most conventional candidate. But it is a story that has seared into my genetic make-up the idea that this nation is more than the sum of its parts – that out of many, we are truly one."* (Barack Obama: *A More Perfect Union)*

rhetorical question	A rhetorical question is one to which no answer is expected; instead, the listener is asked to think about the question and its relevance, e.g. *“How long should this suffering continue?”*
irony	Irony is the use of a statement in which the literal meaning is very different, often even the opposite of the intended meaning; usually, the recipient is made aware of the intended meaning through context or verbal and non-verbal cues, e.g. *hugging oneself in a thunderstorm, saying, „Lovely weather!“*

Glossary – Vocabulary for Analysing Speeches

By telling the listeners something about himself he attempts to establish a personal relationship with his audience.	Er bemüht sich, eine persönliche Beziehung zu seinen Zuhörern aufzubauen, indem er seinem Publikum etwas über seine persönliche Geschichte erzählt.
She attempts to win her listeners over to her side.	Sie versucht, das Publikum auf ihre Seite zu ziehen.
He draws a comparison between ... and ...	Er zieht einen Vergleich zwischen ... und ...
He puts emphasis on the meaning of his words by using parallelism/ repetition in line X.	Durch den in Zeile X verwendeten Parallelismus / die in Zeile X verwendete Wiederholung verleiht er seinen Worten Nachdruck.
He refers to well-known historical events such as ...	Er bezieht sich auf allgemein bekannte historische Ereignisse wie z. B. ...
He wants to call/draw the audience’s attention to the fact that ...	Er möchte die Aufmerksamkeit des Publikums auf die Tatsache lenken, dass ...
His frequent use of rhetorical questions is intended to show that ...	Sein häufiger Gebrauch rhetorischer Fragen soll verdeutlichen, dass ...
His use of metaphorical language is intended to make his speech more lively and interesting.	Sein metaphorischer Sprachgebrauch soll seine Rede interessanter und lebendiger machen.
In line X he directly criticises his political opponents.	In Zeile ... kritisiert er offen seine politischen Gegner.
The frequent use of personal pronouns such as “we”, “us” and “our” gives the audience the impression that he does not regard himself as superior to them but as one of them.	Der häufige Gebrauch der Personalpronomen „wir“, „uns“ und „unser“ soll dem Publikum das Gefühl geben, dass er sich als einer von ihnen und nicht als eine höher gestellte Person sieht.
The speaker appeals to the audience’s emotions by ...	Der Redner / Die Rednerin spricht die Gefühle des Publikums an, indem er/sie ...

The speaker begins by ...	Der Redner / Die Rednerin beginnt mit ...
The speaker makes frequent use of metaphors/similes/symbols/examples to point out / to underline that ...	Der Redner / Die Rednerin macht regen Gebrauch von Metaphern/Vergleichen/Symbolen/Beispielen, um herauszustellen / zu unterstreichen, dass ...
The speaker tries to convince his/her audience of his/her point of view by ...	Der Redner / Die Rednerin versucht sein/ihr Publikum von seinem/ihrem Standpunkt zu überzeugen, indem er/sie ...
The speaker aims to convince/persuade/manipulate the audience.	Es ist das Anliegen des Redners / der Rednerin, das Publikum zu überzeugen/überreden/manipulieren.

Expository Texts: How to Deal with Essays

Keyword

Essay: There are various kinds:
a) essays which reflect the author's opinion on a certain topic (**comment**)
b) essays in which the author weighs up the pros and cons of a particular subject (**argumentative essay**)
c) essays in which a topic is presented in a clear and logical way and which do not contain the author's opinion (**expository essay**)

How to proceed

First you have to find out which kind of essay you are being asked to analyse.
For details on how to analyse **comments** you can refer to the section on **political speeches** above.
Here we will focus on the **argumentative essay.**

Structure

- In the **introduction** the author expresses the main idea of the essay. Instead of giving a personal opinion, she/he might choose to provide the reader with some background information or start with a question which will serve as a guideline and be answered in the course of the essay.
- For the **main part** of the essay, the author can decide on a dialectical or an enumerative approach.
- In an **enumerative approach** the author will enumerate all the aspects of the topic in a neutral way. A **dialectical approach** can either present all the arguments in favour of a position before focusing on the counterarguments (or vice versa), or it can present the pros and cons alternately. The latter is usually considered more skilful.
- Each **new aspect** is usually presented in a new paragraph. The various **arguments** can be backed with examples from real life, established facts, an expert opinion or

other reliable sources. These pieces of evidence are very important as they enable the author to make his/her argument convincing and thus to persuade the reader.
- In the **conclusion** the author sums up the arguments, frequently also restating his/her own opinion and referring to what could happen in the future.

Glossary – Vocabulary for Analysing Essays

The author discusses the pros and cons of ...	Der Verfasser / Die Verfasserin diskutiert die Vor- und Nachteile von ...
The author gives his/her personal opinion on the problem of ...	Der Verfasser / Die Verfasserin äußert seine/ihre eigene Meinung zum Thema ...
He/She believes / is convinced / presumes that ...	Er/Sie glaubt / ist überzeugt / nimmt an, dass ...
She/He wants to persuade the reader ...	Sie/Er möchte die Lesenden überreden ...
One can easily follow his train of thought.	Man kann seinen Gedankengang leicht nachvollziehen.
At the end of her essay she draws / comes to the conclusion ...	Am Ende ihres Essays kommt sie zu dem Schluss ...
His/Her arguments are (not) convincing/well-chosen.	Seine/Ihre Argumente sind (nicht) überzeugend/gut gewählt.
The main topic of the essay is ...	Das Hauptthema des Berichts ist ...
The tone of this essay is humorous/neutral/ironic/serious.	Der Ton des Berichts ist humorvoll/neutral/ironisch/ernst.
The author uses real examples to convince her readers.	Die Verfasserin verwendet reale Beispiele, um ihre Leserschaft zu überzeugen.
The author's choice of words shows/emphasises that he is for/against ...	Die Wortwahl des Verfassers zeigt/unterstreicht, dass er für/gegen ... ist.
In the introductory paragraph of her essay, she asks a rhetorical question, which serves as a thread.	Im einleitenden Abschnitt ihres Berichts stellt sie den Lesenden eine rhetorische Frage, die sich wie ein roter Faden durch den Bericht zieht.
The author uses adjectives with positive/negative connotations to support his/her point of view.	Der Verfasser / Die Verfasserin verwendet Adjektive mit einer positiven/negativen Konnotation, um seinen/ihren Standpunkt zu verdeutlichen.
Her attempt to persuade the readers backfires / works very well.	Ihr Versuch, die Lesenden zu überreden, misslingt/gelingt.

Narrative Texts: How to Deal with Reports

Keyword
Report: This is a special kind of newspaper article.
It provides answers to the five "W" questions *(Who? What? Where? When? Why?)*, as well as the *How* question. Its aim is to inform its readers and NOT to manipulate or influence them.
A report deals with current events and only contains facts.

Sometimes students have problems when it comes to differentiating between a *report* and an *article*, which can also deal with current events but which is usually a mixture of both fact and opinion.
The style of an **article** is usually more personal and its main aim is to entertain the reader. This is ensured by using many adverbs and adjectives to make the article lively and by addressing its readers directly, often by asking them a hypothetical question, e.g. *How would you feel if you discovered that someone had stolen your brand-new car?*
The main characteristics of a **report** are outlined below.

Elements of a report

Structure

- To arouse the reader's curiosity, reports have **headlines** containing basic information without providing too much detail.
- The basic information is generally provided in the first paragraph, which serves as an **introduction.**
- The **main body** of a report consists of a number of paragraphs, which contain one piece of information each.
- The last paragraph serves as a kind of **conclusion.**

Language and style

- A report is written in a factual style and neither reflects the author's personal opinion nor contains any kind of speculation.
- Individual paragraphs are relatively short and consist of short sentences, aiming to ensure that the reader understands the information presented.
- Experts – or people who have first-hand experience of the topic in question – are often quoted, but no authorial comment is given on what they say.

Glossary – Vocabulary for Analysing Reports

The report [title] written by [author] deals with / is about / relates to / describes ...	Der Bericht [Titel] von [Verfasser] beschäftigt sich mit / handelt von / berichtet von / beschreibt ...
The topic(s) of the report is (are) ...	Das Thema / Die Themen des Berichts ist/sind ...
In the introduction the reader learns about / gets to know ...	In der Einleitung erfährt der Leser / die Leserin ...
The report can be divided into ... paragraphs.	Der Bericht kann in ... Absätze gegliedert werden.
The report consists of ... paragraphs.	Der Bericht besteht aus ... Absätzen.
It is the author's aim to inform the reader about ...	Es ist das Anliegen des Autors / der Autorin, die Lesenden über ... zu informieren.
The 2nd/3rd paragraph contains information on ...	Der zweite/dritte Absatz enthält Informationen über ...
The author quotes an eye-witness/ expert who says that ...	Der Autor / Die Autorin zitiert einen Augenzeugen/Experten, der sagt, dass ...
The author describes how ...	Der Verfasser / Die Verfasserin beschreibt, wie ...
The author does not give his/her personal opinion on the topic/problem/question but merely relates facts.	Der Verfasser / Die Verfasserin äußert nicht seine/ihre eigene Meinung zum Sachverhalt / Problem / zu der Frage, sondern gibt Fakten wieder.
The factual style of writing shows that it is the author's aim to inform the reader and not to entertain him/her.	Der sachliche Sprachgebrauch verdeutlicht, dass es das Anliegen des Autors / der Autorin ist, die Lesenden zu informieren und nicht, sie zu unterhalten.

Visuelle Materialien

Any kind of picture can be considered a type of text: it contains information that can be read and interpreted. This requires knowledge of the language of pictures, which is different for each medium: a cartoon must be approached differently from a photograph, for example. A complete account of every kind of visual material cannot be offered here, but some central aspects will be listed and explained.

INFO A note on visual texts in the Abitur

Pictures have often been used in the Zentralabitur. They generally appear as additional material illustrating a certain text and picking up its issues or introducing new aspects for the student to react to. During the written exam, visual texts are limited to printable material; oral exams may occasionally also feature short video sequences.

Common Types of Pictures Used

- **photographs:** often illustrate an issue or problem; their aesthetic qualities should be considered
- **advertisements:** mostly use photographic material combined with text to promote a certain product/service; the intention of the ad must be considered and reflected on; political ads also belong to this category
- **cartoons:** reflect an issue from a critical point of view; the cartoonist's intention to criticise a social or political problem plays a central role
- **works of art:** rarely used; can reflect a society's state of mind and ideals during a certain period (e.g. early American paintings); their aesthetic qualities are essential to an understanding of their message
- **film stills:** a special type of photograph which enables the viewer to analyse the composition of a scene and its meaning/intention
- **films/videos:** this may include formats such as movie scenes, vines and vlogs; for legal reasons these are not likely to be shown in the Abitur but are used in the classroom for film analysis as well as comprehension tasks and as central study texts
- **statistics:** used to prove or explain a certain issue scientifically

Steps for Approaching Visual Material

Step 1: Describe the picture and its content. Do not begin by analysing or interpreting it, but state clearly and briefly what can be seen in the picture. The central question to be answered is, "What type of picture are you dealing with and what can be seen?"
Step 2: Analyse the content and form. The method of analysis depends on the picture. Ask yourself: "What information does the picture convey?" and (except for statistics) "Why was the picture created in this way and not differently?" End by stating what the picture aims to reveal, illustrate, criticise or otherwise convey.

Step 3: Interpret and evaluate the meaning or importance of the picture and the possible intention(s) of its creator. You may ask yourself whether the picture gives a truthful reflection of a certain issue or aspect, whether it distorts or exaggerates reality or whether it is meant to manipulate the viewer.

INFO A note on tasks given to discuss pictures in the Abitur

Many tasks in the Abitur that involve the use of pictures do not specifically ask for an analysis or interpretation but imply that this must be provided. Usually, visual materials have been used to illustrate an issue already introduced in a longer text. In such cases, you will be asked to react to the picture and relate it to the text or to a certain general topic discussed in class.

Examples of Types of Pictures

Cartoons

When analysing cartoons, pay attention to the following aspects:
context: the circumstances in which it was created: when and in what type of magazine or newspaper it was published (historical, political context), connection to a particular article or reference to a current topic, position of its creator
content: the details of what it shows:
- **target:** who or what is it aimed at, what issue does it discuss/criticise?
- **message:** what point does the cartoon aim to make or what ideas does it propose?
  - Has the cartoonist taken sides? Is he/she biased?
  - Is the cartoon's humour ironic, satirical, aggressive ...?

style: How is this message put across? Consider visual and textual elements.

visual elements	**textual elements**
Do visual items display incongruities by means of size, contrast, exaggeration, distortion, personification, etc.?	Has the cartoonist used labels/speech bubbles/captions? What words are made up to convey sounds? (onomatopoeia)
What facial features are used to convey expressions?	Does the cartoon use formal or informal language?
Do the images have symbolic meaning?	Does it play with words?
Does it use contrasts to convey certain issues of the main topic?	Does it use technical or specific terms?
Note: Almost every form of humour is based on incongruity. Things that are juxtaposed or compared in a strange way make us laugh.	

Key elements of cartoons

- **visual metaphors:** Cartoons use simplified visual symbols to carry meaning. The viewer can usually quickly decode them without any effort, e.g. when seeing a grey, dissolving shape one can imagine that this represents smoke.
- **caricature** (noun/verb): usually an exaggerated drawing or picture of a well-known person that makes them seem ridiculous but also easy to recognise
- **onomatopoeia** (noun): a word that sounds similar to the thing it describes, for example "hiss", "bang", "pow" (adj: onomatopoeic)

Advertisements

When analysing ads, pay attention to the AIDA principle (see below) and ask how the ad achieves the following points:
Attention: Ads aim to attract the consumer's attention quickly, for example by showing an appealing, provocative or shocking image or message.
Interest: This initial attention must be kept, thus the ad must create a further interest in the product.
Desire: Once the consumer is interested, the advertisement must spark a desire to buy the product which is advertised.
Action: The desire to own or use the product must lead to action by the consumer; he/she must seek ways to buy or access the product.

These aspects apply to all ads in general even if they do not directly aim to sell a specific product. Campaign ads in politics aim to "sell" a programme or candidate, whereas campaigns published by organisations such as Greenpeace seek to make viewers change their way of living or become politically involved. One must always consider the context in which an ad tries to affect its audience.

Photographs

When analysing and interpreting photographs, it is important to remember that even if a photograph shows a real environment at a certain time, it is still a fabrication of sorts. All photography is influenced by a) the photographer's choice of perspective, frame and timing and b) the camera itself, which can only show a limited view.
Photographers make choices when taking a picture in order to convey a specific effect or impression of their object. So a photograph must be considered in the same way as a painting – always ask yourself why the photographer chose this specific object, perspective, frame (what can and cannot be seen), moment in time and rendition (e.g. colour, black and white, sepia).

Modern means of digital photography have also led to increasing manipulation. Thus, even though we still tend to believe that pictures show reality, it can no longer be taken for granted that a photograph shows an aspect of the real world and/or has not been digitally altered.

Glossary – Vocabulary for Analysing Visual Material

viewer	Betrachter
picture, image	Bild
painting, drawing	Gemälde, Zeichnung
photograph/photo	Fotografie (Vorsicht: nicht Fotograf)
photographer	Fotograf
portrait	Porträt
landscape painting/photograph	Landschaftsgemälde/-fotografie
bird's eye view	Vogelperspektive
worm's eye view	Froschperspektive
incongruity	Widerspruch, Widersprüchlichkeit
background	Hintergrund
foreground	Vordergrund

Basic phrases for a description

In the picture/advertisement one can see ...
In the foreground/middle ground/background ...
The theme / topic / main motif of the advertisement is ...
It's an image of ... (place, person, scene)
The picture shows ... (place, person, scene) close up / from a medium/long distance view.
You look at ... (place, person, scene) from ... (above/behind/...)
The picture was taken in/at ... (place)
Above/On top of ... one can read / it says / one can see a short text ...

Basic phrases to express intention/message/aim

The picture/advertisement is aimed at / is meant to attract / is intended to / appeals to a / shows a/an (exaggerated, illustrative, provocative, unrealistic, flattering/beautified) depiction/image of ...
It expresses/criticises/suggests/reveals/claims/manipulates/influences ...

Basic phrases to express stylistic means / how aims are achieved

The photographer/painter/cartoonist achieves his/her aim by presenting ... in an objective / artistic / exaggerated / limited / digitally manipulated way/style.
By using contrasts / incongruities such as ... / differences in colour/focus, ... the artist/photographer/cartoonist illustrates/emphasises/shows ...
The perspective / point of view suggests that ...
The motif was chosen deliberately because it illustrates the issue well / evokes emotions / stands for / represents a larger, more complex issue ...

Die sprachliche Leistung im Abitur

Die integrative Sprachbewertung

Mit der **integrativen Sprachbewertung** entfallen sowohl die früher getrennte Bewertung von Ausdrucksvermögen und Sprachrichtigkeit als auch die entsprechenden Fehlerindex-Tabellen.
Nun gibt es nur noch eine Gesamtzensur für die sprachliche Leistung, wobei sich die Bewertung an klar umrissenen Kriterien orientiert. Hierbei hat sich ein grundlegender Wandel vollzogen. Wurden früher insbesondere die fehlerhaften Äußerungen einer Klausur als Bewertungsgrundlage herangezogen, so steht jetzt eine sogenannte **Positiv-Korrektur** im Vordergrund. Zwar werden die Mängel der sprachlichen Leistung nach wie vor rot markiert, jedoch sollen besonders gelungene Teile einer Klausur in grüner Farbe hervorgehoben werden. Beispiele für eine positive, grüne Markierung wären etwa der richtige Gebrauch von Präpositionen, Gerundien oder Konnektoren (zur Satzverknüpfung).
Es wird bewertet, ob und in welchem Umfang die Verstöße gegen die sprachliche Richtigkeit die Kommunikation zwischen der/dem Schreibenden und der/dem Lesenden der Klausur beeinträchtigen und ob die Häufigkeit den Gesamteindruck des Textes bestimmt, inwiefern die Fehler störend wirken und ob sie auf eine Nichtbeherrschung grammatischer Regeln schließen lassen. Dabei wird auch berücksichtigt, ob der Prüfling einen komplexeren, idiomatischen Sprachgebrauch angestrebt hat.
Zur integrativen Leistungsbewertung im sprachlichen Bereich werden folgende Kriterien betrachtet:

Texterstellung

- Ist der Text übersichtlich gegliedert und für die Leserschaft damit leicht zu erfassen?
- Ist der Textumfang angemessen?
- Werden sogenannte *linking words* (Konnektoren) zur Verknüpfung von Satzteilen und Ideen sinnvoll und abwechslungsreich eingesetzt?
- Ist das Ausdrucksvermögen anspruchsvoll und wird evtl. das Risiko von möglichen Fehlern akzeptiert, um einen flüssigen und idiomatisch ansprechenden Text zu produzieren?
- Werden textsortenspezifische Formulierungen verwendet (z. B. wird eine private E-Mail anders formuliert als ein Leserbrief)?
- Werden Zitate sinnvoll integriert (treffend gewählt, nicht zu lang)?

Syntax

- Wird der Satzbau variiert oder werden hauptsächlich gleiche Strukturen verwendet?
- Wird auch komplexerer Satzbau beherrscht oder werden bei den Versuchen, nicht nur einfache Strukturen zu verwenden, viele Fehler gemacht?

Lexik

- Sind sowohl der allgemeine als auch der themenspezifische Wortschatz reichhaltig?
- Wird der Wortschatz treffsicher eingesetzt?

Grammatik

- Ist die Fehlerzahl eher gering und beeinträchtigt sie die Kommunikation eher nicht, oder führt eine Häufung zu einer eingeschränkten Verständlichkeit?
- Deuten die Fehler auf eine Unkenntnis oder Unsicherheit hinsichtlich relevanter grammatischer Regeln hin?

Kommunikative Relevanz typischer Fehler

Die folgenden Beispiele zeigen **Fehler, die die Kommunikation beeinträchtigen** und somit zu Abzügen führen. Die Auflistung ist nicht vollständig, sondern vermittelt einen exemplarischen Überblick:

- korrupte Syntax durch Fehlerhäufung
- falsche Bezüge
- uneinheitlicher bzw. falscher Tempusgebrauch (vgl. *summary*)
- falscher Tempusgebrauch bei eindeutigen Signalwörtern (z. B. *last year*)
- fehlende Umschreibung mit *to do* bei Frage und Verneinung
- falsche Präpositionen in *phrasal verbs*
- Germanismen
- falscher Gebrauch von Infinitiv und Gerundium
- *contact clause* im nicht notwendigen Relativsatz
- *that* im nicht notwendigen Relativsatz

Folgende Fehler beeinträchtigen die Kommunikation nicht oder nur in geringem Umfang:

- Rechtschreibfehler, wenn deutlich wird, welches Wort gemeint ist
- falsch gesetztes oder fehlendes Apostroph (**Peters bike; its/it's*)
- fehlerhafte Partizipialkonstruktionen
- Flüchtigkeitsfehler wie gelegentliches Fehlen des *3rd-person singular present -s* oder Plural-s
- ungebräuchliche Präposition bei klarer Aussageabsicht (z. B. **typical for*)
- *progressive* anstatt *simple* (z. B. **The author is dealing with …*)
- fehlerhafte Zeichensetzung

Diese Übersicht ist ein Auszug aus der Bewertungsskala des Niedersächsischen Kultusministeriums.[1]

		sehr gut **15-13 Notenpunkte**	**ausreichend** **6-4 Notenpunkte**
Lexik	Bandbreite	– in hohem Maße präzise und variable Wortwahl – zielsprachentypische Wendungen	– eingeschränkte, noch angemessene Wortwahl
	Korrektheit	– in hohem Maße lexikalisch korrekt – durchgängig verständlich	– teilweise lexikalisch unkorrekt – Verständlichkeit stellenweise beeinträchtigt
Grammatik	Bandbreite	– in hohem Maße variabler Satzbau – durchgängig funktionaler Einsatz der gewählten Strukturen	– wenig variabler Satzbau – noch angemessene Strukturen
	Korrektheit	– in hohem Maße grammatikalisch korrekt – durchgängig verständlich	– teilweise grammatikalisch unkorrekt – Verständlichkeit stellenweise beeinträchtigt
Textgestaltung	Textaufbau	– in hohem Maße zielgerichteter Text mit durchgängig funktionalem Einsatz textstrukturierender Mittel (Kohäsion)	– ansatzweise zielgerichteter Text mit eingeschränkt funktionalem Einsatz textstrukturierender Mittel (Kohäsion)
	Angemessenheit	– in hohem Maße Umsetzung der geforderten sprachlichen Textsortenmerkmale – in hohem Maße situations- und adressatengerechte Sprachverwendung – in hohem Maße eigenständige sprachliche Gestaltung	– ansatzweise Umsetzung der geforderten sprachlichen Textsortenmerkmale – ansatzweise situations- und adressatengerechte Sprachverwendung – ansatzweise eigenständige sprachliche Gestaltung

[1] Quelle: Institut zur Qualitätsentwicklung im Bildungswesen, 08.11.2021, https://bildungsportal-niedersachsen.de/fileadmin/4_Allgemeinbildung/Zentrale_Arbeiten/2025/1_Bewertung_sprachliche_Leistung_EN-FR.pdf (Zugriff: 01.03.2024)

Aufgabenarten

Es können auch Aufgaben gestellt werden, die eine **kreative Lösung** erfordern, um dem Anforderungsbereich III zu genügen. Denkbar sind u. a. das Schreiben eines Briefes oder einer E-Mail an einen Freund oder an die Herausgeberin einer Zeitung, ein Schreiben zur Erlangung von Informationen oder auch ein Beschwerdebrief.
Weiterhin sind Aufgabenstellungen möglich, die das Verfassen eines Artikels, eines **Berichtes**, eines **Drehbuches,** eines **Tagebucheintrags** oder eines **Dialogs** erfordern. Das Schreiben einer **Fortsetzung** oder eines **alternativen Endes einer Geschichte** ist ebenso eine mögliche Aufgabenstellung wie die **Schilderung einer Begebenheit** aus einer anderen Perspektive, um nur einige mögliche Beispiele zu benennen.

Strukturiertes Vorgehen in der Abiturprüfung

Bei der Bearbeitung der Aufgaben in der Abiturprüfung empfiehlt sich ein systematisches Vorgehen in klar definierten Einzelschritten:
Lesen Sie sich zunächst den Text in Ruhe durch und unterstreichen Sie mit Bleistift Wörter, die Sie nachschlagen möchten. Konzentrieren Sie sich dabei auf solche Wörter, die bedeutungsrelevant und zentral für Ihr Verständnis des Textes sind. Verlieren Sie keine wertvolle Zeit mit dem Nachschlagen von Füllwörtern. Schlagen Sie dann die wichtigsten Wörter nach und lesen Sie den Text ein zweites Mal – nun zügiger – durch. Wenden Sie sich danach den Aufgaben zu: Lesen Sie zuerst alle Teilaufgaben genau durch. Machen Sie sich nochmals klar, dass die Bearbeitung der *comprehension task* (Anforderungsbereich I) weitgehend am Ausgangstext orientiert erfolgen soll, gegebenenfalls unter Einbindung vorhandenen Hintergrundwissens. Die *analysis* (Anforderungsbereich II) erfordert die detaillierte Betrachtung von Einzelaspekten unter Anwendung Ihrer Kenntnisse aus dem Bereich Zitieren und Argumentieren. In der *evaluation* (Anforderungsbereich III) wird schließlich nach Ihrer persönlichen Einordnung und Bewertung gefragt.
Konzentrieren Sie sich anschließend auf die erste Teilaufgabe und kennzeichnen Sie gezielt unmittelbar relevante Textpassagen mit einem Marker. Machen Sie sich auf einem separaten Blatt stichpunktartige Notizen zur Bearbeitung der ersten Aufgabe und verfahren Sie so mit allen weiteren Teilaufgaben. Strukturieren Sie nun Ihre Stichpunkte durch Nummerieren und prüfen Sie unmittelbar vor dem Ausformulieren noch einmal die Aufgabenstellung, um sich rechtzeitig zu vergewissern, dass Ihre Bearbeitung auf den Kern der Frage abzielt. Nehmen Sie sich genug Zeit für diese Vorarbeiten (etwa ein Drittel der Zeit ist nicht zu viel), da Sie mit gut vorsortierten Inhalten umso schneller schreiben und sich dabei stärker auf die sprachlichen Aspekte im Englischen konzentrieren können.
Es wird als positiv im Sinne der Textkohärenz bewertet, wenn Sie sich bemühen, Ihre Antworten zu den einzelnen Teilaufgaben sprachlich miteinander in Verbindung zu setzen. Betrachten Sie nicht jede Aufgabe als isolierten Einzelaspekt, der jeweils mit einem Satz für Leserinnen und Leser ohne Vorwissen eingeleitet wird.

TIPP zum Punktesammeln

Gehen Sie professionell vor und lesen Sie Ihre gesamte Arbeit vor der Abgabe noch einmal gründlich durch. Planen Sie dafür etwa 15 bis 20 Minuten ein. Bei diesem Arbeitsgang werden Ihnen selbst ganz sicher sprachliche Fehler auffallen. Achten Sie besonders auf die Bezüge bei den Pronomina, das -*s* in der 3. Person Singular Präsens, die Zeitenfolge sowie Rechtschreibung und Zeichensetzung.

TIPP zur Zeitplanung

1. Schritt: Text lesen, bedeutungsrelevanten Wortschatz klären	20 Min
2. Schritt: Fragen lesen, Stichpunkte machen und vorsortieren	20 Min
3. Schritt: Fragen unter Verwendung der Gliederung beantworten	80 Min
4. Schritt: Korrekturlesen	15 Min

(Diese zeitlichen Richtlinien gelten für Grundkurse; bei Prüfungen im Leistungskurs verlängern sich die Zeiten entsprechend.)

Wortschatzerschließung

Viele scheinbar unbekannte Wörter lassen sich problemlos ableiten. Hierzu kann man den Kontext oder andere bekannte Wörter aus derselben Wortfamilie zurate ziehen. In manchen Fällen helfen auch fächerübergreifend die Kenntnisse in anderen Fremdsprachen oder der Muttersprache. Insbesondere auf das Lateinische bzw. Französische kann man hier häufig zurückgreifen.

Textgestaltung

Kohärenz, Adressatenorientierung, Leserleitung

Kohärenz

TIPP zum Punktesammeln

Bemühen Sie sich, Ihren Text kohärent, also auch sprachlich zusammenhängend, zu gestalten. Schaffen Sie sinnvolle inhaltliche Verknüpfungen zwischen Satzteilen, Sätzen und Sinnabschnitten. Verwenden Sie dazu die sogenannten **Konnektoren,** die als Verbindungsglieder zum besseren Textverständnis beitragen.

Hier ist eine Liste der wichtigsten Konnektoren, geordnet nach ihrer Funktion im Satz.

Reihung von Argumenten

and	und
first(ly)/second(ly)/third(ly)	erstens/zweitens/drittens
furthermore/moreover	außerdem / darüber hinaus / überdies

in addition to	zusätzlich zu
not only ... but also ...	nicht nur ..., sondern auch
as well as	sowie
finally	schließlich

Gegensatz

but	aber/sondern
although	obwohl
however	jedoch
despite the fact that	trotz der Tatsache, dass
in spite of	trotz
nevertheless/nonetheless	nichtsdestoweniger
even so	selbst dann
on the contrary	im Gegensatz dazu
on the one hand, ... on the other hand,	einerseits ..., andererseits
unlike	anders als
whereas	während/wogegen/indessen
while/whilst	während (dagegen)
yet	dennoch

Bedingung

if	falls/wenn
unless	wenn nicht
otherwise	ansonsten

Folge

because	weil
since	da
so	daher
consequently	folglich
as a result	demzufolge
therefore	daher/deshalb
due to	infolge
according to	zufolge
that is why	deshalb

Vergleich

like	wie
in comparison to/with	im Vergleich zu
similarly	ähnlich
equally	gleichermaßen

Zielgruppenorientierung

Schneiden Sie Ihren Text genau auf den Adressaten zu und drücken Sie sich präzise aus. Bewegen Sie sich in der Abiturklausur auf einer neutralen Sprachebene, vermeiden Sie also Stilbrüche wie Slangwörter und *spoken English*. Auch *contracted forms (they're, he's got)* sind nur in privater Kommunikation angebracht.

Lesendenleitung: *Writing a paragraph/comment*

Hier soll insbesondere der *argumentative comment* näher betrachtet werden, in dem Argumente für und gegen eine Behauptung erläutert werden. Die Form des *comment*, der eine These stützt bzw. nur antithetisch arbeitet, ist ein Teilbereich eines *argumentative comment.*

TIPP zum Punktesammeln

Entwickeln Sie in Ihrem Text eine für die Lesenden nachvollziehbare Argumentation.

Ein *comment* folgt einer klaren Struktur: Er beginnt mit einem *topic sentence* zur Einleitung, in dem eine Aussage zum Thema gemacht wird. Anschließend führt er das Argument aus **(These)**, geht über zur Darstellung der Gegenargumente **(Antithese)**, um mit einer **Schlussfolgerung** bzw. der **Darstellung der eigenen Meinung** abzuschließen. In jedem Teil sollten spezifische Formulierungen zur logischen Verknüpfung eingesetzt werden, um den Lesenden die Redeabsicht zu signalisieren.

Eine Sicherheit ausdrücken

The fact is that ...	Es ist eine Tatsache, dass ...
It cannot be denied that ...	Man kann nicht leugnen, dass ...
It goes without saying that ...	Selbstredend ...
Undoubtedly, ...	Zweifellos ...
I am convinced that ...	Ich bin überzeugt davon, dass ...
It is indisputable/obvious that ... There is no doubt that ...	Es ist unbestreitbar / offensichtlich / nicht zu bezweifeln, dass ...
It is inevitable that ...	Es ist unvermeidbar, dass ...

Eine Vermutung ausdrücken

Apparently, …	Anscheinend …
They will probably …	Sie werden wahrscheinlich …
It seems highly likely that …	Es scheint äußerst wahrscheinlich, dass …
It may be the case that …	Es kann sein, dass …

Einen Zweifel ausdrücken

It is doubtful whether …	Es ist zweifelhaft, ob …
I wonder if …	Ich frage mich, ob …
There is no proof/evidence that …	Es gibt keine Beweise, dass …

Einen Sachverhalt betonen

In order to stress that …	Um hervorzuheben, dass …
to emphasise	betonen
I would like to make it clear that …	Ich möchte klarstellen, dass …

Eine Meinung ausdrücken

In my opinion, … / In my view, …	Meiner Meinung nach …
My thoughts on the subject are …	Meine Meinung zu diesem Thema ist …
Personally, I think that …	Ich persönlich denke, dass …
As far as I am concerned, …	Was mich angeht …
From my point of view, …	Aus meiner Sicht …
I assume that …	Ich vermute, dass …
I am (not) convinced that …	Ich bin (nicht) überzeugt davon, dass …
I cannot help thinking that …	Ich kann nicht umhin zu denken, dass …
I get the impression that …	Ich habe den Eindruck, dass …
I am afraid that …	(abschwächend) Ich fürchte, dass …
Honestly, … / To be honest, …	Ehrlich gesagt …
I cannot judge whether/if …	Ich kann nicht beurteilen, ob …
I am in no position to say …	Es steht mir nicht zu, zu sagen …

Einen Widerspruch einräumen

in contrast to …	im Gegensatz zu …
On the contrary, …	Ganz im Gegenteil …

whereas	(gegenüberstellend) während
I strongly object to ...	Ich spreche mich deutlich gegen ... aus.
One could argue that ..., but ...	Man könnte argumentieren, dass ... , aber ...
Although it is true that ... it would be wrong to claim that ...	Obwohl es wahr ist, dass ..., wäre es falsch zu behaupten, dass ...

Zustimmung ausdrücken

Fortunately, ...	Glücklicherweise ...
I entirely agree with / I share the opinion that ...	Ich stimme vollkommen mit ... überein.
I support his view.	Ich unterstütze seine Meinung.
I share her views.	Ich teile ihre Meinung.
I am of the same opinion (as) ...	Ich bin der gleichen Meinung (wie) ...
I approve of his/her opinion.	Ich bin mit seiner/ihrer Meinung einverstanden.
I take your point about ...	Ich akzeptiere Ihre Meinung über ...
I am in favour of ...	Ich bin für ...
He rightly mentions that ...	Zu Recht betont er, dass ...
I will not object to ...	Ich widerspreche ... nicht.
It cannot be justified that ...	Es gibt keine Rechtfertigung für ...
Nobody would disagree with that statement.	Niemand würde dieser Behauptung widersprechen.
This statement is very convincing.	Diese Aussage ist sehr überzeugend.
I have to admit that the author ...	Ich muss zugeben, dass der Autor / die Autorin ...

Ablehnung ausdrücken

It is only partly true that ...	Es entspricht nur teilweise der Wahrheit, dass ...
I disagree completely with ...	Ich muss widersprechen.
I see things differently.	Ich sehe den Sachverhalt anders.
I must/have to disagree on this matter.	Ich bin in dieser Angelegenheit anderer Meinung.
One cannot possibly accept that ...	Man kann unmöglich akzeptieren, dass ...
I must object to ...	Ich muss ... widersprechen.

I have to criticise strongly that ...	Ich muss scharf kritisieren, dass ...
I doubt whether ...	Ich bezweifle, dass ...
This statement entirely contradicts ...	Diese Behauptung widerspricht ganz und gar ...
However, ...	Jedoch ...
It is not as simple as it seems.	Es ist nicht so einfach wie es scheint.
Unlike the author, I think ...	Anders als der Autor / die Autorin glaube ich ...
I cannot share the author's view on ...	Ich kann die Meinung des Autors / der Autorin über ... nicht teilen.

Einen Grund angeben

As/Since ...	Da/Weil ...
In view of the fact that ...	Angesichts der Tatsache, dass ...
The reason for this lies in ...	Der Grund dafür liegt bei ...
This causes confusion.	Das sorgt für Verwirrung.
That is why ... / Therefore / For this reason ...	Aus diesem Grund ... / Deshalb
Given that ...	In Anbetracht der Tatsache, dass ...
That was caused by ...	Das wurde verursacht durch ...

Eine Folge darstellen

Consequently, ... / As a consequence, ...	Folglich (am Satzanfang)
In view of this statement, ...	In Anbetracht dieser Behauptung ...
in order to	um zu
as a result of	als Folge von

Vergleiche anstellen

to be comparable	vergleichbar sein
compared to / in comparison with	im Vergleich zu
to be different from	sich unterscheiden von
distinguish between (A and B)	(A von B) unterscheiden
to be considerably better than	wesentlich besser sein als
to get more and more difficult	immer schwieriger werden
Nowadays, it is less and less common ...	Heutzutage ist es immer weniger üblich ...
superior/inferior to	überlegen/unterlegen
The former ..., the latter	Der erstere ..., der letztere ...

They have little in common.	Sie haben wenig gemeinsam.
They are equal in price.	Sie haben den gleichen Preis.

Beispiele anführen

for example/instance	zum Beispiel
Let me give you an example.	Lassen Sie mich ein Beispiel anführen.
such as	wie (zum Beispiel)
Look at ...	Sehen wir uns einmal ... an.

Conclusion

To sum up, ... / To summarise, ...	Zusammenfassend kann man sagen ...
I come to the conclusion that ...	Ich komme zu dem Schluss, dass ...
in short	kurz gesagt
To put it in a nutshell ...	Um es auf einen Nenner zu bringen ...
I can support the author's view on ...	Ich kann die Ansicht des Autors / der Autorin über ... unterstützen.
All in all, I believe that ...	Insgesamt glaube ich ...

Intention der Autorin / des Autors

An mehreren Stellen in Ihrer Abiturklausur werden Sie Ihre eigenen Aussagen in Relation zur Meinung der verfassenden Person setzen müssen. Dafür empfiehlt es sich, eine Reihe von sprachlichen Ausdrücken parat zu haben, z. B.:

He/She points out / argues that ...	Er/Sie weist darauf hin / führt an, dass ...
He implies/claims/states that ...	Er behauptet, dass ...
He/She believes/suggests ...	Er/Sie glaubt/schlägt vor ...
He/She lays emphasis on ...	Er/Sie betont ...
His/Her idea was to ...	Er/Sie wollte ...
He/She writes with the intention of *(+ gerund)* ...	Er/Sie schreibt mit der Absicht, ...
His/Her aim is to ...	Sein/Ihr Ziel ist es ...
His/Her attitude towards ...	Seine/Ihre Einstellung gegenüber ...
When he/she says/writes ..., he/she means that ...	Wenn er/sie sagt/schreibt ..., meint er/sie ...
According to the author, ...	Dem Autor / Der Autorin zufolge ...

Verweise und Zitate

Um Ihre Aussagen zu belegen, fügen Sie geeignete Zitate aus dem Originaltext in Ihre Antworten ein. Setzen Sie diese in englische Anführungszeichen – diese beginnen und enden oben. Da es sich in der Abiturklausur um einen relativ kurzen Ausgangstext handelt, genügt als Quellenangabe die Zeilennummer in Klammern direkt hinter dem Zitat.

Beispiel zu Shakespeare, Romeo and Juliet:
In his speech Prince Escalus speaks about the Montagues and the Capulets as "enemies to peace" (l. 1) and finishes by even menacing them with "pain of death" (l. 23).
Verwenden Sie nicht das ganze Zitat, können Sie die ausgelassenen Passagen mit eckigen Klammern kennzeichnen. Genauso können Sie ein Bezugswort in eckigen Klammern einfügen, wenn dies aufgrund der Satzkonstruktion notwendig ist.
Die wörtliche Übernahme von Formulierungen aus dem Ausgangstext bzw. einem anderen Text ohne entsprechende Kennzeichnung ist nicht zulässig und wird negativ bewertet.
Da mit Zitaten Aussagen belegt oder gefestigt werden, stehen sie normalerweise nach der entsprechenden Behauptung. Diese sollten Sie zunächst mit eigenen Worten paraphrasieren. Nehmen Sie dabei Ihr einsprachiges Wörterbuch zur Hilfe, um nach Synonymen zu suchen.

Textstruktur und Absätze

Formalia

TIPP zum Punktesammeln

Achten Sie darauf, dass Sie formale Nachlässigkeiten vermeiden. Hier Punkte zu verschenken, ist unnötig.

Zunächst eine generelle Bemerkung: Die Lesenden Ihrer Englischprüfung werden Ihnen grundsätzlich wohlgesonnen sein und werden Sie gerecht bewerten wollen. Dazu ist es natürlich gerade in einer Fremdsprache eine wichtige Voraussetzung, dass Ihre Handschrift gut lesbar ist, sowie dass die Buchstaben und die Wortgrenzen deutlich erkennbar sind, damit die Lesenden nicht raten müssen, ob Sie nun das für den jeweiligen Kontext passende Wort benutzt haben oder nicht. Wenn Sie also wissen, dass Ihre Handschrift schlecht lesbar ist, bemühen Sie sich zu Ihrem eigenen Vorteil darum, besonders groß und deutlich zu schreiben! Reduzieren Sie nachträgliche Ergänzungen auf ein Minimum. Lassen sich diese nicht vermeiden, nummerieren Sie sie fortlaufend und deutlich und listen Sie den eingefügten Text entweder jeweils am Seitenende oder nach Abschluss des Textes in chronologischer Reihenfolge auf.
Rücken Sie zur besseren Lesbarkeit zwei bis drei Zentimeter ein, wenn Sie einen neuen Absatz beginnen. Erlauben Sie wie gefordert die Hälfte der Seite als Rand für Korrekturzeichen und Bemerkungen der Lehrkraft.

Satzzeichen

Natürlich sollen Sie in der Englischprüfung im Abitur zeigen, dass Sie mit komplexen Satzgefügen umgehen können. Vermeiden Sie allerdings Schwerfälligkeit! Allzu lange Sätze mit vielen Nebensätzen machen Ihren Text schwer lesbar und erhöhen die Wahrscheinlichkeit, dass Sie sich in Ihrer Satzkonstruktion verzetteln. Achten Sie auf sinnvolle Strukturierung durch Satzzeichen; sie helfen dem Leser / der Leserin, Ihren Gedanken zu folgen und sich in Ihrem Text zurechtzufinden. Wechseln Sie ab: Verwenden Sie nicht nur Punkt und Komma, sondern auch Strichpunkt oder Gedankenstrich. Auch durch den Einsatz von Fragen können Sie Ihre Texte ansprechender gestalten.
Interpunktion wird in den Bewertungskriterien nicht aufgeführt und in der Schule großzügig gehandhabt. Bedeutungstragende Satzzeichen, z. B. bei *non-defining relative clauses,* werden jedoch verlangt.

Ausdrucksvermögen / Verfügbarkeit sprachlicher Mittel

Klarheit und Präzision

Die Formulierung der Abituraufgaben folgt klar definierten Regeln. So kommen als Arbeitsanweisungen nur bestimmte Verben in Frage, die sogenannten **Operatoren**. Eine Aufstellung der Operatoren finden Sie auf den Seiten 95 f. in diesem Buch.
Lesen Sie die Formulierung der Fragen genau und machen Sie sich klar, welche Art der Antwort von Ihnen im konkreten Fall erwartet wird. Der Operator drückt deutlich aus, was von Ihnen verlangt wird.
Nachdem also die Art der Fragestellung aufgrund der Formulierung mittels der Operatoren klar definiert ist, können Sie Ihre Antwort entsprechend ausrichten. Achten Sie beim Verfassen auf Fehlerquellen, die leicht vermieden werden können. Im Folgenden werden einige typische Fehlerquellen genannt und erläutert. Diese Hinweise mögen auf den ersten Blick selbstverständlich erscheinen, doch durch die notwendige Konzentration auf den Inhalt oder das Arbeiten unter Zeitdruck schleichen sich oft unnötige Fehler ein.

Textökonomie

Schreiben Sie nach dem Grundsatz der Textökonomie „Jeder Satz ein Statement". Vermeiden Sie Wiederholungen im Wortschatz und umständliche inhaltliche „Schleifen". Zum einen leidet darunter der Stil und zum anderen wird die korrigierende Person diese Taktik wahrscheinlich durchschauen.
Vermeiden Sie die Formulierung von Allgemeinplätzen.
(Beispiel: *It is well-known that Europe is suffering from many problems these days.)*

Stellen Sie sicher, dass die sprachlichen Bezüge korrekt sind: Wählen Sie also bewusst die passenden Personal-, Possessiv-, Demonstrativ- und Relativpronomen, um Ihre Leserschaft eindeutig durch den Text zu führen. Verwenden Sie zusätzlich **signal words** *(Firstly, secondly, thirdly, ...)* als Gliederungssignale, um den Text sinnvoll zu strukturieren. Achten Sie auf die Verwendung der Zeiten! Wenn Sie im **past tense** beginnen, müssen Sie diese Zeitebene auch durchgängig beibehalten.

Wortschatz

Der in Ihren Texten verwendete Wortschatz sollte sachlich und stilistisch angemessen sein. Demonstrieren Sie, dass Sie über einen differenzierten allgemeinen Wortschatz verfügen, und variieren Sie in Ihrem Ausdruck.

Ausdrucksmöglichkeiten im Wortfeld „sagen“
to say, to tell, to relate, to describe, to let somebody know, to state, to speak, to talk, to answer, to respond, to reply, to inform, to advise, to recommend, to brief, to update somebody, to promise, to lie, to whisper, to shout, to scream, to yell, to report, to repeat, to argue, to converse, to allude to something, to articulate, to suggest, to demand, to insist, to urge, to ask, to question

Achten Sie dabei besonders auf gängige Fehlerquellen. Die Beispiele sollen Sie für die Problematik sensibilisieren, aus Platzgründen werden jeweils nur einige genannt.

Seien Sie in Alarmbereitschaft bei potenziellen **false friends.** Hier einige Beispiele:

deutsch	**englisch**	**false friend**
bekommen	to get	*nicht:* become
die Kritik	criticism	*nicht:* critic – die Kritikerin / der Kritiker
die Politik	politics	*nicht:* policy – persönliche Strategie, *außer in Begriffen wie* foreign policy – Außenpolitik
sensibel	sensitive	*nicht:* sensible – vernünftig
meinen/ glauben	to think	*nicht:* mean – bedeuten *(oder Adj.* mean – gemein)
aktuell	current	*nicht:* actually – in der Tat
also	so	*nicht:* also – auch
Chef	boss	*nicht:* chef – der Küchenchef
engagiert	committed	*nicht:* engaged – verlobt; besetzt
eventuell	possibly	*nicht:* eventually – schließlich
Handy	mobile phone (AE: cell phone)	*nicht:* handy – handlich, praktisch
Konfession	denomination	*nicht:* confession – die Beichte
Konkurrenz	competition	*nicht:* concurrence – Übereinstimmung
konsequent	consistent	*nicht:* consequently – folglich
mobben	to bully	*nicht:* mob – das gemeine Volk
prägnant	concise	*nicht:* pregnant – schwanger
prinzipiell	fundamentally, basically, in/on principle	*nicht:* principally – hauptsächlich
Prospekt	brochure, leaflet	*nicht:* prospect(s) – die Zukunftsaussichten

Protokoll	minutes	*nicht:* protocol – die Etikette (außer bei EDV)
Publikum	audience	*nicht:* public – die Öffentlichkeit
rentabel	profitable	*nicht:* rentable – zu mieten
Rückseite	back	*nicht:* backside – Hinterteil
spenden	to donate	*nicht:* to spend – ausgeben

Verwendung der richtigen Präposition nach Verben oder Adjektiven
Orientieren Sie sich nicht am Deutschen, das kann schnell in die Irre führen.

Collocations
Bestimmte Wörter treten immer in einer **festen Verbindung** auf, einer **Kollokation**. Der Austausch eines der Bestandteile ist nicht möglich. (Beispiele: *a quick shower, strong tea, to drive so. crazy, fully aware)*

Darüber hinaus wird von Ihnen die Verwendung eines angemessenen **thematischen Wortschatzes** erwartet. Prägen Sie sich die Glossare zu den lehrplanrelevanten Themen der vorangegangenen Kapitel ein, um den thematischen Wortschatz bei Bedarf zur Verfügung zu haben (vgl. Kapitel „Basiswissen", S. 14 ff.).
Zu guter Letzt sollten Sie über einen präzisen **fachmethodischen Wortschatz** verfügen. Das Handwerkszeug dazu bekommen Sie im Kapitel „Methoden der Textarbeit" (S. 94) dieses Buches, wo Sie geeignetes Vokabular zum Thema finden. Sie sollten sich sowohl Vokabular für literarische Texte als auch für Sach- und Gebrauchstexte aneignen.

Differenzierte Satzgestaltung

Neben der Gewandtheit im Wortschatz wird natürlich auch Ihr Können im Bereich Syntax bewertet. Wechseln Sie also je nach Kontext ab zwischen Parataxe und Hypotaxe, d. h. einer Reihung von Hauptsätzen bzw. komplexen Satzgefügen mit Nebensätzen. Verbinden Sie diese entsprechend mit Konnektoren (s. Liste S. 127 f.); erwähnen Sie Bezüge in temporaler, kausaler, konzessiver, konditionaler und resultativer Hinsicht.

Übersicht über die möglichen Konjunktionen

temporal	while, before, after, until
kausal	since, because, as, for
konzessiv	(al)though, while/whilst, whereas
konditional	if, unless
resultativ	so (that)

Integrieren Sie Partizipial-, Gerundial- und Infinitivkonstruktionen sowie Passivkonstruktionen. Wechseln Sie zusätzlich durch Inversion sowie gelegentliche Verwendung von (rhetorischen) Fragen mit anderen Satzformen ab.

Eigenständigkeit (Paraphrase)

In der Abiturklausur werden Ihr Textverständnis und Ihre Ausdrucksfähigkeit bewertet. Ihr Ziel muss es deshalb sein, der korrigierenden Person ein umfassendes Bild Ihrer Ausdrucksfähigkeit im Englischen zu geben. Greifen Sie dabei häufig auf längere Passagen des Originaltexts zurück, kann die Eigenständigkeit der Leistung nicht ausreichend bewertet werden. Verwenden Sie daher Zitate nur zum Belegen Ihrer eigenen Thesen.

Sprachliche Richtigkeit (Fehlerschwerpunkte vermeiden)

Orthografie, Grammatik

Orthografie

Rechtschreibfehler passieren leicht als Flüchtigkeitsfehler beim Schreiben. Um dem entgegenzuwirken, sollten Sie sich eine funktionierende Zeitplanung aneignen, die Ihnen genug Spielraum lässt, nach Abschluss der produktiven Phase den Text noch einmal durchzulesen und eventuelle Rechtschreibkorrekturen vorzunehmen. Achten Sie dabei besonders auf Interferenzen mit dem Deutschen.

Grammatik

Wie bereits zu Eingang des Kapitels erwähnt, kann in diesem Rahmen keine umfassende Grammatikwiederholung stattfinden. Gehen Sie also Ihre individuellen Problempunkte selbst an.
Trotzdem können an dieser Stelle einige gängige Fehlerquellen genannt werden, auf die Sie ein besonderes Augenmerk legen sollten:

Verben
Sehen Sie sich vor der Prüfung noch einmal die Liste der unregelmäßigen Verben an und prägen Sie sich die Formen ein, die keinem gängigen Schema folgen, z. B. *lie, lay, catch.*

Denken Sie darüber hinaus auch an *phrasal verbs,* deren Bedeutung zum Teil nicht aus den Bedeutungen der Einzelwörter erschließbar ist, z. B. *turn down* (etwas ablehnen).

Adverbien
position of adverbs in the sentence: Adverbien können im englischen Satz an verschiedenen Stellen stehen, die oft nicht mit dem Deutschen übereinstimmen. Sie können folgende Positionen einnehmen: Satzanfang oder -ende sowie vor und nach dem Verb, das sie näher bestimmen (bei zusammengesetzten Verbformen nach dem Hilfsverb).

<u>Beispiele:</u>
Unfortunately, *the turnout for the country's first free election was very low.*
They had counted the votes ***carefully.***
Nevertheless, *the bad news weighed* ***heavily*** *on them.*
I ***often*** *wonder what became of him.*
My sister ***also*** *came. / We must* ***also*** *consider the opposite case.*

Beispiele für Prüfungsaufgaben

Die Beispielaufgaben sind vom Umfang und vom Schwierigkeitsgrad her teilweise für Leistungskurse, teilweise für Grundkurse konzipiert.
Um den verschiedenen Vorgaben für die beiden Kursarten gerecht zu werden, wurden überwiegend Texte ausgewählt, die den Vorgaben beider Kursarten entsprechen. Von Fall zu Fall werden Aufgabenstellungen ergänzt oder angepasst. Eine gute Möglichkeit, sich auf diesen Teil der Prüfung vorzubereiten, sind die TED Talks: www.ted.com.

Aufgaben mit Beispiellösungen

Hörverstehen

Beispielklausur: „Do we need a monarchy?"

You can listen to the audio file by scanning this QR Code:

Source: "The Today Debate: Do we need a monarchy?", *BBC Sounds,* 25 April 2023, https://www.bbc.co.uk/sounds/play/p0fjs1j8 (00:05–04:53) (accessed on 1 April 2024)

> You will hear a radio programme called *Best of Today,* dealing with the future of the royal family. While listening, tick the right answer (a, b, c or d). Do not tick more than one answer. You will hear the recording twice. You have two minutes to look at the task. You will have 30 seconds to finalise your answers after the second listening.

1. The host wonders whether
a) we should celebrate the coronation of the king. ☐
b) historical periods should be named after their monarchs. ☐
c) the monarchy links us to our past. ☒
d) royal children are strange. ☐

2. The audience
a) are invited to join in the debate. ☐
b) didn't know what the topic of the debate would be. ☒
c) boo some of the people on the stage. ☐
d) had to book their places far in advance. ☐

3. Billy Bragg doesn't regard himself as
a) a left-winger. ☐
b) an anti-monarchist. ☐
c) a Republican. ☒
d) an anti-Republican. ☐

4. Juliet Samual points to the beauty of the monarchy in
a) the symbolism of the rose and the thistle.
b) the allegory "The Pilgrim's Progress".
c) the painting of the unicorn and the magician.
d) every-day experiences such as traffic jams and call centres.

5. What has *The Guardian* recently been investigating?
a) the uselessness of the British monarchy
b) the power of the monarchy
c) fake stories about the British monarchy
d) the wealth of the British monarchy

6. Charles Moore claims that Queen Elizabeth was a role model for
a) good management.
b) ceremony.
c) leadership.
d) restraint.

7. Which topic doesn't Jason Arday work on?
a) education
b) gender
c) race
d) inequality

8. According to Jason Arday, Britain doesn't need a monarchy because
a) some aspects are not appropriate any more.
b) it is useless in 21st-century society.
c) it isn't affordable any more
d) it doesn't make a difference in today's society.

Lösung

1. c	5. d
2. b	6. c
3. c	7. b
4. a	8. c

Beispielklausur: „How to survive the digital age"

You can listen to the audio file by scanning this QR Code:

Source: "BBC Trending: How to survive the digital age", *YouTube*, 2 July 2019, https://www.youtube.com/watch?v=l-ZJNGuEP4U (00:18–04:37) (accessed on 1 April 2024)

You will hear a podcast dealing with recent technological developments and the rise of social media. While listening, complete the table below. Write your answers in the boxes. You do not have to write complete sentences. There is one example answer (0). You will hear the recording twice. You have 90 seconds to look at the table. You will have 2 minutes to finalise your answers after the second listening.

0	Douglas Rushkoff can be called …	*an intellectual of the digital world.*	
1	"Team Human" is a book about what Rushkoff calls …	anti human machinery	✓
2	Rushkoff wrote his book after …	in response to panel he was on with one of the famous trans humanist	✓
3	Other scientists argue that human beings had to accept that …	digital community was a new way to talk	✗
4	In what way are humans special, according to Rushkoff? (Give two examples)	*a)* embrace embracery *b)* ~~diffrent~~ ~~diffrent~~ social	0,5 ✓
5	According to Rushkoff, human beings get their power from …	connecting with one another	✓
6	Rushkoff fears that the digital world we are creating …	isolates us	✓
7	The problem for social media companies was that …	took too much money	✓
8	In order to grow fast enough, social media companies …	do increasingly manipulative things	✓

7,5/9

Lösung

1. anti-human machinery.
2. he spoke on a panel (with a famous transhumanist).
3. we will be succeeded by technology.
4. social; able to deal with ambiguity and paradox; able to experience liminal/transitional states
5. connecting with one another.
6. isolates us. / prevents us from connecting with each other.
7. they needed too much money.
8. became manipulative. / manipulated their users.

Beispielklausur: „Plastic Fantastic“

You can listen to the audio file by scanning this QR code:

Source: “Plastic Fantastic: What’s the Solution”, *BBC Sounds*, 29 May 2018, https://www.bbc.co.uk/sounds/play/b0b42z8k (00:00–05:05) (accessed on 1 April 2024)

You will hear a podcast dealing with the topic of solutions to the plastic pollution. While listening, complete the table below. Write down your answers in the boxes. You do not have to write complete sentences. There is one example answer (0). You will hear the recording twice. You have 90 seconds to look at the table. You will have 2 minutes to finalise your answers after the second listening.

0	What plastic is called?	*the workhorse of the economy*
1	Why is plastic such a valuable material? (Name three reasons.)	*a)* *b)* *c)*
2	The programme investigates the question whether all packaging ...	
3	Why it is not realistic to go plastic-free?	
4	More environmentally friendly forms of plastic currently aren’t a good solution because ...	
5	Plastic bottles shouldn’t be recycled but ...	
6	The government is discussing the introduction of ...	
7	Which two economic systems is Purnell talking about?	
8	What is the key aspect of the economy Purnell wants to transition to?	
9	The main problem of designers is that they feel ...	

Lösung

1. flexible, durable, cheap, disposable
2. should be biodegradable.
3. Because everything around us is plastic.
4. we don't have the right infrastructure. / it isn't recycled/composted properly.
5. reused.
6. a deposit return scheme for bottles.
7. linear and circular
8. Products return to the value they had before they were used.
9. that they have no sense of responsibility.

Kombinierte Aufgabe – Sachtext und politische Rede

Part 1: Mediation

AUFGABENSTELLUNG

Together with your English partner school, you are participating in an international project on climate change. Your task is to write an article on the results of the Glasgow Climate Change Conference 2021 (COP 26) to be published on the project's website. Write this text using the article below and focussing on the perspective of the African nations.

Materialgrundlage

M1 Andrea Böhm, „Klimaschutz oder grüner Kolonialismus? – Eine Kolumne von Andrea Böhm", *ZEIT online*, 06.01.2022, https://www.zeit.de/politik/ausland/2022-01/cop-26-globaler-sueden-klimawandel-gerechtigkeit-5vor8 (Zugriff: 01.04.2024, gekürzt).

M1 „Klimaschutz oder grüner Kolonialismus?" *Andrea Böhm*

[...]

Die Konferenz in Glasgow im vergangenen November, in Deutschland schon fast wieder vergessen, hat in Staaten des globalen Südens enorme Verbitterung hinterlassen. Erneut wurde ihre zentrale Forderung abgebügelt: Klimagerechtigkeit.

Natürlich war COP26 kein totaler Reinfall. Der schrittweise Abschied aus der Kohleenergie steht im Abschlusspapier, über 140 Regierungen haben den Schutz und die Wiederaufforstung der Wälder versprochen, über 100 Länder wollen bis 2030 den Methanausstoß um ein Drittel reduzieren und alle sollen ihre Klimaziele bis zur nächsten Konferenz nachbessern. Was in Glasgow nicht passierte: die Verantwortung für die Erhitzung unseres Planeten ehrlich zu benennen und Rechenschaft abzulegen.

Dass die Ärmsten am wenigsten zur Erderwärmung beigetragen haben, aber schon seit Langem den höchsten Preis zahlen, ist längst eine Binsenweisheit. Bloß empfindet sie in unseren Breitengraden kaum jemand als Skandal. 23 reiche Staaten mit heute zwölf Prozent der Weltbevölkerung (darunter die USA, Deutschland, Kanada und Japan) haben seit Beginn der Industrialisierung die Hälfte aller CO_2-Emissionen ausgestoßen.

Die andere Hälfte verteilt sich auf über 150 andere Länder – und wird angeführt von China, das inzwischen fast 14 Prozent der Emissionen verursacht hat. Subsaharaafrika ist für gerade mal 1,85 Prozent verantwortlich, wird aber schon seit Jahrzehnten weit dramatischer von den Folgen der Klimakrise getroffen als Europa. Gleiches gilt für die kleinen Inselstaaten, denen buchstäblich der Untergang droht.

Deswegen fordern ärmere Staaten seit Jahren einen Fonds für Schäden und Verluste (*loss and damage*) gefüllt von den Hauptverursachern des Klimawandels. Aus diesem Fonds sollen von Dürren, Fluten, Hungersnöten oder Unwettern Betroffene im Zusammenhang mit der Erderwärmung unterstützt werden. Der Außenminister von Bangladesch, AK Abdul Momen, hat das Konzept unlängst mit dem Vorgehen gegen die Tabakindustrie in den Neunzigerjahren verglichen, als sich die US-Regierung von den Konzernen vor Gericht einige der Milliarden Dollar zurückholte, die durch die Gesundheitsschäden des Rauchens entstanden waren.

Die Entwicklungsländer fühlen sich verprellt

Nun, der Fonds wurde in Glasgow nicht beschlossen, vor allem aufgrund des Widerstands der USA und der EU, die fürchten, für Klimaschäden haftbar gemacht zu werden. Auch bei anderen Zahlungen fühlen sich Entwicklungsländer verprellt. 100 Milliarden US-Dollar jährlich ab 2020 wollten Industrienationen für Klimaprojekte im globalen Süden bereitstellen, um beim Übergang zu grüner Energie und bei der Anpassung an die Krise zu helfen – zum Beispiel durch Frühwarnsysteme oder Küstenbefestigungen. Die Summe wird frühestens 2023 zum ersten Mal erreicht.

Zum Vergleich: Der Hilfsfonds für die Opfer des Hochwassers in Rheinland-Pfalz und Nordrhein-Westfalen ist auf 30 Milliarden Euro angelegt.

Viel des internationalen Geldes wird laut einer Studie von Oxfam auch gar nicht als Zuschuss geleistet, sondern als Kredite, die oft mit Zinsen zurückgezahlt werden müssen. Soll heißen: Was vonseiten der Industriestaaten als Hilfe angeboten wird, ist für die Empfänger oftmals eine Schuldenfalle.

Natürlich gibt es auch kleine Lichtblicke: So gaben die EU, Großbritannien, Deutschland und Frankreich während der Glasgower Konferenz bekannt, Südafrika mit 8,5 Milliarden Euro beim Ausstieg aus der Kohle helfen zu wollen.

Prima. Aber es mindert nicht die Wut unter Politikern wie Aktivistinnen auf dem Nachbarkontinent über europäische und US-amerikanische Heuchelei. In Glasgow versprachen westliche Industrienationen, die Finanzierung weiterer Projekte zur Öl- und Gasförderung zu stoppen. Im Ausland, aber nicht daheim. Großbritannien subventioniert weiter seine Erdölindustrie, die USA wollen ihre Inlandsproduktion sogar noch steigern.

Kein afrikanisches Land sieht seine Zukunft in fossilen Energieträgern

Und während westliche Staaten sowie internationale Finanzinstitutionen den Geldhahn für Erdgasförderung in afrikanischen Ländern zudrehen, stempelt sich die EU Atomkraft und Gas klimafreundlich. Der Vorwurf des "grünen Kolonialismus" afrikanischer Aktivisten mag in europäischen Ohren harsch klingen, verständlich ist er allemal: Hier warten Abermillionen darauf, dass endlich Strom aus der Steckdose kommt. Gerade Afrika braucht Erdgas für seine wirtschaftliche Entwicklung – als Übergang. Denn kein afrikanisches Land sieht seine Zukunft in fossilen Energieträgern. Kenia oder Sambia beziehen schon heute über 50 Prozent ihrer Energie aus nachhaltigen Quellen. Das Ölland Nigeria, das 2050 mehr Einwohner haben wird als die USA, will seine Stromproduktion bis dahin verachtfachen – überwiegend mit Solarenergie. Zur Absicherung braucht es, wie gesagt, Erdgas. Und mehr finanzielle Hilfe.

Die Forderung nach einer gerechteren Beteiligung und Entschädigung durch Industriestaaten wird nach Glasgow nicht leiser, sondern lauter werden. Immerhin: Die Deutschen sehen ihr Land in der Verantwortung. Über 70 Prozent erklärten in einer Umfrage des Instituts für Demoskopie Allensbach im vergangenen Sommer, dass die Industrieländer eine "große" oder "sehr große" Verantwortung für die Klimakrise in Entwicklungsländern tragen.

[...]

Part 2: Politische Rede

AUFGABENSTELLUNG Writing

1 Outline the main points in Kamala Harris' speech. (30 %)

2 Analyse the stylistic means Kamala Harris uses to persuade the audience of her position. (30 %)

3 Choose ONE of the following tasks.

a) Assess Kamala Harris' statement from her speech: "And while this virus touches us all [...] [i]t is not an equal opportunity offender". Include additional materials studied in class in your considerations.

– or –

b) You are an exchange student at an American high school, where you covered Harris' speech in class. Being inspired, write a blog entry commenting on the importance of leadership in times of crisis, using the speech as a starting point. (40 %)

Materialgrundlage

M2 „Senator and Vice-Presidential Nominee Kamala Harris' 2020 Democratic National Convention (DNC) speech on August 19", 19.02.2020, *General Counsel, Austin;* https://www.rev.com/blog/transcripts/kamala-harris-2020-dnc-speech-transcript (Zugriff: 01.04.2024, gekürzt)

M2 Kamala Harris: 2020 Speech at the Democratic National Convention (extract)

Aug 20, 2020

That I am here tonight is a testament to the dedication of generations before me, women and men who believed so fiercely in the promise of equality, liberty, and justice for all. […]

My mother instilled in my sister Maya and me the values that would chart the course of our lives. She raised us to be proud, strong Black women, and she raised us to know and be proud of our Indian heritage. She taught us to put family first, the family you're born into, and the family you choose. […]

And even as she taught us to keep our family at the center of our world, she also pushed us to see a world beyond ourselves. She taught us to be conscious and compassionate about the struggles of all people, to believe public service is a noble cause, and the fight for justice is a shared responsibility. […]

I accept your nomination for Vice President of the United States of America.

I do so committed to the values she taught me, […] and to a vision passed on through generations of Americans, one that Joe Biden shares. A vision of our nation as a beloved community, where all are welcome, no matter what we look like, no matter where we come from, or who we love. A country where we may not agree on every detail, but we are united by the fundamental belief that every human being is of infinite worth, deserving of compassion, dignity, and respect. A country where we look out for one another, where we rise and fall as one, where we face our challenges and celebrate our triumphs together.

Today, that country feels distant. Donald Trump's failure of leadership has cost lives and livelihoods. […] And while this virus touches us all, we got to be honest. It is not an equal opportunity offender. Black, Latino, and Indigenous people are suffering and dying disproportionately. And this is not a coincidence. It is the effect of structural racism, of inequities in education and technology, healthcare and housing, job security and transportation. […]

So we're at an inflection point. The constant chaos leaves us adrift. The incompetence makes us feel afraid. The callousness makes us feel alone. It's a lot, and here's the thing. We can do better, and deserve so much more. We must elect a president who will bring something different, something better, and do the important work. A president who will bring all of us together, Black, White, Latino, Asian, Indigenous, to achieve the future we collectively want. We must elect Joe Biden. […]

Right now, we have a president who turns our tragedies into political weapons. Joe will be a president who turns our challenges into purpose. Joe will bring us together to build an economy that doesn't leave anyone behind, where a good paying job is the floor, not the ceiling. […]

That's the vision that our parents and grandparents fought for. The vision that made my own life possible. The vision that makes the American promise, for all its complexities and imperfections, a promise worth fighting for. So make no mistake, the road ahead is not easy. We may stumble. We may fall short, but I pledge to you that we will act boldly and deal with our challenges honestly. We will speak truths, and we will act with the same faith in you that we ask you to place in us. We believe that our country, all of us, will stand together for a better future. [...]

In this election, we have a chance to change the course of history. We're all in this fight. You, me, and Joe, together. What an awesome responsibility. What an awesome privilege. So let's fight with conviction. Let's fight with hope. Let's fight with confidence in ourselves, and a commitment to each other, to the America we know is possible, the America we love. And years from now, this moment will have passed, and our children and our grandchildren will look in our eyes. And they're going to ask us, "Where were you when the stakes were so high?" They will ask us, "What was it like?" And we will tell them. We will tell them not just how we felt. We will tell them what we did. [...]

Beispiellösung

Part 1: Mediation

North vs. South: The Climate Injustice of COP 26

The conference in Glasgow may seem a success story for a lot of states in the Northern hemisphere: 140 countries signed a treaty to phase out of fossil fuels, to protect forests and to reduce methane emissions by a third.

However, in her review of COP 26 in the German newspaper *ZEIT*, Andrea Böhm points out that the conference has left many nations in the South feeling bitter, as the conference once again failed to address one pressing issue: climate justice. While 23 states with 12 % of the world population are responsible for half of all carbon dioxide emissions, these suffer comparatively little from the effects of climate change. On the other hand, sub-Saharan nations, for example, which contribute less than 2 % of global CO_2 emissions, are hit particularly hard by climate change. Hence, these southern nations demand that those mainly responsible for carbon dioxide emissions create a special fund to pay for the damages caused by climate change.

Due to resistance from the US and the EU, COP 26 failed to implement this fund. In addition, financial aids promised by these richer nations for climate projects in the global south not only appear relatively small compared to money that is spent on climate-related damages nationally. A lot of these payments are also planned as loans, making further debt likely.

Another injustice has led some African activists to speak of "green colonialism": While the EU labels natural gas as climate-friendly within its sphere, it has stopped financial support for its exploitation further south. This decision hits African nations hard since they rely on gas for their economic growth, even though some of these states already gain over 50 % of their energy from sustainable sources and no African country sees its future in fossil fuels.

In any case, the calls for more climate justice are growing louder even in western nations such as Germany. Luckily, the next COP is just around the corner.

Part 2: Politische Rede

Aufgabe 1

The text is from Senator Kamala Harris's acceptance speech, given at the Democratic National Convention on 20 August 2020 after her nomination as Democratic vice presidential candidate for the forthcoming election. As the first woman of colour to run for

vice presidency of the USA, she emphasises her pride in her Indian heritage and her gratitude to her mother, who brought her up to be compassionate and conscious of other people's problems.
Harris touches upon liberty, equality and justice for all: this is the "shared responsibility" she and Joe Biden accept. She pictures the USA as a "beloved community" where everybody is welcome, irrespective of ethnic heritage or sexual orientation. Everyone deserves respect; every individual is of inestimable value.
Harris calls on her fellow Democratic Party members to show unity and loyalty to Joe Biden and herself in the task of reversing Trump's white-supremacist policy, which has politically polarised and socially divided the country. She holds out the prospect of Joe Biden as a healing and unifying head of state, building an economy that provides jobs for all and in this way re-establishes the "American promise". But at the same time she admits that this may be a path of trial and tribulation.
Harris ends her speech by emphasising her belief in the country standing together to achieve a better future for all American citizens and by again invoking Democratic Party unity. Underlining the opportunity to change the course of history by winning the Presidency, she calls the election a "fight" which should be undertaken confidently and convincingly.

Aufgabe 2
Kamala Harris employs a variety of stylistic means to persuade her audience, weaving together personal narrative, appeals to shared values and direct criticism of opposing viewpoints.
She uses antithesis to juxtapose ideas to highlight contrasts, as seen in her remarks about the current state of the country versus her vision for its future. For example, she places "Donald Trump's failure of leadership has cost lives and livelihoods" (ll. 40–42) in opposition to the idea of electing Joe Biden to bring about positive change (cf. ll. 56–62). This device sharpens the differences between her and her opponents, clarifying the choice for the audience.
Similes and metaphors convey complex ideas in a relatable way in Harris' speech. Referring to America as "a beloved community" (l. 29) invokes a sense of unity and warmth and serves to inspire and evoke a sense of belonging and togetherness among the audience. Likewise, her metaphor of "a good paying job [being] the floor, not the ceiling" (ll. 69–71) easily simplifies the idea of financial prosperity without delineating these concepts more sharply.
Most frequently, Harris uses the anaphora and parallelism to emphasise her points and to build rhythm. For instance, the frequently repeated "she taught us" (ll. 12, 15, 18) highlights the values instilled by her mother but also creates a rhythmic flow that enhances the memorability and impact of her words. The parallelism of "a vision" and "a country" (ll. 26–39) again gives the text a rising cadence and links the US with her political ideas.
Harris also employs inclusive language to create a sense of unity and belonging. This is most obviously stressed in the frequent use of "we", "us" and "our" (ll. 30–39, 43, 51–62, 78–102). This inclusivity reinforces her vision of a united nation and appeals

to a broad audience by emphasising diversity and acceptance, but it also points to a shared responsibility.
In the same vein, Harris directly addresses the audience, seeking to build rapport. In stating, "I accept your nomination for Vice President of the United States of America" (ll. 23 f.), Harris engages with the audience directly, making her message more personal and powerful. The same holds true for her assurance of action in lines 80 f. that is prefaced by "I pledge to you" (l. 79).
Each of these stylistic devices serves to strengthen Harris' message, making her speech more persuasive, memorable and emotionally resonant. By skillfully combining these elements, she not only communicates her vision but also motivates her audience to support her and the values she represents.

Aufgabe 3a
In her 2020 acceptance speech for the vice-presidential nomination, Kamala Harris eloquently addresses the profound challenges facing America, underscored by the COVID-19 pandemic. However, her speech transcends the immediate crisis, touching upon a more enduring and pervasive issue: structural racism. Pointing out that "this virus [...] is not an equal opportunity offender", Harris not only highlights the uneven toll of the pandemic but also uses it as a lens to expose the broader, systemic inequalities that have long plagued American society.
The pandemic has starkly revealed and intensified pre-existing health disparities among minority communities. These disparities, as Harris points out, are not accidental but are deeply rooted in structural inequities that limit access to healthcare, quality housing and economic opportunities and hence lead to higher rates of mortality. This argument underscores the urgent need to address this systemic neglect and discrimination.
Harris's critique extends into the realm of economic disparities and job insecurity, where marginalised communities are overrepresented in precarious, low-wage jobs without adequate protections. The pandemic has exacerbated these economic vulnerabilities, highlighting the intersection of systemic racism with economic injustice. The disproportionate economic impact on these communities underscores the necessity of systemic reforms.
The transition to digital learning has also magnified the educational divide due to unequal access to technology and resources, affecting primarily Black, Latino and Indigenous students. Similarly, housing inequities, manifesting in higher rates of homelessness and inadequate living conditions, made it challenging for people from these communities to adhere to public health measures during the pandemic.
An additional dimension of structural racism is the disproportionate impact of police violence on Black, Latino and Indigenous communities. This form of systemic injustice is a vivid manifestation of the racial bias embedded within law enforcement and the broader criminal justice system. The call for reform in policing practices and the demand for accountability and justice reflect a critical aspect of the broader struggle against systemic racism.
Kamala Harris's speech, while anchored in the context of the COVID-19 pandemic, thus offers a profound critique of structural racism in America. Her assertion that "[i]t is not an equal opportunity offender" serves as a powerful reminder of the systemic inequalities

that pervade US society. Harris' vision for America – a vision of equity, justice and unity – demands a collective commitment to dismantling structural racism, ensuring that the promise of equality and liberty is realised for all.

Aufgabe 3b

Leadership in Times of Crisis: A Reflection Inspired by Kamala Harris' Speech

As an exchange student at an American high school, I've had the unique opportunity to observe and engage with the political and social dynamics of the United States from a fresh perspective. Recently, our class covered Kamala Harris' acceptance speech for the vice-presidential nomination, and it left a profound impact on me. The speech provides a compelling starting point for discussing the importance of leadership in times of crisis.

The current global landscape is marred by crises that test the very fabric of our societies: the ongoing war in Ukraine, the escalating, man-made climate catastrophe and the enduring Israeli-Palestinian conflict, to name a few. Harris' emphasis on empathy as a cornerstone of effective leadership is particularly relevant in these contexts.

The ability to understand and share the feelings of those suffering – be it from war, environmental devastation or longstanding conflict – is crucial for leaders tasked with guiding their nations through these turbulent times. By acknowledging the disproportionate suffering of Black, Latino and Indigenous communities during the pandemic, she not only sheds light on systemic inequalities but also illustrates the leader's role in recognising and addressing the pain of those they serve. Empathy, as Harris' speech demonstrates, is about more than understanding; it's about taking action to mitigate the struggles of the most vulnerable. As Harris says, it is not merely about how we feel, but also about what we do.

Another aspect of Harris' speech that struck me was her unwavering commitment to a vision of unity and inclusivity. In times of crisis this is vital because we confront global challenges that require cooperation across borders. The climate catastrophe, for example, demands a unified approach to mitigate its impact and adapt to its inevitable consequences. Harris' call for a nation "where all are welcome" is a powerful reminder of the need for leaders who can see beyond the present challenges to a future in which everyone has a place.

Perhaps the most compelling message I took from Harris' speech is the idea that leadership is not the sole responsibility of those in high office. She speaks of public service as a noble cause and the fight for justice as a shared responsibility. This perspective invites us to con-sider our role in shaping the future, encouraging each other to engage in civic life and work towards the kind of society we want to live in.

Kamala Harris' speech, while anchored in the American political landscape, offers valuable insights for understanding and addressing the global crises of our time. Her message of empathy, unity and shared responsibility resonates deeply in a world grappling with environmental devastation and conflict. As I reflect on her words from my unique vantage point as an exchange student, I am inspired by the potential for leadership – both within and beyond political realms – to guide us through these challenges.

Cartoon – Globalisation

AUFGABENSTELLUNG

Globalisation and globalised economy – a fair chance for everyone?
With an international group of university students, you are preparing a weekend seminar on the effects of globalisation, communicating with the other students via email.
You are responsible for the opening session and have been given the task of choosing a cartoon as an opener. You have found the cartoon at hand. Explain how it will best suit the purpose of introducing the issue and why it can be given to the participants as a means of stimulating discussion.
After describing the cartoon, analyse what the students can take from it and give your partners some idea of the main points you want to make.
Write this email.

TIPP zur Beschreibung von Bildmaterial

Auch bei Aufgaben, in denen das Material nur eingebettet ist, ist es sinnvoll, dieses an der entsprechenden Stelle im Text zu beschreiben. In unserem Beispiel ist es notwendig, die Beschreibung des Bildes in der Einleitung aufzugreifen, um anschließend darauf eingehen zu können. Bei der Betrachtung von Bildern ist es ebenso wie bei Texten entscheidend, die Position des Fotografen, Künstlers, Karikaturisten etc. zu berücksichtigen. Bei jedem Bild sollte man sich die Frage stellen, mit welcher Absicht es angefertigt worden ist, und sollte dies sprachlich in der Darstellung berücksichtigen.

Lösungshinweise

- introduction: reasons for choosing this cartoon as eye-opener for weekend seminar
- possibly cover speech bubble to stimulate participation
- description: man on the right is sitting at a desk talking to a woman on the left; behind the woman, open door leads to a room with many people working, seemingly folding/packaging some sort of product; room is labelled "sweat shop floor", indicating that the people there are working long hours for little money; sign in office indicates that this is a factory for leisure clothing; man on the right says that they located their production to this country because they have no word for "leisure" in their language
- analysis: skin colour and clothing identify man on the right as Westerner, probably a manager; woman in the middle places the setting most likely in a developing nation; "sweat shop floor" sign indicates exploitation of cheap labour; graph on the wall on the right insinuates that manager/company only cares for profit and not their employees' wellbeing; irony of producing leisure products in a country where people have no word for this concept; globalisation exclusively interested in profit
- companies want to cut labor costs but exploit human resources, especially in Asia in order to do so; globalisation exploiting man power, cultural idiosyncrasies and most likely also natural resources
- fast fashion has become a phenomenon that is facilitated to large degree by globalisation
- because of lacking regulation, workers often suffer from low pay, a poor and dangerous working environment and physical abuse

Sachtext – Politischer Zeitungsartikel

AUFGABENSTELLUNG

1 Summarise the main reasons Southern Co-op uses live facial recognition technology (30 %)

2 Contrast the view of Southern Co-op with the opposing perspectives on the necessity and benefits of facial recognition technology. (30 %)

3 Choose ONE of the following tasks.

a) Discuss the potential and risks of technology in crime prevention, considering the given article as well as material covered in class.

– or –

b) Write a blog commenting on the fast-paced development of technology in fighting crime, incorporating the article as well material covered in class. Use the following quotation as a starting point:
„Privacy is rarely lost in one fell swoop. It is usually eroded over time, little bits dissolving almost imperceptibly until we finally begin to notice how much is gone."
(Daniel J. Solove, 2011) (40 %)

Materialgrundlage

Shanti Das, „Facial recognition cameras in supermarkets ‚targeted at poor areas' in England", *The Guardian,* 27.01.2024, https://www.theguardian.com/uk-news/2024/jan/27/facial-recognition-cameras-in-supermarkets-targeted-at-poor-areas-in-england. Copyright Guardian News & Media Ltd 2024. (Zugriff: 01.03.2024, gekürzt)

„Facial recognition cameras in supermarkets 'targeted at poor areas' in England" *Shanti Das*

[...]

Facial recognition cameras installed by a supermarket chain to tackle shoplifting disproportionately target people in poorer areas, according to a privacy rights group.

Southern Co-op, which uses Facewatch live recognition cameras in 34 branches, typically has shops in richer-than-average neighbourhoods. But just five of the stores in which it uses Facewatch are in the richest third of neighbourhoods in England, while 14 are in the poorest.

Professor Pete Fussey, director of the Centre for Research into Information, Surveillance and Privacy at University of Essex, said the findings raised concerns about the targeting of people on the "margins of society". "This is another example of the many ways in which surveillance is more intensely focused on minorities and those who are disadvantaged socioeconomically," he said.

Southern Co-op [...] said it did not consider how deprived an area was, or other demographic information, when deploying the technology. The cameras were in locations considered high-risk based on "our crime data and stock loss reports".

Fussey said police and businesses often claimed decisions on where to use facial recognition were an "objective judgment" based on crime levels. "But the issue is that it's not clear at all," he said. "We're going to find crime in the areas we look at most heavily. And we look most heavily at suspect populations, those who are seen as threatening or outsiders, and the urban poor."

Analysis by the privacy group Big Brother Watch used data supplied by Southern Co-op cross-referenced with the England-wide 2019 Indices of Multiple Deprivation. The index ranks more than 30,000 neighbourhoods across seven areas, including income and employment, to calculate their relative deprivation – with the number one ranked neighbourhood being the most deprived.

An average Southern Co-op store is in an area ranking at 19,835 out of 32,844, putting it in the best-off third of neighbourhoods. But supermarkets where facial recognition is deployed are in neighbourhoods ranked at 14,453 on average, placing them in the most deprived half.

Jake Hurfurt, the head of research at Big Brother Watch, said: "This data shows that AI supermarket surveillance is being directed at poorer communities, who are more likely to suffer excessive invasions of their privacy and unfair treatment as a result."

Increasingly used by police and private firms, live facial recognition operates in real-time to compare camera feeds with faces on a predetermined watchlist, to identify people of interest. Each time a match is found, the system generates an alert.

Advocates including police chiefs and the government say the technology deters crime and helps identify offenders. But concerns have been raised over a lack of oversight and transparency as its use becomes more mainstream.

On Friday, the House of Lords Justice and Home Affairs committee wrote to the home secretary, James Cleverly, calling on him to urgently address concerns about live facial recognition use by police, which it said lacked "clear legal foundation".

The committee said there were "no rigorous standards or systems of regulation" in place for monitoring the technology's use and "no consistency in approaches to training" among police forces. "The committee accepts that live facial recognition may be a valuable tool in apprehending criminals, but it is deeply concerned that its use is being expanded without proper scrutiny and accountability," it said.

[...]

Nick Fisher, the chief executive of Facewatch, said the technology was used to protect stock and staff and to deter crime. "Retailers across the UK use Facewatch in those stores where it is necessary to do so because other crime prevention methods have been tried and failed," he said. "Their lawful use of Facewatch reduces crime between 30% and 70% in every location it is deployed in."

A Southern Co-op spokesperson said its use of the technology was "limited and targeted", and had helped cut crime. It recorded 38,262 incidents in 2022, including "shoplifting, violence and physical and verbal abuse". Internal figures showed a 34% reduction in violence against staff in 2021 compared with 2020 at shops using the technology. It acknowledged that this was due to "a range of measures we are using to tackle crime, as well as a number of external factors".

[...]

In October, human rights groups including Liberty and Amnesty International wrote to leading UK retailers urging them to quit a police-led scheme that aims to use facial recognition to tackle shoplifting. In a letter to companies including John Lewis, Tesco, Boots and M&S about the "Pegasus" initiative, the charities said: "Facial recognition technology notoriously misidentifies people of colour, women and LGBTQ+ people, meaning that already marginalised groups are more likely to be subject to an invasive stop by police, or at increased risk of physical surveillance, monitoring and harassment by workers in your stores."

A government spokesperson said facial recognition a "sound legal basis" and had helped police catch "a large number of serious criminals" including people wanted for murder and sexual offences. "The police can only use facial recognition for a policing purpose, where necessary, proportionate and fair, in line with data protection and human rights laws," they said.

ONS figures last week put shoplifting at record levels, with more than 402,000 offences in the year to September 2023, up from 304,459 the year before.

Annotations:

16 suspect – verdächtigt; **19 deprivation** – Benachteiligung; **64 ONS** – Office for National Statistics; Behörde, die mit der Erhebung und Publikation statistischer Daten beauftragt ist

Lösungshinweise und Beispiellösungen

Aufgabe 1

- introductory sentence, incl. title, text form, author, source, date
- technology protects personnel (e. g. from physical/verbal abuse) and inventory (e. g. from shoplifting, damage, etc.), deters crime
- operates in real time, thus immediate reaction possible
- in-store data: crime reduction of 30–70 % after deployment
- validation: deployment based only on in-store crime and stock loss data. not on demographic data

Aufgabe 2

Southern Co-op's perspective:

- Validation: live recognition cameras in 34 branches, (allegedly) solely based on "crime data and stock loss reports" (l. 28)
- Effectiveness: "limited and targeted" deployment (ll. 103 f.), aimed at protecting staff/ customers and inventory; effectiveness evident (34% reduction in violence against staff after installation (cf. ll. 107 ff.); proven effectiveness in policing (cf. ll. 128 ff.)
- "Last Resort": Facewatch succeeds where other methods have failed (cf. ll. 96 ff.)
- "sound legal basis" (l. 130), only allowed to be used "where necessary, proportionate and fair, in line with data protection and human rights laws" (ll. 136 ff.)

Opposing perspective:

- Validation: use of facial recognition cameras in Southern Co-op shops is biased towards demographically deprived areas (cf. ll. 9 f.)
- crime disproportionately sought (and found) within "suspect population" (ll. 35 f.)
- Unreliability: human rights organisations argue that the technology "notoriously misidentifies people of colour, women, and LGBTQ+ people" (ll. 123 ff.)
- minority groups and disadvantaged people are victim to increased invasion of privacy (cf. ll. 18 ff.), unfairness (cf. ll. 67 ff.), "monitoring and harassment" (ll. 128 f.)
- Legal framework: House of Lords Justice and Home Affairs committee highlighting the absence of legal foundation and regulation (cf. ll. 81 ff.)

Aufgabe 3a

Potential:

- Efficiency: can significantly improve security measures by analysing patterns to predict crime hotspots and times; allows for more efficient allocation of law enforcement resources (cf. crime reduction between 30% and 70% according to Facewatch CEO; 34% reduction in violence against staff at Southern Co-op)
- can increase success rates of investigations; behavioral patterns can be established so frequent offenders can be recognised and prosecuted more easily (cf. pre-determined watchlist); could also help identify non-threatening situations (cf. "Heads of the Colored People": Riley's and Richard's dispute could have been identified as a mere quarrel, the alleged weapon as a book, thus preventing police from shooting them)
- mere presence of surveillance technologies can deter potential offenders

Concerns and Criticisms:

- Privacy and surveillance: expansion of surveillance technologies can lead to overreach, where monitoring and collection of data infringe on personal privacy and civil liberties, creating a surveillance state
- technology has been criticised for potentially misidentifying people, particularly those from marginalised groups (cf. Liberty and Amnesty International in article); biased implementation against marginalised groups (cf. Fussey in article)
- Dependence on technology: reliance on technological solutions undermines traditional policing methods and skills; vulnerability to cyberattacks
- Lack of regulation and oversight: concerning lack of clear legal frameworks and rigorous standards (cf. House of Lords Justice and Home Affairs committee in article)
- Manipulation and misinformation: advanced technologies like AI-generated content can be used to create false evidence or misinformation
- Ethical and societal implications: technologies that appear to predict criminal activity based on historical data can reinforce biases and lead to discriminatory practices towards disadvantaged or marginalised communities, worsening social inequalities and contributing to a climate of mistrust and discrimination. (cf. "Heads of the Colored People": unfavourable depiction of both innocent victims in the press)

Aufgabe 3b

<u>The Double-Edged Sword of Technological Advances in Crime Prevention</u>

In the rapidly evolving landscape of crime prevention, technology stands as both a beacon of hope and a source of heated discussions. Daniel J. Solove's insight that "[p]rivacy is rarely lost in one fell swoop. It is usually eroded over time, little bits dissolving almost imperceptibly until we finally begin to notice how much is gone" rings especially true in light of a recent report by Shanti Das in *The Guardian* on 27 January 2024, detailing the deployment of facial recognition cameras by a British supermarket chain, notably targeted at poorer areas. In my opinion, this development serves as an example of the broader dialogue on the balance between security and privacy in the digital age.

The adoption of technology in the fight against crime is a double-edged sword, a sentiment echoed by Southern Co-op's widespread use of facial recognition cameras. Nick Fisher, the CEO of Facewatch, champions this approach, boasting substantial crime reduction rates of 30% to 70% wherever implemented. However, the enthusiasm for these achievements must be tempered with caution, as the ramifications for personal privacy and societal fairness loom large and unsettling.

The heart of the matter here isn't just the creeping loss of privacy, something we're all vaguely aware of but often choose to ignore until it slams us in the face. It's about how this invasion, subtle as it might seem at first, reveals itself in stark reality when technologies like facial recognition are unleashed upon deprived neighborhoods. Such actions don't just smell of bias; they reek of a deliberate targeting that could deepen the chasms within our society. A spokesperson for Southern Co-op casually mentions the deployment in "high-risk" areas, but one can't help but wonder who decides what "high-risk" means and whether it's just a euphemism for economic profiling.

Diving deeper into this quagmire, we're faced with a regulatory landscape that's as barren as a desert. The criticism from bodies like the House of Lords Justice and Home Affairs committee about the lack of robust frameworks isn't just academic – it's a red flag signaling the potential for rampant misuse and an unchecked spread of surveillance tactics. This wild west of surveillance technology underscores an alarming disregard for individual rights, practically inviting a dystopian future where privacy is a concept as outdated as dial-up internet.
Then there's the Achilles' heel of these technologies: their disturbingly high failure rates, particularly in accurately recognising individuals from diverse backgrounds. This isn't just a glitch; it's a systemic flaw that risks wrongful accusations and exacerbates tensions between the public and those wielding this digital power. The repercussions extend beyond mere errors – they erode the very trust that's essential for any form of governance.
So, where do we go from here? The solution isn't to demonise technology or halt its progress in crime prevention; after all, the benefits it brings to the table are too significant to ignore. However, it's high time for a more opinionated, vocal public discourse that demands accountability and transparency in how these tools are used. The internet is awash with experts calling for tighter regulations and oversight, not to stifle innovation but to ensure it serves the greater good without trampling over our rights to privacy and fairness.
Reflecting on Daniel J. Solove's poignant words, I think it is evident that our quest for security shouldn't lead us down a path where we're left with a hollow shell of what privacy once was. The balancing act between leveraging technology in fighting crime and preserving our fundamental liberties is delicate and requires constant vigilance. After all, in the pursuit of a safer society, we mustn't lose sight of the values that define our humanity and justice.

Aufgaben mit Bewertungskriterien

Kombinierte Aufgabe – Sachtext und Romanauszug

Part 1: Mediation

Aufgabenart

Zielgruppengerechte Sprachmittlung – keine Übersetzung! Für die Aufgabe stehen 60 Minuten Zeit zur Verfügung. Es darf ein Wörterbuch verwendet werden. Nach Ablauf der Bearbeitungszeit wird der zweite Prüfungsteil ausgehändigt.

AUFGABENSTELLUNG

Your English partner school is planning an international work experience programme, which also welcomes applications from German students. The programme's supervising teacher found the article below online and has asked you for a contribution to the school's homepage. Write this text, summarising the article's key information.

Materialgrundlage

M1 Roland Preuß, „Anonyme Bewerbungen: Inkognito zum neuen Job", *Süddeutsche Zeitung*, 17.04.2012, https://www.sueddeutsche.de/karriere/anonyme-bewerbungen-inkognito-zum-neuen-job-1.1334284 (Zugriff: 01.04.2024, gekürzt)

M1 „Anonyme Bewerbungen: Inkognito zum neuen Job" *Roland Preuß*

[...]

Ein Pilotprojekt zeigt nun auf, wie mehr Chancengleichheit in die Personalabteilungen einziehen kann. Eineinhalb Jahre lang haben fünf Unternehmen und drei öffentliche Arbeitgeber anonymisierte Bewerbungen getestet, unter ihnen die Deutsche Post, L'Oréal und das Bundesfamilienministerium. An diesem Dienstag stellt die Antidiskriminierungsstelle des Bundes in Berlin die Ergebnisse vor. In dem Bericht, der der *Süddeutschen Zeitung* vorliegt, kommen die Autoren [...] zu dem Schluss, dass anonyme Bewerbungen denen, die sonst unter Pauschalurteilen leiden, zugutekommen.

[...]

Bei dem Großversuch mit gut 8500 Bewerbungen hatten die Arbeitgeber zunächst auf Angaben wie Foto, Name, Alter und Geschlecht verzichtet. Mal mussten die Aspiranten einen Online-Fragebogen ausfüllen, mal wurden verräterische Zeilen geschwärzt. Für die Vorentscheidung zählten also nur die Fakten wie Abschlüsse und Berufserfahrung. Erst vor dem Bewerbungsgespräch durften die Chefs Namen und Zeugnisse sehen. Dann aber haben die Bewerber nach Einschätzung der Forscher bereits die entscheidende Hürde überwunden, denn im persönlichen Gespräch wucherten Klischees weniger.

„Das Projekt hat gezeigt, dass anonymisierte Bewerbungen den Fokus auf die Qualifikation lenken", sagt die Leiterin der Antidiskriminierungsstelle des Bundes, Christine Lüders. Zudem habe sich das Verfahren als praktikabel erwiesen. Laut Bericht sehen die Personalverantwortlichen das neue Verfahren „durchgängig positiv", nur das Schwärzen von Unterlagen wird als aufwendig kritisiert. Auch die Jobsuchenden befürworten das Verfahren überwiegend, allerdings glaubt ein gutes Viertel von ihnen, dass ihre Chancen bei herkömmlichen Bewerbungen höher sind.

Vier Arbeitgeber des Pilotversuchs haben sich bereits dafür entscheiden, weiter auf anonymisierte Bewerbungen zu setzen, darunter der Geschenkedienstleister Mydays und das Bundesfamilienministerium. [...]

Part 2: Literarischer Text – Zadie Smith, *White Teeth*

Aufgabenart

Analyse und Interpretation eines literarischen Textes im Rahmen eines situativen Kontextes.

AUFGABENSTELLUNG

1 Summarise the excerpt. (30 %)

2 Analyse how Zadie Smith portrays the impact of multiculturalism in London through the characters' experiences. (30 %)

3 Choose ONE of the following tasks.

a) Discuss the fears and hopes of immigrants as shown in the extract, considering historical and contemporary contexts of immigration as well as personal experiences and/or material covered in class.

– or –

b) In an article for your school's website, evaluate the significance of cultural diversity in shaping individual identities. Use the given text as well as personal experiences and/or material covered in class. (40 %)

Materialgrundlage

M2 Zadie Smith, *White Teeth*, London: Hamish Hamilton, 2000. S. 326 f. (346 Wörter)

M2 White Teeth (excerpt) *Zadie Smith*

The following text is an extract from the novel "White Teeth" by Zadie Smith, which is set in contemporary London. The story focuses on three families with different cultural backgrounds whose lives become intertwined because of their children. One of the characters (Irie Jones, l. 8) has an English father and a Caribbean mother. She has fallen in love with a boy called Millat Iqbal, whose parents are from Bangladesh.

This has been the century of strangers, brown, yellow, and white. This has been the century of the great immigrant experiment. It is only this late in the day that you can walk into a playground and find Isaac Leung by the fish pond, Danny Rahman in the football cage, Quang O'Rourke bouncing a basketball, and Irie Jones humming a tune. Children with first and last names on a direct collision course. Names that secrete within them mass exodus, cramped boats and planes, cold arrivals, medical checkups. It is only this late in the day, and possibly only in Willesden, that you can find best friends Sita and Sharon, constantly mistaken for each other because Sita is white (her mother liked the name) and Sharon is Pakistani (her mother thought it best – less trouble). Yet, despite all the mixing up, despite the fact that we have finally slipped into each other's lives with reasonable comfort (like a man returning to his lover's bed after a midnight walk), despite all this, it is still hard to admit that there is no one more English than the Indian, no one more Indian than the English. There are still young white men who are angry about that; who will roll out at closing time into the poorly lit streets with a kitchen knife wrapped in a tight fist. But it makes an immigrant laugh to hear the fears of the nationalist, scared of infection, penetration, miscegenation, when this is small fry, peanuts, compared to what the immigrant fears – dissolution, disappearance. Even the unflappable Alsana Iqbal would regularly wake up in a puddle of her own sweat after a night visited by visions of Millat (genetically BB; where B stands for Bengaliness) marrying someone called Sarah (aa where 'a' stands for Aryan), resulting in a child called Michael (Ba), who in turn marries someone called Lucy (aa), leaving Alsana with a legacy of unrecognizable great-grandchildren (Aaaaaaa!), their Bengaliness thoroughly diluted, genotype hidden by phenotype. It is both the most irrational and natural feeling in the world.

Annotations:

8 to hum: summen; **10 to secrete:** to hide; **14 Willesden:** an area in North West London;
33 miscegenation: Rassenmischung; **36 unflappable:** unerschütterlich;
46 diluted: verdünnt; **46 f. genotype/phenotype:** genetische Veranlagung / äußere Erscheinung

Bewertungskriterien und Beispiellösungen

Teil 1: Sprachmittlung

Dieser Teil wird in Abhängigkeit von Qualität und Klarheit der sprachlichen Vermittlung integrativ bewertet. Es erfolgt keine getrennte Wertung von Sprache und Inhalt.

Sprachmittlung
Die Schülerin / Der Schüler stellt im Rahmen der geforderten Textsorte zielgruppengerecht und sprachlich angemessen die wesentlichen Punkte des Textes dar: – pilot scheme that included the German mail service and companies like L'Oreal tested anonymous applications for 18 months – proved that otherwise disadvantaged applicants profit from this process – applicants either blacked out details like name, gender and age or completed an online application; these details were only provided to the potential employer shortly before interviews – process put greater focus on an applicant's qualifications instead of clichés – while a quarter of the applicants believed to have a better chance with a regular application, four of the five participating employers decided to continue with the anonymous application process

TIPP zum Punktesammeln

In Mediationsaufgaben wird generell erwartet, dass das Material nicht wortwörtlich übersetzt, sondern sinngemäß einbezogen wird. Dies erfordert einen souveränen Umgang mit der englischen Sprache, sodass deutsche Ausdrücke und Redewendungen nicht wörtlich übernommen, sondern in richtiges Englisch umgesetzt werden. Auch die kulturellen Unterschiede können bei diesem Aufgabentyp von Bedeutung sein, sodass beachtet werden muss, ob typisch deutsche Gepflogenheiten ggf. geklärt werden sollten oder ob es, wie in diesem Fall, darauf ankommt, auf im englischen Sprachraum bekannte Themen zurückzugreifen.

Teil 2: Schreibaufgabe

Aufgabe 1
Die Schülerin / Der Schüler gibt die wesentlichen Inhalte sinngemäß zusammenfassend wieder. Folgende Aspekte können angeführt werden:
– The novel *White Teeth* by Zadie Smith, written in 2000, is set in present-day London, focusing on three culturally diverse families interconnected through their children.
– Irie Jones, of mixed English and Caribbean descent, is in love with Millat Iqbal, whose parents are Bangladeshi immigrants.
– The excerpt describes an age of change, highlighting the mix of cultures and the common sight of children with diverse ethnic names playing together.
– It depicts fragments of the immigrant experience, marked by journey hardships, integration challenges and the quest for identity amidst a multicultural backdrop.
– Despite an increased intercultural blending, there are still a lot of (white) nationalists scared of this development.
– In comparison, however, it is said that immigrants fear said blending even more, as it inevitably leads to a cultural dilution and loss of heritage.
– Alsana Iqbal is one of those, fearing an identity loss of what it means to be Bengali for her grand- and great-grandchildren through intermarriage.

Aufgabe 2
Die Schülerin / Der Schüler erläutert die folgenden Aspekte des multikulturellen Zusammenlebens in Smiths Text:
– names as symbols of cultural intersection: Zadie Smith describes an age of different ethnicities coming into contact and intermingling, illustrated by a blending of ethnic names, such as Danny Rahman or Quang O'Rourke. These embody their tribulations as immigrants and the following cultural intersection. The example of Sita and Sharon repeatedly being mistaken for one another serves as a microcosm of the broader themes of identity and belonging.

– cultural and racial identities in conflict: Through characters like Irie Jones and Millat Iqbal, Smith explores the internal and external conflicts faced by individuals navigating multiple cultural identities. Irie's mixed heritage and her relationship with second generational immigrant Millat, against the backdrop of their families' histories, underscore the ongoing negotiation of identity in a multicultural context.
– reactions to multicultural integration: London becoming increasingly multicultural leads to societal integration, acceptance and appreciation (cf. playground scene), as well as fear, loss of identity and acts of xenophobia (cf. white nationalists).
– fear and anxiety about cultural dilution: The character Alsana Iqbal embodies the fears of first-generation immigrants about losing their cultural identity and heritage. Her nightmares about her lineage becoming "diluted" through intermarriage with individuals of different ethnic backgrounds highlight the emotional and psychological impact of multiculturalism on individuals who worry about their cultural legacy.
– immigrant experience and societal fears: Through Alsana's fears and the juxtaposition of immigrant anxieties with nationalist fears, Smith critiques societal attitudes towards immigration and multiculturalism, highlighting the irony in nationalist fears of "infection" when compared to the immigrants' fear of disappearing within the dominant culture.

Aufgabe 3a

The excerpt from Smith's novel vividly portrays Alsana Iqbal's fear of her descendants losing their cultural heritage. This fear epitomises a broader concern among immigrants about the gradual loss of their cultural identity in the melting pot of their new homeland. Immigrants have always faced pressure to assimilate and abandon their native traditions, languages and values in favour of those of the dominant culture, leading to a sense of cultural erosion. This is also shown in Safraz Manzoor's ***Greetings from Bury Park,*** where he illustrates the immigrant experience through the father's apprehension about losing their cultural heritage amidst the pressures of assimilation. The father is consequently reluctant to fully embrace western customs, and his insistence on preserving their native language, religion and traditions serves as a constant reminder of the immigrant community's struggle to maintain their cultural distinctiveness while navigating the challenges of integration.

Additionally, Smith's novel underscores the xenophobia and racism generations of immigrants have faced and still do, as their presence is perceived as a threat to the cultural and economic status quo. This is echoed in the text in the young white men who resent the changing racial and cultural landscape, a sentiment that resonates with contemporary debates on immigration and nationalism. It is also an issue in Nafissa Thompson-Spires' **"Heads of the Colored People",** where police kill two Black men who are engaged in an innocent brawl. No apology is given, and the media portrays them unfavourably in racially charged stereotypes. There are more subtle examples, for example in Camille Acker's **"Cicada",** where young protagonist Ellery Cook is, as the only black competitor, subjected to Lori's racist remarks and demeanor at a piano

recital. Constance, in Acker's **"Mambo Sauce",** finds it difficult to tolerate racist remarks about "ghetto sauce" by her partner's white college friends.
Moreover, Alsana's nightmare of her family's "Bengaliness" being diluted over generations captures a profound fear of disappearance – not just in a physical sense, but in the effacement of cultural and genetic legacy. This fear reflects historical instances where immigrant communities have struggled to maintain their identities against forces of assimilation and erasure, from the enforced cultural assimilation of Native Americans and Aboriginal Australians to the experiences of African slaves stripped of their cultural identities. This fear is also exemplified in Manzoor's *Greetings of Bury Park*, where Manzoor's parents insist on arranging marriages within their ethnic community. From a different perspective, Acker's Constance, too, continually struggles to come to terms with her interracial relationship. In her short story **"Fatima, the Biloquist",** Thompson-Spires addresses the issue from yet another point of view, that of Fatima, who constantly struggles for a sense of identity, as she feels neither Black nor white enough to belong to either ethnic group. Consequently, all of these authors poignantly illustrate the fear of cultural erasure, resonating with the profound longing to preserve a sense of identity and belonging in a rapidly changing world.
Despite these fears, Smith's novel also reflects a hope for integration and acceptance. The multicultural playground scene, with children of diverse backgrounds playing together, symbolises the potential for a society where cultural differences are not just tolerated but celebrated. In "Heads of the Colored People", Richard Simmons and Paris Larkin play with their identity through cosplay, thus transcending cultural barriers. Manzoor's passion for Bruce Springsteen's music also serves as a bridge between his Pakistani upbringing and his British surroundings. His pursuit of education and career opportunities also represents broader aspirations for integration and acceptance within British society. Through these examples, a hopeful narrative of cultural harmony and acceptance is emphasised.
Furthermore, the blending of cultures, as uneasy and complex as it may be, carries the hope of cultural exchange and enrichment. Immigrants bring with them traditions, knowledge, variety and perspectives that, when shared, have the potential to enrich the cultural tapestry of their new home. One such example is food, such as the eponymous mambo sauce. However, there is also a dark side to this blending, such as cultural appropriation as illustrated by Wally in "Fatima", as well as evidenced throughout in Jasmine-Lee Jones play ***seven methods of killing kylie jenner*****,** which heavily focuses on the exploitation of Black culture.
In conclusion, Smith's novel as well as the texts mentioned above, offer a poignant exploration of the fears and hopes that have characterised the immigrant experience throughout history and into the contemporary era. These characters mirror the broader human stories of struggle, adaptation and the enduring quest for community and identity in the face of change.

Aufgabe 3b

<u>Celebrating Our Tapestry: The Role of Cultural Diversity in Shaping Identities</u>

In the vibrant streets of contemporary London, as depicted in Zadie Smith's novel *White Teeth*, the rich tapestry of cultural diversity comes alive, painting a world where indivi-

dual identities are as much a product of personal experiences as they are of the myriad cultural backgrounds that influence them. This serves as a starting point for a further exploration of the significance of cultural diversity in shaping our identities, illuminating the complexities and the beauty inherent in our increasingly interconnected world.
Various characters in literature, such as Smith's Irie Jones and Millat Iqbal, Safraz Manzoor in the autobiography ***Greetings from Bury Park,*** or Cleo and Kara in Jasmine Lee-Jones' ***seven methods of killing kylie jenner*** embody the confluence of cultures that characterises modern urban life. They represent the new generation for whom identity is not singular but plural, a blend of traditions, histories and narratives. This mosaic of identity reflects the lived reality of many in our school community, where students come from diverse backgrounds, bringing with them stories and influences that enrich our collective experience.
The playground scene Smith describes – a microcosm of cultural diversity, where children of different ethnicities play side by side – mirrors the environment we strive to foster within our school. It's a reminder that cultural diversity is not just about coexistence but about interaction, learning and growing together. Each day, we as students can learn from one another, can discover the stories behind names that carry within them tales of migration, aspiration and resilience and consequently enrich our own self-conception. Furthermore, Smith's narrative goes beyond the superficial aspects of diversity, delving into the fears and hopes that accompany the immigrant experience. It speaks to the fear of losing one's cultural identity and the hope of finding acceptance and integration in a new world. The downside of this experience is shown in literary figures such as Nafissa Thompson-Spires' **"Fatima",** who constantly struggles to come to terms with her ethnic identity in a predominantly white environment, eventually turning to literal codeswitching, or Constance in Camille Acker's **"Mambo Sauce",** whose fears affect and potentially end her relationship with her white partner.
These themes resonate within our school community, where we also witness the journey of students navigating the challenges of fitting in while holding onto their cultural heritage, especially after the refugee crises following the wars in Syria, Afghanistan, Iraq and most recently the war waged on Ukraine. It's a delicate balance, one that teaches empathy, respect and the value of diversity, in consequence also shaping our identities. However, said diversity of our school community, much like the London depicted in *White Teeth*, can be considered our strength. It provides a rich ground for the exchange of ideas, for innovation and for fostering a global perspective among our students. It challenges us to think beyond our own experiences.
As we look to the future, the lessons from Zadie Smith and other authors as well as the experiences within our school walls inspire us to continue building an environment of inclusion, safe spaces and multiplicity. Our collective identity is shaped by the diversity of our individual stories, and it is through embracing this multifacetedness that we prepare ourselves for the world beyond. In conclusion, the significance of cultural diversity in shaping individual identities cannot be overstated. It is a journey of discovery, of learning to navigate the myriad influences that make us who we are.

Aufgaben zur Sprachmittlung mit Beispiellösungen oder Bewertungskriterien

Sachtext – *Gun debate*

AUFGABENSTELLUNG

You have just come back from an exchange year at an American high school in Massachusetts. Since your English class is discussing the American self-perception at the moment, your teacher has asked you to do a short presentation on the American self-image in terms of the gun debate. While searching the internet, you have found the following article online.
Write that part of the presentation that deals with this article.

Materialgrundlage

David Signer, „Nur ein bewaffneter Amerikaner ist ein richtiger Amerikaner", in: *Neue Zürcher Zeitung* (Zürich), 13.07.2022, https://www.nzz.ch/meinung/amoklaeufe-in-den-usa-die-liebe-zu-waffen-ist-teil-der-kultur-ld.1692477 (Zugriff: 01.04.2024, verändert)

„Nur ein bewaffneter Amerikaner ist ein richtiger Amerikaner"
David Signer

[...]

„Hey Joe, wohin gehst du mit dem Gewehr in deiner Hand?", heißt es in dem alten amerikanischen Song, der in der Version von Jimi Hendrix berühmt wurde. „Ich erschieße meine Alte, weil sie mit einem andern rumgemacht hat." Nach vollbrachter Tat macht sich der Rächer im Lied auf in den Süden, „wo ein Mann noch frei sein kann".

Da ist alles drin, was der Hälfte der Amerikaner heute solche Sorgen macht: Die Gewaltverherrlichung, der Preis [des] Waffenkult[s], die „toxische Männlichkeit", die Frauenverachtung und eine seltsame Auffassung von Freiheit. Die andere Hälfte der Amerikaner sieht jedoch kein Problem darin, und das ist das wahre Problem.

[...]

Zwar führt ein Vorfall wie die Tötung von sieben Zuschauern einer Parade in Chicago, ausgerechnet am amerikanischen Unabhängigkeitstag, zu Schock und Empörung. Aber es wäre erstaunlich, wenn sich irgendetwas ändern würde. Die Pattsituation bei den Gesetzgebern ist lediglich ein Spiegel der Bevölkerung. Unter Millionen von Amerikanern ist der „Kult um den Colt" tief verankert; schließlich ist das Recht, eine Waffe zu besitzen und zu tragen, schon im Zweiten Zusatzartikel der Verfassung festgehalten. Für viele ist dieses Grundrecht praktisch gleichbedeutend mit Freiheit an sich. [...] Die Beziehung vieler Amerikaner zu ihrer Waffe ist geradezu mythisch, vor allem auf dem Land und in kleinstädtischen Verhältnissen.

In diesem konservativen Milieu, „wo die Welt noch in Ordnung ist", und nicht in den Großstädten, finden die meisten Massenschießereien statt. Die Knaben wachsen dort mit Spielzeugpistolen auf, spielen Cowboys, die Jagd auf Indianer machen, und später bekommen sie von ihrem Vater feierlich ein Gewehr als Geschenk überreicht. Wenn man Erwachsene von diesem Moment erzählen hört, wird man an Initiationsrituale erinnert, an Konfirmation, Bar Mizwa[1], Matura[2] oder Rekrutenschule, die aus dem Knaben angeblich einen richtigen Mann machen.

Der Archetyp des amerikanischen Waffenträgers ist der Revolverheld, wie er in unzähligen Filmen gefeiert wurde und wird. Die klassische Ausprägung ist der einsame Cowboy mit seinem Colt, der sich im Wilden Westen in einer gottverlassenen Frontier-Siedlung und in der Prärie gegen Indianer und andere Bösewichte verteidigen muss. Jüngere Versionen werden verkörpert von Rambo und anderen Einzelkämpfern, zugleich Helden und Antihelden, die das Gesetz in die eigenen Hände nehmen, weil auf keinen anderen Verlass ist. […]

Übrigens werden auch oft Hip-Hop-Videoclips mit ihrer Verherrlichung von Gangsta-Kultur und Machismo für die Bandenkriminalität vor allem unter Afroamerikanern verantwortlich gemacht. Am Phänomen selbst gibt es nichts zu rütteln, aber es handelt sich dabei um eine Subkultur. Der Kult um Waffenbesitz und Waffentragen als Ausdruck einer uramerikanischen Freiheit betrifft hingegen vor allem die Mainstream-USA und wird in erster Linie von weißen Männern (und auch Frauen) getragen.

Die verbreitete Kriminalität und die Brutalität der Polizei vor allem gegen Afroamerikaner, der konservativ-patriotische Stolz der „Rechtschaffenen" auf ihre Waffe und die Gewaltorgien der Amokschützen, die sich in ihren irren Manifesten oft zu furchtlosen Kämpfern hochstilisieren, gehören zusammen; sie sind die zwei Seiten derselben unglückseligen Medaille.

Die Bibel in der einen, das Gewehr in der anderen Hand

Erstaunlich ist die Symbiose, die die „gun culture" oft mit christlichem und vor allem evangelikalem Gedankengut eingeht, verkörpert in dem weitverbreiteten Bild des „rechtschaffenen Amerikaners" mit dem Gewehr in der einen und der Bibel in der anderen Hand. Eigentlich kann man sich den Jesus der Bergpredigt kaum als Revolverhelden vorstellen.

Davon abgesehen passt der Kult ums Töten auch nicht recht zur vehementen Ablehnung der Abtreibung in denselben Kreisen. Schutz des Lebens? Pro Life für Ungeborene, Pro Death für Geborene? Und die militante Verteidigung der individuellen Freiheit und der Selbstbestimmung kollidiert eigentlich mit der Jagd auf sexuelle Minderheiten, zu der die Konservativen zunehmend blasen. Aber Stringenz und Widerspruchslosigkeit waren noch nie typische Kennzeichen von Ideologien.

Wenn die Anbetung der Waffe tatsächlich so tief verwurzelt ist in der amerikanischen Geschichte, Mythologie und Kultur, bedeutet das, dass sie kaum verändert werden kann? Nicht unbedingt. In Ländern wie Kanada, Australien oder Neuseeland herrschte und herrscht vor allem unter der ländlichen Bevölkerung ein ähnlich konservativer, individualistischer und staatskritischer Unabhängigkeits- und Pioniergeist. Trotzdem ist es diesen Ländern nach ähnlich aufsehenerregenden Schießereien wie in den USA gelungen, die Waffengewalt einzudämmen. Die USA sind heute das einzige Land auf der Welt, in dem diese Art von Massenmorden, vor allem an Schulen, regelmäßig vorkommt.

[…]

Dieser Text wurde aus didaktischen Gründen gekürzt und verändert.

Annotations:

1 **Bar Mizwa:** jüdische Feier, die das Erreichen der religiösen Mündigkeit im Alter von 13 Jahren zelebriert

2 **Matura:** schulische Abschlussprüfung in der Schweiz, die etwa dem Abitur entspricht

Beispiellösung

Dear class,
I've just come back from my exchange year in the US, where the right to bear arms is a very controversial topic. But before I tell you about my own experience, I would like to talk about an article I recently found in the *Neue Zürcher Zeitung*.
So let's start with the fact that it's an erroneous assumption that the majority of Americans rejects stricter gun laws. Many detest their country's arms policy and see it as a symbol of toxic masculinity. Furthermore, it reflects a strange concept of freedom for many people. However, half of the Americans see no problem in the handling of weapons, which is an even bigger issue according to David Signer, the author of the article. Even though incidents such as the killing of seven spectators at a parade in Chicago on Independence Day lead to shock and public outcry, it doesn't change anything. The public holds on to the Second Amendment to own a gun, in particular in rural areas. In these places one is likely to find a conservative environment in which boys grow up surrounded with toy guns. As little children they play cowboys hunting Native Americans and are solemnly presented with a gun by their fathers later on.
Furthermore, the archetype of American arm bearers seems to be the gunslinger, who is presented in pop-cultural contexts such as the lonely cowboy who has to defend himself against various villains. In general, these characters take the law into their own hands because no one else can be relied upon.
Weapon ownership is most likely to be seen as a cultural tradition and the ultimate expression of freedom among white men and women. African-Americans, on the other hand, are often victims of white police violence, while hip-hop subculture that glorifies violence is often wrongly mistaken as characteristic for the whole Black population.
Another inherent aspect of American identity forms an interesting symbiosis with gun culture, namely the religious faith of many Americans. Singer points out that the righteous American carries a gun in his one and a bible in his other hand. This seems to contradict the call for protecting life in all its stages.
But does this mean that gun control and gun culture cannot be changed because it is rooted deeply in American history and culture? Signer points out that the rural populations of Canada, New Zealand and Australia share certain similarities with their American counterpart, namely their conservative and individualistic pioneer spirit. However, those countries were able to drastically reduce cases of gun violence. So far, the United States remain the only country where mass killings occur frequently.
From my personal experience I may add that guns belong to a cultural tradition that is shared by many Americans and is considered to be self-evident ...

Sachtext – *Migration*

AUFGABENSTELLUNG

You are taking part in an international youth conference tackling immigration. As the participants share information about different approaches within their countries, you are asked to write an article to be read by the other participants, presenting the situation in Cottbus, Germany. Write this text, summarising the article's key points.

Materialgrundlage

Sonja Vogel, „Geflüchtete? Geile Soft Skills!“, *taz,* 31.01.2018, https://taz.de/Kolumne-German-Angst/!5477958/ (Zugriff: 01.03.2024).

„Geflüchtete? Geile Soft Skills!“ *Sonja Vogel*

In Cottbus regiert die rechte APO. Dabei wäre es doch einfach, geflüchtete Menschen positiv rüberzubringen: Als teamfähig und stressresistent!

„Schnauze voll!“ steht auf den Schildern. Viele Hundert Cottbusser demonstrierten so gegen Geflüchtete in ihrer Stadt. Dem Brandenburger Innenministerium war ihr Wunsch Befehl. Es verkündete einen Flüchtlingsstopp. Schön, wenn eine APO noch etwas bewegen kann.

Aber haben die Cottbusser wirklich etwas gegen alle Geflüchteten? Vielleicht sind ja nur die falschen gekommen, nämlich – hört man ihnen zu – Arbeitsscheue, Asoziale, Kriminelle?

Eine ehrliche Haut, das ist die, in der der Wille zur Arbeit steckt. Deutsche Tugenden wie Fleiß und Ordnung. Hört sich an wie von der Müllhalde der Geschichte. Heißt aber heute nur anders: Soft Skills, die Rekrutierung der gesamten Erfahrungswelt zur Optimierung des eigenen Marktwerts. In der freien Wirtschaft hat man diesen Gedanken weitergesponnen. Wenn Menschen hier Menschen in Not nicht als Menschen akzeptieren wollen, verkaufen wir sie ihnen als Arbeitskräfte!

Es ist aber so eine Sache mit dem Kapitalismus. Nichts kann er allein, und darum muss es immer Deppen geben, die sich mit frischen Ideen in seinen Dienst stellen.

Kapitalismus kann nichts allein

In diesem Fall war es die Agentur Social Bee. Mit Plakaten, auf denen Geflüchtete aus Eritrea, Syrien oder der Türkei abgebildet sind, wirbt sie für deren Einstellung. Aber nicht, weil es eine gute Sache wäre, Menschen unabhängig zu machen – noch immer werden die Hürden im Bürokratiedschungel von „ungesichertem“ Aufenthalt bis Arbeitsverbot besonders hoch gesetzt. Nein. Weil sie geile Soft Skills haben! Unter jedem Plakat steht ein Spruch wie „Ich bin stressresistent – Auf der Flucht wurde ich verhaftet und mehrere Tage verhört“ oder „Ich bin zielorientiert – Auf der Flucht war ich drei Monate lang zu Fuß unterwegs“. Das ist doch mal praktisch gedacht, und man kann sich den Sachbearbeiter der Agentur für Arbeit vorstellen: „Sie haben es in einem überladenen Gummiboot über das Mittelmeer geschafft, ohne zu ertrinken? Dann sind Sie ja teamfähig und stressresistent!“

So wird es sicher gehen: Kapitalismus sticht strukturellen Rassismus.

Ganz egal wie „provokativ“ oder „witzig“ die Kampagne gemeint ist: Sie zeigt, was in den letzten Monaten in Deutschland geschehen ist. Sie spricht einige an, die dem Weg der Kanzlerin seit 2014 gefolgt sind: von rhetorisch moderat (= gegen die Schließung der Grenzen) bis fundamental gegen die Einwanderung und das Asylrecht (= Schließung der Grenzen jenseits Deutschlands, in der Türkei und Libyen). Der Diskurs über massenhafte Flucht und Einwanderung ist komplett nach rechts gerutscht, hin zu Zahlenspielen und Obergrenzen – ein Menschenrecht auf Asyl hat keinen Platz mehr.

Und das ist das Fatale an dieser Kampagne. Es ist ganz sicher nicht die Aufgabe von Asylsuchenden, „unsere Gesellschaft (zu) bereichern“, wie es einer der Social-Bee-Gründer sagt. Das Recht auf Asyl ist deshalb ein Menschenrecht und universell, weil es die Unterscheidung zwischen nützlich und unnütz nicht kennt.

Annotations:

1 APO – Außerparlamentarische Opposition; locker organisierte, ursprünglich insbesondere studentische Aktionsgemeinschaft, die versucht, ihre politischen Interessen außerhalb des Parlaments durchzusetzen

9 Müllhalde der Geschichte – *hier insbesondere:* Zeit des Nationalsozialismus

Bewertungskriterien

- introduction (occasion, context, adressees, author, source)
- Brandenburg Ministry of the Interior announced a stop to reception of refugees after right-wing rallies in Cottbus
- criticises the notion that refugees are first and foremost classified according to their employability
- campaign by marketing agency Social Bee that promotes refugees by emphasising their “soft skills” such as stress resistance and goal orientation
- suggests (potentially provocatively) that capitalism can exploit refugees‘ skills and work ethic, despite bureaucratic barriers to their employment
- campaign reflects a broader shift in German discourse on immigration towards right-wing ideologies, characterised by a focus on numbers and limits
- article concludes by asserting that asylum seekers should not be expected to enrich society but rather be granted asylum as a universal human right

Original-Prüfungsaufgaben 2022/2023 gA

Quelle der Aufgabenstellung

Niedersächsisches Kultusministerium
Hinweis: Bei den Musterlösungen zu den Prüfungsaufgaben handelt es sich um nicht amtliche Lösungen.
Aus rechtlichen Gründen kann die Hörverstehensaufgabe sowie die Textaufgabe 2 des grundlegenden Anforderungsniveaus aus dem Jahr 2023 an dieser Stelle nicht veröffentlicht werden. Sie finden daher im Folgenden die jeweiligen Prüfungsteile aus dem Jahr 2022 vor.

Hinweise:

Die zentrale schriftliche Abiturprüfung im Fach Englisch besteht aus einer kombinierten Aufgabe:

Prüfungsteil 1: a) **Hörverstehen** b) **Sprachmittlung**	**Prüfungsteil 2:** **Textaufgabe**

Ablauf und Bewertung der Prüfung:

Ausgabe der **Aufgaben für den Prüfungsteil 1a**	
Prüfungsteil 1a:	**Hörverstehen**
Gewichtung:	20 %
Bearbeitungszeit:	30 Minuten
	Abgabe sämtlicher Unterlagen des **Prüfungsteils 1a**
Ausgabe der **Aufgaben für den Prüfungsteil 1b** und der zugelassenen **Hilfsmittel**	
Prüfungsteil 1b:	**Sprachmittlung**
Gewichtung:	25 %
Bearbeitungszeit:	60 Minuten
	Abgabe sämtlicher Unterlagen des **Prüfungsteils 1b**
Ausgabe der **Aufgaben für den Prüfungsteil 2**	
Prüfungsteil 2:	**Textaufgabe**
Gewichtung:	55 %
Prüfungszeit:	210 Minuten
	Die Prüfungszeit setzt sich zusammen aus 30 Minuten Auswahlzeit und 180 Minuten Bearbeitungszeit.

Hilfsmittel für alle Prüfungsteile:

Den Prüflingen stehen einsprachige sowie für den schulischen Gebrauch geeignete zweisprachige Wörterbücher der Allgemeinsprache (Deutsch–Englisch/Englisch–Deutsch) zur Verfügung (s. Erlass zur Nutzung von [elektronischen] Wörterbüchern in Prüfungen: https://www.nibis.de/uploads/mk-bolhoefer/2022/202111ElektronischeWoerterbuecher.pdf).

Hinweis

- Jedes einzelne Blatt ist mit dem Namen zu versehen.

Hinweise zum Prüfungsteil 2

- Von den zwei Aufgaben ist eine auszuwählen und zu bearbeiten.
- Bei jeder Teilaufgabe ist die inhaltliche Gewichtung angegeben.

gA Listening Comprehension **24 BE**

AUFGABENSTELLUNG

You will hear each recording twice. After each listening, you will have time to complete your answers.

Task 1: Turning Pollution into Art **9 BE**

Preparation time: 1:30 minutes

You will hear an interview with Angela Haseltine Pozzi, an artist living in Oregon. While listening, tick the correct answer (a, b, or c). There is only one correct answer.

1. The Southern Oregon coast is known for its

a	flat islands.	☐
b	dramatic scenery.	☐
c	recreational value.	☐

2. It is Angela's aim to

a	gather lots of plastic.	☐
b	make people collect plastic on shore.	☐
c	locate plastic items bitten into by animals.	☐

3. Angela's pieces of art feature

a	extinct sea animals.	☐
b	fantasy sea animals.	☐
c	endangered sea animals.	☐

4. Angela's intention of creating large sculptures is that

a	people notice them.	☐
b	stability can be ensured.	☐

c	a lot of waste is used up.	☐

5. With her project, Angela hopes

a	to encourage other artists.	☐
b	to appeal to society as a whole.	☐
c	to cooperate with youth workers.	☐

6. Angela's organisation Washed Ashore

a	gathers plastic waste from all over the US.	☐
b	puts together exhibitions throughout the nation.	☐
c	supports global campaigns for plastic-free oceans.	☐

7. The Beijing Olympics is mentioned to show that

a	plastic is a long-lasting problem.	☐
b	sports events create a lot of plastic trash.	☐
c	people find plastic products with logos attractive.	☐

8. Angela is aware that plastic

a	can be necessary.	☐
b	has to be replaced.	☐
c	should be disposed of properly.	☐

9. When it comes to single-use plastic items, Angela suggests that

a	they should be banned.	☐
b	engineers must solve the problem.	☐
c	the public is warned about the long-term effects.	☐

Now listen to the recording again.

Source:
Kirk Siegler, "On The Oregon Coast, Turning Pollution Into Art With A Purpose", *npr*, 4 December 2019, https://www.npr.org/2019/12/04/784416386/on-the-oregon-coast-turning-pollution-into-art-with-a-purpose (accessed on 1 April 2024).

Task 2: Sugar

5 BE

Preparation time: 30 seconds

You will hear five people talking about regulating sugar consumption.
Choose from the list (A–G) which heading best applies to which statement (1–5). For each statement there is only one correct answer. There are two more headings than you need.

Headings	
A	Harming minors
B	Business principles
C	Prolonging life expectancy
D	Attitude towards authorities
E	Lowering the cost for health care
F	Impact of prices on consumer groups
G	Varied public health measures required

Statement	1	2	3	4	5
Heading					

Now listen to the recording again.

Sources:
- "Health Report: Is it time for a sugar tax?", *ABC*, 18 December 2017, http://www.abc.net.au/radio national/programs/healthreport/is-it-time-for-a-sugar-tax/9224258 (accessed on 1 April 2024)
  Statement 1: 13:16–13:41
  Statement 2: 08:07–08:31
  Statement 4: 04:54–05:16 + 05:37–05:41
  Statement 5: 04:04–04:34
- "Inside Health: Preventive HIV therapy, Sugar tax, Bowel cancer, Surgery", *BBC Radio 4*, 22 March 2016, https://www.bbc.co.uk/programmes/b07414dg (accessed on 1 April 2024).
  Statement 3: 02:43–03:11

Task 3: Modernising the Royal Family

10 BE

Preparation time: 1 minute

You will hear a radio programme on changes in the British Royal Family since 1992. Lucy Burns from the BBC speaks to Charles Anson, the former press secretary of the Royal Family.

While listening, answer the questions. You need not write complete sentences. Unless otherwise specified, name one aspect.

1	What did the Royal Family do in reaction to the situation in the early 1990s?	
2	How does the Queen remember 1992?	
3	What family matters affected the Royals in 1992? (Name one.)	
4	How did the media react to the royal events? (Name two examples.)	• ______ • ______
5	What issue did the public raise?	
6	What happened in November 1992?	
7	What made Charles Anson's job more challenging at the time?	
8	How does Anson characterise the Queen during her long reign?	
9	Which change did Queen Elizabeth declare that affected the public directly?	

Now listen to the recording again.

Source:
"The Way Ahead group: Modernising the Royal Family", *BBC World Service*, 27 January 2020, https://www.bbc.co.uk/sounds/play/w3csywyp (00:09–04:08) (accessed on 1 April 2024).

Lösungen

Task 1: Turning Pollution into Art

1	2	3	4	5	6	7	8	9
b	a	c	a	b	b	a	a	c

Task 2: Sugar

1	2	3	4	5
D	B	F	G	A

Task 3: Modernising the Royal Family

No.	BE	*Lösungsvorschlag:*
1	1	set up group to plan for the future
2	1	as a difficult/horrible year
3	1	separations/divorces
4	1 1	*two of the following:* relentless interest / leaked tapes of intimate phone calls / offered phone lines to listen to recordings
5	1	cost of royal family to taxpayers
6	1	fire at Windsor Castle
7	1	people wanted to talk about private lives of royal family, which they were not allowed to discuss
8	1	offered steadiness / very calm
9	1	started paying income tax / public would not need to pay for certain members of royal family

gA Sprachmittlung mit Beispiellösung

Max Hunger, „Jugend. Macht. Politik." (2019)

AUFGABENSTELLUNG

Your English friend is a member of the UK Youth Parliament and asks you about young Germans in local politics. Write an email to your friend in which you present the Muldestausee youth council and its accomplishments.

Materialgrundlage:

Max Hunger, „Jugend. Macht. Politik.", *Mitteldeutsche Zeitung* (Halle), 24.11.2020, S. 3, zitiert nach: https://www.mz.de/lokal/bitterfeld/jugend-macht-politik-wieso-ein-teenie-parlament-aus-sachsen-anhalt-erfolg-hat-3153418
(Zugriff: 1. April 2024)

Hilfsmittel:

Ein- und zweisprachiges Wörterbuch der Zielsprache

„Jugend. Macht. Politik." *Max Hunger*

EHRENAMT: In der Gemeinde Muldestausee mischen Teenager in der Kommunalpolitik mit. Und das mit Erfolg: Projekte für eine halbe Million Euro hat der Jugendgemeinderat bereits umgesetzt. Dafür wurde er für einen bundesweiten Preis nominiert. Warum das Konzept auch für Konflikte sorgt.

Für seine Arbeit ist der Jugendgemeinderat Muldestausee jüngst für den Deutschen Engagementpreis nominiert worden. Unter den 383 von den Organisatoren nominierten Personen und Initiativen schaffte es das Teenie-Parlament aus Sachsen-Anhalt bei einer ersten Bürgerabstimmung auf Platz 32. Über die Verleihung des mit 10.000 Euro dotierten Preises entscheidet in einem zweiten Schritt am 3. Dezember eine Fachjury.

Dass die Jugend in Muldestausee so erfolgreich ihren Ort mitgestaltet, hat einen Grund: Anders als in den meisten Jugendbeiräten im Land haben sie hier nicht nur beratende Funktion. Die Jungpolitiker haben ein festes Antrags- und Rederecht im Gemeinderat. Außerdem steht ihnen ein jährliches Budget von 6.000 Euro zur Verfügung. Den Vorsitz des Rates hat Bürgermeister Ferid Giebler (parteilos) – ein Stimmrecht hat er allerdings nicht. „Man muss uns zuhören und mit uns reden", sagt Maximilian Frey.

Er selbst hat im vergangenen Jahr den bisher wichtigsten Antrag des Jugendrates im Gemeinderat eingebracht: Auf einem 8.200 Quadratmeter großen Gelände der Kommune wollen die Jugendlichen ein Freizeitzentrum für knapp 400.000 Euro bauen lassen. Skaterbahn, Fitnessstrecke, Parkanlage. Es soll ein Treffpunkt für alle werden, wo man auch mal laut sein kann. Der Kniff: Das Projekt belastet den knappen Gemeindehaushalt mit keinem Cent. Der Großteil des Budgets stammt aus Fördertöpfen von Land und Bund. 70.000 Euro haben Bürgermeister und Jugendrat selbst an Spenden gesammelt. „Das ist mit Abstand unser bisher größtes Projekt“, sagt Frey. Und ein besonders wichtiges.

Der 20-Jährige – Brille, Gelfrisur, eleganter Mantel – ist in der Gemeinde östlich von Bitterfeld aufgewachsen. Eine Kernstadt gibt es nicht. Stattdessen verbinden Landstraßen die 13 Ortsteile, winden sich entlang des namensgebenden Stausees, des großen Goitzschesees, feuchter Wiesen und saftiger Wälder. „Es ist eine echt schöne Gegend“, schwärmt Frey. Doch für Jugendliche gebe es hier nicht viel: Das nächste Kino? Eine Stunde Autofahrt entfernt. Eine Disco? Gibt es nicht. Abends Freunde zu treffen, das bedeute meist stundenlange Busfahrten. Wenn der Bus überhaupt noch fährt. Viele Jugendliche treffen sich daher an Bushaltestellen und verbringen dort ihre Abende. „Wenn man sich abends fragt: Wohin sollen wir überhaupt? Dann läuft was schief.“

Probleme, die im Gemeinderat oft nicht zur Sprache kommen. Das weiß auch Bürgermeister Giebler. Um die Interessen der Jugendlichen besser vertreten zu können, hat der 2016 neu gewählte Gemeindechef als eine seiner ersten Amtshandlungen den Jugendgemeinderat gegründet. „Die haben sonst einfach keine Stimme“, sagt der 37-Jährige. Denn im Gemeinderat entscheiden meist Menschen jenseits der 60 über die Geschicke der Orte. Die Jugendlichen wären bei ihnen zu Beginn nicht auf offene Ohren gestoßen. Mehrfach hätten sich Ortsbürgermeister über die Einmischung beschwert. Denn die Jugendvertretung agiert hier auf Augenhöhe mit allen anderen Ausschüssen und Gremien. „Das war ein Riesenproblem.“ Aber mit den Erfolgen seien auch die Kritiker nach und nach verstummt. Eine halbe Million an Förder-, Preis- und Spendengeld hat der Jugendgemeinderat laut Bürgermeister in den vergangenen drei Jahren in die Gemeinde geholt. Doch dem studierten Politikwissenschaftler geht es nicht nur um die Zahlen: „Das ist auch politische Bildung.“

Denn im Jugendgemeinderat läuft alles so wie bei den Großen – oder besser: den Älteren. Bei der nächsten Wahl im Dezember bekommen alle Zwölf- bis 25-Jährigen der Gemeinde offizielle Briefwahlunterlagen zugeschickt. 14 Jugendliche haben sich zur Wahl gestellt. Bei den Sitzungen einmal pro Quartal gilt eine feste Tagesordnung. Dabei fungiert der Bürgermeister als Übersetzer zwischen Bürokratiedschungel und Jugendsprache. Beschlüsse fällen die Mitglieder demokratisch.

(585 Wörter)

Beispiellösung

Dear Jasmine,

In your last email you asked me about young Germans in local politics.
Concerning this topic, I found a very interesting article in a German newspaper dealing with a youth council in Muldestausee, a rural community in Saxony-Anhalt. I chose this article because it shows that even people at a very young age can participate actively in politics in order to advocate for their needs and interests.
Because the area doesn't have a lot to offer for young people, Muldestausee's mayor established the youth council as an initiative for people aged 12–25 in 2016. It meets

on a regular basis, having the same procedures as the city council. It's chaired by the mayor, who supports the young people in various ways. The youth council, which aims to make Muldestausee a better place for young people, has the right to bring up their concerns in the city council. It allows them to spend a fixed budget of € 6,000 on projects supporting the interests of young people in Muldestausee. For example, it has planned to build a new youth recreation centre and will receive most of its funds from federal and state coffers.
The successful youth council of Muldestausee has also slowly gained respect in local politics as well as received nationwide recognition, as it was nominated for a national award for social commitment.
I hope this was useful to give you a broader picture of young Germans in local politics. Please let me know if you have further questions. Looking forward to hearing from you soon!

Best,
xxx (260 words)

gA Aufgabe I mit Beispiellösung

Text: Ling Ma, "Peking Duck" (excerpt, 2022)

AUFGABENSTELLUNG

1 Sum up the excerpt. (30 %)

2 Examine the relationship between the narrator and her mother. (30 %)

3 You are taking part in a summer literature course offered by Boston University for international students on "Identity and the Migrant Experience." For the course's blog, all participants have to contribute an entry in which they discuss the statement by U.S. writer Greg Poehler about his migrant experience: "[T]he longer you stay in a country, you almost lose your former self and become this third-party person who is caught in between two worlds."
Write the blog entry, also referring to the text at hand and materials studied in class, such as the short stories by Levy and Pandit. (40 %)

Materialgrundlage:

Ling Ma, „Peking Duck“, *The New Yorker* (New York), 04.07.2022, zitiert nach: https://www.newyorker.com/magazine/2022/07/11/peking-duck
(gekürzt; Zugriff: 1. April 2024)

Hilfsmittel:

Ein- und zweisprachiges Wörterbuch der Zielsprache

"Peking Duck" (Excerpt) *Ling Ma*

The narrator, a seven-year-old girl, has moved to the U.S.A. from China to live with her parents, who she has not seen since she was five years old. For the last two years she lived with her grandparents, who remain in China.

It's December, possibly, off the top of my memory, when I arrive. There are sensations that exist for me only in English, many associated with winter, that I experience for the first time when I move to Utah. There is the sensation of walking underneath pine trees, of wearing a too big puffy coat [...]. The sensation of my mother dragging a wet towel across my face to wipe off dried congee, and the sensation of wet skin drying in the stiff, cold air outside. We live in a one-bedroom apartment that is very tidy, but sometimes ants come in through the bathroom. I sleep in the living room, where, at night, I still hear my grandma's phantom snores.

In someone else's home, a two-story mansion nestled in the mountains outside Salt Lake, a VHS cassette of "Bambi" plays on the TV while actual deer come through the back yard, pulling at the garden foliage with their teeth, and we are separated from them only by a sliding glass door.

My mother points outside. *Deer. Tree. Teeth. Eats.*

I repeat the words, then put them in sentence order: *Deer eats tree with teeth.*

The English lessons take place inside the mansion, where my mother is employed as a nanny to a toddler named Brandon. The home, which has a lobby-like foyer and an elevator, is imposing enough that not even Mormon missionaries bother us. Either that, or it's too isolated from anywhere else to be worth the trek. When I first arrive in the U.S., my mother takes me with her to work every day, my father driving us half an hour outside the city before swinging back to campus to resume his grad studies. At the mansion, our days are geared around my learning English. We watch "Sesame Street," though it's too babyish for me even then, so I can learn the alphabet. I keep a daily journal and write three to five sentences in English every day.

When her charge is napping, my mother goes through E.S.L. workbooks with me at the kitchen table, books she's found at school-supply stores. One question set asks you to come up with the first letters of similar-sounding words. *Mouse, house, blouse. Pill* and *hill. Bell* and *knell. Pail* and . . . She gives me hints. "The letter you feel in your nose," she says, and I understand that she is talking about "n." *Nail. Pail* and *nail.*

[...]

I'm not sure how my mother teaches me English, when her facility with the language is hesitant and halting. Unlike my father, she didn't learn English in China, and even after living in the States for years she is not fluent or even proficient. Cashiers at grocery stores stare at her blankly, the Mormon missionaries who show up at our apartment give up trying to convert us, and the sellers at yard sales shake their heads and over-enunciate, saying loudly, "I can't understand you." Despite this, her imperfect, broken English serves as a scaffolding for my own.

The winter that I touch snow for the first time, I also taste ice cream. In the kitchen, we review the fridge and pantry foods in English. My mother names every item, foods I've never heard of: Minute Maid orange-juice concentrate, Yoplait strawberry-banana yogurt, Farley's Dinosaurs Fruit Snacks, Lay's potato chips, Surfer Cooler Capri Sun, Lunchables. I repeat each word after her. They hover in a vacuum, with no Chinese correlation. And we're not allowed to eat anything, so I can't associate word with taste.

There is, however, *bing ji ling,* which up until this point I have seen only on TV. My mother sneaks me some from a rectangular paper carton. Breyers French Vanilla. It's denser and sweeter than I expected, eggy in flavor, fuzzy with freezer burn. To my surprise, I don't like it at all and feel nauseated by its smell. But I have to like it, because I saw ice cream on TV back home, where all my friends and I fantasized about how wonderful it must taste.

Ice cream is my favorite food. I write these words in the journal my mother gives me to record my first days in the U.S. English is just a play language to me, the words tethered to their meanings by the loosest, most tenuous connections. So it's easy to lie. I tell the truth in Chinese, I make up stories in English. I don't take it that seriously. When I'm finally enrolled in first grade, I tell classmates that I live in a house with an elevator, with deer in the back yard. It is the language in which I have nothing to lose, even if they don't believe a thing I say.

(789 words)

Annotations

9 **congee** – rice porridge

18 **VHS cassette** – video cassette

32 **Mormon missionaries** – members of a religious group who go from door to door to spread their faith

38 **grad studies** – university studies for a master's degree or higher

41 **Sesame Street** – American educational television show for young children

45 **charge** – *here:* the child that her mother takes care of

46 **E.S.L.** – abbreviation for "English as a second language"

88 **freezer burn** – when food changes taste and structure after being in a freezer for too long

Beispiellösung

Aufgabe 1

The excerpt from "Peking Duck", written by Ling Ma in 2022 and published in *The New Yorker*, deals with the experiences of a seven-year-old Chinese girl, the narrator of the story, who has not seen her parents for two years and recently moved to the United States.

After her arrival, the narrator settles into a tiny apartment with her parents. While her father studies, her mother works as a nanny in a mansion and is usually accompanied by her daughter. Her mother, who speaks only little English, uses every opportunity to teach her daughter as much of the language as possible. She buys language-learner books for her, lets her watch children's TV programmes and points out individual words to her. Meanwhile, the narrator keeps a daily journal, in which she writes down some English sentences every day.

One day, the narrator is secretly given some ice cream by her mother, but does not like it at all. Yet, she writes in English into her journal that it is her favourite food. The narrator reveals that she uses her two languages, Chinese and English, in different ways: while she tells the truth in Chinese, she sees English as a toy to play with and make up stories in. (208 words)

Aufgabe 2

Overall, the mother-daughter relationship can be described as very pragmatic as well as lacking an outward show of emotion and affection.

This can be seen when the mother takes care of the narrator's needs in a somewhat rough manner ("dragging a wet towel across my face to wipe off dried congee", l. 8 f.). Also, she doesn't give her daughter a toy or a stuffed animal as a welcoming gift but rather a practical present in order to help her learn English ("the journal my mother gives me to record my first days", ll. 95 f.). The mother doesn't have a lot of time to spend with her daughter at home, but uses every opportunity she has at the mansion where she works for educational purposes ("our days are geared around my learning English", l. 39 f.). Teaching her daughter English thus serves as an important bond in their relationship.

Furthermore, their relationship is delineated by very traditional roles: while the mother is persistent and reassuring ("she gives me hints", l. 51 f.), the daughter is obedient and executes her mother's ideas even though she might not be interested in them ("We watch 'Sesame Street,' though it's too babyish for me even then", ll. 40–42; "I repeat each word after her", l. 78 f.). Also, she uses the journal given by her mother quite frequently (cf. ll. 42–44).

It is easy to see that, having been separated from one another for two years still has an impact on the mother-daughter relationship because the narrator does not seem to be emotionally attached to her mother. Instead, she misses her grandmother in China ("I still hear my grandma's phantom snores," l. 14 f.). Arguably, the mother, too, struggles with those years of separation. Nonetheless, her commitment to her daughter's future is unwavering: not only does she invest considerable amounts of money (the diary and the ESL books, cf. l. 46) and time (cf. l. 39 f.), but also risks her employment in order to allow her daughter the taste of ice cream (cf. ll. 80–82) – presumably because the family wouldn't be able to afford buying it themselves.

It can therefore be argued that the mother-daughter relationship is defined by their status as immigrants and their continuous search for a better life, and therefore mostly practical rather than emotional. The parents' precarious financial situation serves as much as "scaffolding" (l. 68) for a better future for the daughter as the mother's rudimentary knowledge of English. Accordingly, the daughter dutifully acquiesces to the mother's instructions, even though, as a child, she does not see much worth in them. (432 words)

Aufgabe 3

Writing an entry based on Greg Poehler's statement about his migrant experience is very challenging. Many of us may feel or have felt like him: the longer you spend time in a foreign country, the more likely it gets for your original identity to vanish, or rather for you to form a new hybrid identity that struggles to retain its true sense of belonging.

One can agree with Poehler because outsiders often experience discrimination, which can lead to insecurity and loneliness. This can be seen in Laylor's experience of rejection in Levy's "Loose Change" as well as the Somali women's confrontation with racism in Pandit's "She Shall Not Be Moved". Being displaced from your original environment likewise often leads to identity problems and social isolation, as one is often cut off from one's family, as it is portrayed in the character of Laylor in "Loose Change".
Another aspect to support Poehler's position is that language – as part of one's identity –and therefore language acquisition are key elements in adapting to new surroundings. Accordingly, the narrator's mother in Ling Ma's text "Peking Duck", in spite of her own difficulties with the English language, strives to enable her daughter to learn English so that she can prosper in American society. The same is true for Laylor, who seeks connection through language in "Loose Change". Not only is language an important aspect of integration, but also of adapting to cultural habits in order to fit in. Again, this can be seen when the narrator in "Peking Duck" pretends to like American food, even though they don't like it. However, it helps them have a sense of belonging. The fact that the narrator uses her two languages differently testifies to the idea that living in a different culture for a long time prevents a true sense of belonging. People can get stuck in between.
Pandit's short story, on the other hand, offers an example quite opposite to Poehler's position. The Somali woman on the bus refuses to be subdued by the racism directed at her. She retains her sense of self and the dignity connected with it. Indeed, the accuses the bus driver of having become a slave in his search for assimilation. Arguably, however, she too remains "caught in between two worlds".
Perhaps the world becoming more and more globalised will make social connections more important than geographic ones, meaning that a true sense of belonging can be forged anytime, anywhere.
Lastly, there might not be a hybrid identity because keeping one's former identity and adding new aspects may be possible. It seems to be a very individual decision and experience that cannot be generalised. It is always about people and their individual life stories. (452 words)

gA Aufgabe II mit Beispiellösung

Marybeth Gasman, "The Shame of My Father's Racism" (2017)

AUFGABENSTELLUNG

1 Outline Marybeth Gasman's reactions to her father's racism. (30 %)

2 Compare the author's father with Walt Kowalski from the movie *Gran Torino.* (30 %)

3 WHYY, a public news and media organization, has invited readers to share their ideas about "Living Cultural Diversity" on its website. You have decided to contribute a blog entry in which you assess the relevance of dealing with questions of cultural diversity for members of your generation. As a starting point, you take the following statement by author Audre Lorde: "It is not our differences that divide us. It is our inability to recognize, accept, and celebrate those differences."
Write the blog entry, also referring to the text at hand and materials studied in class, such as the movie *Gran Torino.* (40 %)

Materialgrundlage:

Marybeth Gasman, „The Shame of My Father's Racism", in: *Independence Mall West* (Philadelphia), 20.05.2017, zitiert nach: https://whyy.org/articles/essay-the-shame-of-my-fathers-racism (Zugriff: 1. April 2024).

Hilfsmittel:

Ein- und zweisprachiges Wörterbuch der Zielsprache

"The Shame of My Father's Racism" (2017) *Marybeth Gasman*

It took me years to talk about the racism perpetuated by my father in public settings. I was ashamed and embarrassed by him most of my early life. He was angry, verbally abusive, and looked down upon others regularly.

When I was a child, he attempted to fill my head with racist ideas about various people. He used racial slurs regularly and called me and members of our family these same names. As I grew older and began to read books in school, I started to push back at him and challenge his racist notions. He told me I was ignorant.

I couldn't understand why my father hated most racial and ethnic minorities, even though he had never met any member of these groups in his entire life. His hate was deep and angry, and he used "evidence" to try to persuade me that whites were better than others. He would tell me that African Americans "caused riots and destroyed cities," and point to pictures from the Civil Rights Movement. He left out most of the details. He would tell me that African Americans were "stupid and preferred to live in poverty," and point to examples that he saw on television in shows such as

"Sanford and Son." He would tell me how cruel Asian Americans were, citing their efforts to defend their own nations during wartime. He neglected to tell me about the cruelty that has cut across our own nation both during wars and at times of peace. He would tell me how Hispanics were "lazy and took advantage of the government," citing stereotypical pictures drawn by whites of Mexican Americans.

My father was an uneducated man, living in dire poverty most of his life. Instead of seeing the commonalities that he had with others oppressed in our nation and looking for ways to bridge those commonalities, he chose to blame others for his poverty and lack of success. It's important to note that my father often worked two jobs – one in a lumberyard and another on our small animal and vegetable farm; he also looked for odd jobs to make extra money. However, he could never get ahead, making less than minimum wage in many cases. Instead of hurling insults at the systems that perpetuated poverty, or becoming more active locally to change these systems, he decided to funnel his anger into hate for racial and ethnic minorities.

I spent years trying to change his mind – talking with him, trying to educate him, sometimes yelling at him. I even pursued a career as a professor who concentrates on race and class issues in American society, to better understand the hate that my father held in his heart. However, it wasn't until my father was older, in a nursing home, and had met someone African American, that he let go of his hate and our nation's original sin.

The pathway for my father was friendship, and the eventual understanding that he and his friend had much in common and were equally frustrated with their lot in life. It was at this point that my father confided in me that he was unhappy with his life and chose to blame racial and ethnic minorities – African Americans in particular – for his pain and failure. It was easier to blame those who so many others blamed rather than take responsibility or fight the systems that had helped maintain his place in society.

My father's story is one of hope in many ways, because he realized his wrongs, but it is also hopeful for me as a scholar. Many of my faculty colleagues throughout the country don't believe that we can make progress on racial issues and racism. However, I do – but only by engaging others in conversation and encouraging them to assist in dismantling systems. People dismantle systems, not systems themselves.

I have spent hours upon hours talking to people on planes, trains, in hotels, at conferences, in classrooms, etc. about race and have with each conversation tried to get people to consider the perspectives of others and examine their own biases. When people ask me if I get tired or frustrated by these conversations, I often respond by noting that I worked with and on my father for nearly 20 years, knowing that eventually he would turn a corner. What I realized in the end, however, is that it was not my intellectual ideas that changed him but the friendship of another and my having heart-to-heart conversations in which I listened to him openly. We need to do more listening to each other's stories to move our nation to a better and more equitable place for all.

(777 words)

Annotations:

29 "Sanford and Son" – American sitcom TV series (1972–1977)

Beispiellösung

Aufgabe 1

In her article "The Shame of My Father's Racism", published on WHYY.org in 2017, Marybeth Gasman recounts how she has been upset by and concerned with her father's obvious racism and hatred towards ethnic minorities for decades.
Forced to endure her father's verbally abusive behaviour towards ethnic minorities in public and even towards his family, she feels unable to understand or address his racism at first. Through her education and as she gets older, however, she begins to take issue with him on his insulting notions and challenges him. She investigates the reasons for his hatred, tracing it back to a lack of education and resulting extreme poverty, which caused him to scapegoat minorities. Finally, driven by her wish to understand her father's attitude, she chooses a career as a professor focusing on race and class issues. Moreover, she dedicates a lot of her time and energy on trying to educate people she meets on these matters. (157 words)

Aufgabe 2

When comparing Marybeth Gasman's father with Walt Kowalski, it becomes clear that both men at first share certain characteristics concerning their hostile convictions about ethnic minorities, but after experiencing unexpected friendship, they eventually change their minds.
Gasman and Kowalski spend most of their lives as inveterate racists, which can be seen in their openly displayed contempt towards other ethnic groups. Gasman uses racial slurs frequently and even abuses his family members with the same insults (l. 9–11). Kowalski likewise despises his Hmong neighbours, treating them with disrespect – for example, when he bangs the door into Thao's face – and slurring insults at them. Both Gasman and Kowalski are quick to draw on stereotypes in order to underline their firm convictions: Gasman "point[s] to examples that he saw on television" (ll. 27 f.), whereas Kowalski accuses Asians as a whole of allegedly eating dogs.
Both men are to some degree alienated from their family. Kowalski is widowed and estranged from his two sons, living alone with his dog. Gasman "was angry, verbally abusive, and looked down upon others" (ll. 4–6), including his own family, whom he also regularly bullied with racist epithets (cf. ll. 9–11). The text does not give any details about Gasman's family life, but most likely it was overshadowed by his antagonising behaviour.
Another similarity is the fact that both of them project their personal frustrations on members of ethnic minorities, which eases their minds about their dissatisfying circumstances of life. Gasman particularly blames African Americans for his poverty (ll. 50–56). Kowalski, on the other hand, seems to be distressed by his changing neighbourhood, where he feels white middle-class families are being replaced by Hmong immigrants, whom he automatically associates with his traumatising experiences in the Korean War and his own lifelong guilt. Therefore, he murmurs insults and shows scornful behaviour like spitting in their direction.
Eventually, both Gasman and Kowalski open their minds to the people they despised so deeply before. The reason for sparking this process in both cases is making friends with a member of a different ethnic group. Gasman does so with an African-American man

he meets in his nursing home (cf. ll. 63–67). Kowalski, on the other hand, is befriended by the Hmong family's daughter, opens up to their culture and becomes a substitute father figure for Thao. As a result, both Gasman and Kowalski eventually admit that their convictions were wrong. They open up and seem to achieve reconciliation, but their ways of doing so are completely different. Gasman confides to his daughter that it was his unhappiness about his life that fostered his racism (ll. 72–80). Kowalski, on the other hand, confesses to Thao to having killed an Asian boy during the Korean War, which has been haunting him ever since.
However, there are also dissimilarities to their situations. Gasman's social background differs from Kowalski's with respect to education and social class. Whereas Gasman belongs to the lower working class and suffers from lack of education (cf. ll. 39 f.), Kowalski is part of the middle class. In addition, their occupations show different qualities. Gasman's menial jobs were badly-paid (cf. ll. 45–49) and so deprived him of a sufficient income, a fact he proceeded to blame on immigrants. Kowalski, on the other hand, is bitter and disaffected by the decline of the automobile industry in Detroit that has also led – in his view – to a social decline of his environment. In addition, his experiences in the Korean War have left him traumatised and battling both guilt and a simplistic world view. Lastly, their ways of redeeming themselves are likewise dissimilar. Gasman recognises the root of his racism and admits his wrongs to his daughter. Kowalski does not directly renounce his racist ideas. Instead, he acts as a mentor for Thao and eventually willingly and calculatingly sacrifices his own life in order to save Thao and his family by making sure that the gang members threatening them will be imprisoned for a long time.
All in all, the conclusion can be drawn that while Gasman and Kowalski share a path from racism to redemption, a closer look at the motives for their hatred and the personal insights causing their respective changes of mind reveals enormous differences.

(708 words)

Aufgabe 3

Dear fellow bloggers,
After reading so many blog entries on "Living Cultural Diversity", I have decided to write an entry based on a statement by Audre Lorde: "It is not our differences that divide us. It is our inability to recognise, accept, and celebrate those differences". I feel that this quote fittingly sums up our topic because it truly expresses the fact that people from different ethnic backgrounds do not easily find their way towards each other because we fear our cultural differences.
Lorde argues that the fact that people are different is of minor importance and that we need to learn to embrace cultural diversity. This seems a valuable idea taking into account that many people are intimidated by the unknown, which unfortunately makes them avoid new experiences. In order to overcome such obstacles and to reduce both apparent and subconscious fears, it is necessary to reconsider our everyday attitudes towards other ethnicities. If we manage to do so, we will be able to accept different cultures more easily and welcome each other with open arms.
Cases of people overcoming their prejudicial or even racist ideas through forming bonds with a person from a different culture can often be found in literature and film. Two such

impressive examples are Marybeth Gasman's father, whose journey she describes in "The Shame of My Father's Racism" (2017), and the protagonist Walt Kowalski in the film *Gran Torino*. Gasman's father, who had been quick to blame his own destitution on other ethnicities, finally makes friends with an African American in his retirement home and realises that people of colour face the same problems as he does. A similar development can be found in Kowalski: After initially showing open contempt towards his new Hmong neighbours, based in part on his own guilt-ridden experiences in the Korean War, he becomes a mentor to one of the family's boys and starts protecting the whole Hmong family, who is terrorised by a gang.

Aside from that, it can be very fortunate to give up one's reservations and approach situations of intercultural contact with open-minded curiosity. For Walt Kowalski, doing so enables him to gradually enjoy the Hmong family's hospitality when he is invited to share their meals and to get to know their customs.

Another advantageous way of approaching other cultures is actively looking for similarities, which definitely brings people together. This is underlined by both Gasman's father, who finds out that he and his African-American friend share a similar economic situation, as well as Kowalski, who eventually considers himself closer to the Hmong family than to his own.

In addition, it is vital that everybody tries to free themselves from prejudices and stereotypes as they represent considerable obstacles to a peaceful coexistence. Accordingly, Marybeth Gasman consistently tries to subvert not only her father's but also others' racist views.

Besides, as cultures of homogeneous ethnic roots are increasingly becoming a phenomenon of the past, it is important to recognise that changing ethnic structures of communities have been on their way for several decades and that we have to accept and assist this development by actively learning about each other's cultures in order to gain a closer insight into others' customs and traditions. Doing so should be considered the norm in order to give everybody an intercultural understanding. This way, we should be prepared to address critical situations, which could otherwise cause cultural conflict, in a constructive way.

However, a much better solution to many problems evoked by cultural clashes is to initiate systemic changes which, at best, could lead to a constant peaceful coexistence of different cultural communities. Movements such as Black Lives Matter can be seen as a significant step towards raising awareness and achieving equality.

And what about us younger people? What can we do for a closely-knit community consisting of various cultures? In my eyes, we must try to make this a better world by vehemently opposing stereotypes and prejudice, as Gasman lays out in her text. We must not let up and keep these issues alive and burning. And we must be fearless to "recognize, accept, and celebrate those differences", as Lorde puts it. It is high time that we, the young generation, took a stand against racism in order to heal painful wounds scarred by history and to prevent future wars. Consequently, we need to stick together in order to enable us all to live together peacefully. (735 words)

Original-Prüfungsaufgaben 2023 eA

Hinweise:

Die zentrale schriftliche Abiturprüfung im Fach Englisch besteht aus einer kombinierten Aufgabe:

Prüfungsteil 1:	a)	**Hörverstehen**
	b)	**Sprachmittlung**
Prüfungsteil 2:	**Textaufgabe**	

Ablauf und Bewertung der Prüfung:

Ausgabe der **Aufgaben für den Prüfungsteil 1a**	
Prüfungsteil 1a:	**Hörverstehen**
Gewichtung:	20 %
Bearbeitungszeit:	30 Minuten
Abgabe sämtlicher Unterlagen des **Prüfungsteil 1a** Ausgabe der Aufgaben für den **Prüfungsteil 1b**	
Prüfungsteil 1b:	**Sprachmittlung**
Gewichtung:	25 %
Bearbeitungszeit:	60 Minuten
Abgabe sämtlicher Unterlagen des **Prüfungsteil 1b** Ausgabe der Aufgaben für den **Prüfungsteil 2**	
Prüfungsteil 2:	**Textaufgabe**
Gewichtung:	55 %
Prüfungszeit:	240 Minuten Die Prüfungszeit setzt sich zusammen aus 30 Minuten Auswahlzeit und 210 Minuten Bearbeitungszeit.

Hilfsmittel für alle Prüfungsteile:

Den Prüflingen stehen einsprachige sowie für den schulischen Gebrauch geeignete zweisprachige Wörterbücher der Allgemeinsprache (Deutsch–Englisch/Englisch–Deutsch) zur Verfügung (s. Erlass zur Nutzung von [elektronischen] Wörterbüchern in Prüfungen: https://www.nibis.de/uploads/mk-bolhoefer/2022/202111ElektronischeWoerterbuecher.pdf).

Hinweis

- Jedes einzelne Blatt ist mit dem Namen zu versehen.

Hinweise zum Prüfungsteil 2

- Von den zwei Aufgaben ist eine auszuwählen und zu bearbeiten.
- Bei jeder Teilaufgabe ist die inhaltliche Gewichtung angegeben.

eA Listening Comprehension **25 BE**

AUFGABENSTELLUNG

You will hear each recording twice. After each listening you will have time to complete your answers.

Task 1: Crime and Law Enforcement **6 BE**

Preparation time: 45 seconds

You will hear six extracts from radio reports on people's experiences with crime and law enforcement.
Choose from the list (A–G) which description best applies to which extract (1–6). For each extract, there is only one correct answer. There is one more description than you need.

Descriptions	
A	Fearing a relapse
B	Doing detective work
C	Facing legal proceedings
D	Examining a crime on the rise
E	Ruling out potential lawbreakers
F	Offering a way out of illegal activities
G	Accepting help from law enforcement

Extract	1	2	3	4	5	6
Description						

Now listen to the recording again.

Sources:
Audio 1: "People fixing the world: Residents turn detective to fight crime", *BBC World Service,* 2 July 2019, https://www.bbc.co.uk/programmes/p07fp90n (02:23–02:51);
Audio 2: "People fixing the world: From prison to star employee", *BBC World Service,* 17 November 2020, https://www.bbc.co.uk/programmes/p08ymfb7 (05:01–05:35);
Audio 3: "People fixing the world: The career where it helps to have a criminal past", *BBC World Service,* 29 June 2021, https://www.bbc.co.uk/programmes/p09mr1br (00:12–00:44);
Audio 4: "Talk of the Nation: What Bystanders Do When They Witness Violence", *NPR,* 29 October 2009, https://www.npr.org/templates/story/story.php?storyId=114287592 (01:15–01:41);
Audio 5: M. L. Kelly, "All things considered: Debris 'as far as the eye can see' along Los Angeles train tracks following thefts", 17 January 2022, https://www.npr.org/2022/01/17/1073661326/thousands-of-empty-boxes-are-strewn-along-los-angeles-train-tracks-following-the (00:17–00:51);
Audio 6: Audio 6: "People fixing the world: The hotel for homeless people", *BBC World Service,* 14 September 2021, https://www.bbc.co.uk/programmes/p09vv0m8 (03:07–03:51).

(All audio files accessed on 1 April 2024.)

Task 2: Baby College

11 BE

Preparation time: 1:30 minutes

You will hear an extract from a radio report about Baby College, a program of the non-profit organization Harlem Children's Zone.
While listening, fill in the missing information. You need not write complete sentences. Unless otherwise specified, name one aspect.

1	Baby College's two target groups	• ______ • ______
2	Time frame of a Baby College course	
3	How the participants express the importance of reading	
4	One positive effect of Baby College for its participants according to an expert	
5	Basic child-rearing principle Baby College promotes	
6	What Edgar Garcia learned	
7	The two ways to find new participants for Baby College	• ______ • ______
8	How participation is made attractive *(Name two.)*	• ______ • ______

Now listen to the recording again.

Source:
A. Starr, "Code Switch: Boosting Education For Babies And Their Parents", *NPR*, 9 May 2015, https://www.npr.org/sections/codeswitch/2015/05/09/405270265/boosting-education-for-babies-and-their-parents (00:00–02:58 + 04:36–04:44) (accessed on 1 April 2024)

Task 3: Costing the Earth

8 BE

Preparation time: 1:30 minutes

You will hear a radio report about American businessman Russ George and his project to supply the world with more seafood.
While listening, tick the correct answer (a, b or c). There is only one correct answer.

1. Russ George tries to increase the quantity of fish by

a	imitating nature.	☐
b	having fishing regulated.	☐
c	using advanced technology.	☐

2. An important part of George's project is

a	monitoring fish size in the Pacific.	☐
b	introducing additives to the Pacific.	☐
c	removing pollutants from the Pacific.	☐

3. George's idea might also support the environment by

a	binding harmful gases.	☐
b	increasing biodiversity.	☐
c	triggering waste decomposition.	☐

4. According to George, plankton that descends to the deep sea

a	adapts to the new habitat over time.	☐
b	remains in the ocean for a very long time.	☐
c	damages the ecosystem in the course of time.	☐

5. According to the reporter, George was hurt most by the claim that

a	his actions were inefficient.	☐
b	his aim was to make money.	☐
c	his project damaged the ecosystem.	☐

6. George cooperated with a musician in order to

a	create public attention for his project.	☐
b	try out the practical aspects of his project.	☐
c	demonstrate the positive effects of his project.	☐

7. An article in a magazine revolves around

a	the innovative funding of the project.	☐
b	the political implications of the project.	☐
c	the academic evaluation of the project.	☐

Now think of the text as a whole:

8. The radio programme focuses on

a	ethical aspects.	☐
b	economic aspects.	☐
c	ecological aspects.	☐

Now listen to the recording again.

Source:
J. Jenkins, "Costing the Earth: 'Greenfinger'", *BBC Radio 4,* 19 May 2021, https://www.bbc.co.uk/programmes/m000w33w (00:00–02:18 + 02:35–03:48) (accessed on 1 April 2024)

Lösungen

Task 1: Crime and Law Enforcement

1	2	3	4	5	6
B	A	F	C	D	G

Task 2: Baby College

No.	BE	*Lösungsvorschlag:*
1	1 1	– anticipating parents / soon-to-be parents – first-time parents / parents with infants and toddlers / parents with kids under 3
2	1	– for nine straight/successive Saturdays / once a week, spanning more than eight weeks
3	1	– they collaborate through musical expression / with the aid of tunes
4	1	– forms a circle of support / reduces feelings of solitude among parents / enhances parents' capability to be empathetic and attentive to their kids / fosters a sense of community
5	1	– non-physical disciplinary methods / without the use of physical force / discipline without hitting
6	1	– emphasising emotional bonds / prioritising guidance / being emotionally available for your child
7	1 1	– ringing doorbells – approaching expectant mothers in public
8	1 1	*two of the following:* – baby gates – books for children – free food – supervision for children while parents visit classes – lottery for those who attend all course dates

Task 3: Costing the Earth

1	2	3	4	5	6	7	8
a	b	a	b	b	b	c	c

eA Sprachmittlung

AUFGABENSTELLUNG

You are going to take part in an international youth conference about sustainable business ideas. To prepare for the discussions, participants share an example from their own country on the conference website.
Write an article for this website in which you present „Lieferrad DA".

Materialgrundlage:

Astrid Ludwig, „Der Spargel kommt per Lastenrad", *Frankfurter Allgemeine Zeitung* (Frankfurt), 29.03.2021, S. 3 (gekürzt)

Hilfsmittel:

Ein- und zweisprachiges Wörterbuch der Zielsprache

„Der Spargel kommt per Lastenrad" *Astrid Ludwig*

Lange schon hegte das Professoren-Trio die Idee für einen Lieferservice der anderen Art. Einen, der die Umwelt schont, den örtlichen Handel stärkt, Mitarbeiter fair bezahlt und trotzdem rentabel ist. Doch die Wirtschafts- und Logistikexperten Johanna Bucerius und Axel Wolfermann von der Hochschule Darmstadt und Kai-Oliver Schocke von der Frankfurt University of Applied Sciences fanden niemanden, der bereit war, das auch auszuprobieren. Dann aber kam Corona. „Als wir gesehen haben, wie schlecht es dem Einzelhandel geht, haben wir den Lieferservice selbst gestartet", berichtet Bucerius. Beim hessischen Wirtschaftsministerium beantragten die drei Forscher Fördergeld. Sie bekamen rund 100.000 Euro, mit denen E-Lastenräder angeschafft und Gehälter für das studentische Team aus Hilfskräften und Kurierfahrern gezahlt werden konnten.

Seit dem Sommer rollen die schwarzen Lasten-Bikes mit dem gelbblauen Aufdruck „Lieferrad DA" durch Darmstadt. Sie bringen Blumen, Bücher, Wein, Lebensmittel, die nicht gekühlt werden müssen, Kleidung, Kosmetik oder auch Medikamente von den Einzelhändlern direkt nach Hause zu den Kunden. „Es lief gut an", sagt Axel Wolfermann – dank Werbung über soziale Medien sowie Kontakten zur Stadt und örtlichen Wirtschaft. Ein Spargelbauer im Stadtteil Arheilgen machte den Anfang. Bei manchem Geschäft fragten die Studenten auch persönlich an.

Mittlerweile nutzen rund 50 Einzelhändler in Darmstadt den unentgeltlichen Lieferservice. Darunter auch große Händler wie das Modekaufhaus Henschel und die Buchladen-Kette Thalia. Armin Pourhosseini, Mitbegründer des Naturkosmetik-Shops „Woodberg", hat sich nach eigenen Worten bewusst für den klimaschonenden Raddienst entschieden. [...] Umweltschutz gehört für ihn zum Geschäftsmodell. Für seine Naturprodukte nutzt er recyceltes Verpackungsmaterial, bei Versand und Bezahlung bietet er Kunden Modelle an, die

Ökoprojekte unterstützen. Rund vier von zehn Bestellungen aus Darmstadt lässt er von Lieferrad DA zustellen.

Die studentischen Radkuriere haben gut zu tun. Wöchentlich fahren sie zwischen 100 und 150 Pakete aus. „Weihnachten ging es deutlich nach oben, da waren es rund 300 Pakete pro Woche. Das war Rekord“, so Wolfermann. Am Valentinstag nahmen die Ausfahrten ebenfalls zu, und Ostern werde sicherlich eine weitere Herausforderung, vermutet Bucerius. Bis Ende 2020 brachte „Lieferrad DA“ montags bis freitags insgesamt 1068 Pakete an die Haustüren. Die zwei studentischen Kuriere radelten mehr als 3000 Kilometer durch die Straßen Darmstadts.

Die Kunden bestellen bei den Händlern, die die Aufträge an das Studententeam weiterleiten. „Wird bis 12 Uhr bestellt, liefern wir am selben Tag aus“, sagt Florian Treiber. Der Dreiundzwanzigjährige, der Logistikmanagement an der Hochschule Darmstadt studiert, ist für die Tourenplanung zuständig. Er pflegt die Bestellungen in die Tourensoftware ein, prüft, ob Händler wegen vieler oder schwerer Pakete mehrfach angefahren werden müssen, checkt Öffnungszeiten, rechnet Pufferzeiten ein und übernimmt die Datenanalyse. Weil Kundendaten sensibel sind, stellt die Hochschule dafür einen gesicherten Laptop zur Verfügung. Treiber ist für die Kuriere erreichbar, „falls ein Kunde nicht da, die Adresse falsch oder der Akku leer ist“. Vor Weihnachten ist er sogar selbst als Fahrer eingesprungen – ein lehrreicher Blick auf die andere Seite. „Das Projekt ist ohnehin eine super Einstiegsmöglichkeit in die Logistikbranche“, findet der Student. Und das ohne Druck und schlechte Bezahlung, über die Paketzusteller immer wieder klagen. Die Lieferrad-Kuriere und Hiwis werden pro Stunde honoriert, nach den Sätzen der Hochschule. Studenten mit Bachelorabschluss erhalten rund 15 Euro. „Sie werden zudem in das Forschungsprojekt einbezogen, bringen ihre Erfahrungen ein“, ergänzt Bucerius. Der Lieferdienst ist auch Gegenstand mehrerer Bachelorarbeiten.

Das Professoren-Trio ist zufrieden mit dem Projekt. Zum Jahresende ist zwar die Förderung ausgelaufen, doch eine Fortsetzung ist in Sicht. Noch ist die Hochschule Darmstadt Betreiberin und der Lieferdienst gebührenfrei. Doch es soll eine neue Rechtsform gefunden werden, damit Lieferrad DA als Verein oder GmbH Gewinne generieren kann. Denn die Forscher wollen auch herausfinden, unter welchen Bedingungen ein derartiger Lieferservice rentabel bestehen kann. Bei voller Auslastung betragen die Kosten je Lieferung derzeit rund vier Euro. Der Einzelhandel, sagt Wolfermann, habe Interesse an dem Lieferdienst, aber angewiesen ist das Projekt auf zusätzliche Kunden wie die Stadt, kommunale Betriebe, Unternehmen oder Wochenmarkt-Beschicker. Andere Kommunen haben schon Interesse am Aufbau eines ähnlichen Lieferdienstes bekundet.

(640 Wörter)

Anmerkungen:

24 DA – Autokennzeichen Darmstadts

91 Hiwi – studentische wissenschaftliche Hilfskraft

Beispiellösung

"Lieferrad DA": The Sustainable Delivery Revolution from Darmstadt, Germany

In the age of climate change and e-commerce boom, the need for sustainable delivery solutions is more urgent than ever. Enter "Lieferrad DA", a German initiative courier service that ticks all the boxes: environmental friendliness, support for local trade, fair employee wages and profitability. The name refers to cargo bikes as well as the licence plate code of the city the service operates in.

"Lieferrad DA" was the brain child of three university professors from Hochschule Darmstadt and Frankfurt University of Applied Sciences, who specialise in economics and logistics. Initially, they struggled to find backers for their idea, but after the COVID-19 pandemic's devastating impact on local retailers they secured financial support from regional government funds, allowing them to purchase electric cargo bikes and recruit a student workforce.

The students carry an assortment of goods – everything from locally sourced food to cosmetics – directly from the shop to the customer's doorstep. But they also assist with route optimisation and data analytics, which offers them valuable work experience.

The local community has been quick to jump on board. Around 50 Darmstadt businesses have opted into this zero-emissions delivery service. The service is also gaining traction among eco-conscious consumers. Currently offered as a free service under the university's wings, there are ambitions to transition it into a self-sustaining model. Meanwhile, the project has sparked interest in other cities.

"Lieferrad DA" is a shining beacon of what sustainable business can look like in the urban context. It demonstrates that thoughtful business models can bring about solutions that are both environmentally sustainable and beneficial to the community, which makes it an insightful case study at this international youth conference. (283 words)

eA Aufgabe I mit Beispiellösung

Yvette Edwards, "Security" (2019, excerpt)

AUFGABENSTELLUNG

1 Describe the situation in the shop. (30 %)

2 Examine Merle's character. (30 %)

3 You want to take part in an online seminar at the University of Houston on the migrant experience titled "The Quest for True Belonging and the Courage to Stand Alone," which is offered by social scientist Brené Brown. As a prerequisite for attendance, you have to hand in an essay commenting on her statement "Fitting in is not belonging."
Write the essay, also referring to the text at hand and materials studied in class, such as the short stories by Lahiri, Levy, Pandit, and Shahraz. (40 %)

Materialgrundlage:
Yvette Edwards, „Security", in: *New Daughters of Africa. An International Anthology of Writing by Women of African Descent.* Hrsg. Margaret Busby. Oxford: Myriad, 2019. 336–340 (gekürzt)

Hilfsmittel:
Ein- und zweisprachiges Wörterbuch der Zielsprache

"Security" (Excerpt) *Yvvette Edwards*

Merle noticed the security guard the moment she stepped through the entrance of Penny World: a tall, heavy-set white man, mid-forties, who had positioned himself on top of a barstool at the front of the store to have an unobstructed view of customers entering; and she knew he'd clocked her, because he stood up straightaway, trying to make the action seem natural by generally surveying the store, as if that had been his intention all along, and it surprised her, the anger she felt – hot and rapid, erupting inside her chest like a volcano come to life – surprised her at a time when she was upset with so many other things, proper problems with longevity attached, that this incident, when she'd just popped out to pick up some Sure deodorant and a roll of clingfilm, was the blow that finally swept her over the edge.

Her flight was tomorrow morning at 11 and arrangements had been made to pick her up at 5 a.m. so she didn't miss it. She'd bought the suitcase last week, had to, because the only one she'd ever owned was the one she'd brought with her when she made the six-week boat journey from Jamaica to England in June 1964, which had for years been reclining on top of her wardrobe, the metal handle broken, clasps defunct, reduced in status to a storage container, nothing more. She'd not been back to Jamaica since arriving here, had never gone on holiday abroad, never had need of a passport, and here she was, at the age of seventy-eight, making the journey back [...]. Seventy-eight years of age, and with the neat and tidy way she always dressed and carried herself, were she a stranger trying to work out what kind of person she might be, the word that would have come to mind is church. Despite this, in the fifty-four years she'd been living in England and spending her money in shops with security guards, she'd regularly been followed around like a thief.

Forty-one of those fifty-four years she'd worked as a care assistant in homes for the elderly, spoon-feeding geriatrics, dressing and undressing them, giving herself back problems that plagued her to this day, from lifting them in and out of bed and bath, on and off seats, toilets, floors; cleaning their dirty behinds and infronts, their soiled bedding, while acting like it was just sticks and stones to have them tell her they didn't want her black hands touching them, their food, their cutlery and medicine cups.

She'd been watched with suspicion by those same people she'd looked after, watched as she mopped up all manner of nastiness, as if the only reason she dressed in the uniform her employers issued, wearing gloves and carrying a mop and bucket, was to rob them of the little shekels in purses and wallets they hid under mattresses and at the back of their drawers. And had she harboured any grudges against them? Nope. She had not. [...]

Merle dawdled as she approached the end of the aisle, handling products she had no intention of buying, touching everything she felt like, without a backward glance. Then, as she rounded the corner, out of the security guard's sight, she began marching briskly, nearly but not quite running, careful not to slip or trip and mash up her seventy-eight-year-old body, hurrying only as fast as she could manage safely, because if she injured herself, they'd probably say she'd done it on purpose to avoid the flight, and God alone knew whether after all the years of paying National Insurance contributions from her wages, she'd be entitled to treatment from the National Health Service. She scurried determinedly down Aisle 2 and around the corner so she was back in Aisle 1, continued swiftly along it, then for the second time rounded the top, slowing only when she spotted the security guard a few feet ahead, facing away from her, body alert, his head pinging back and forth like a meerkat, no doubt wondering where the old lady had vanished. She stopped immediately behind him, and as he turned around in confusion, Merle picked up a column of fifty disposable cups and stared at it, trying to calm her breathing, while joyfully basking in the vibe of his astonishment at discovering the woman he'd been following was now behind him. [...]

She said, “It doesn't feel very nice, does it?”

The security guard's voice was deep, bassy, tinged with a strong accent that Merle couldn't narrow down further than Eastern European. He said, “My job, stop steal.”

The fact of his accent broke her; she didn't know why. It made no difference to what had happened, to this latest affront. Was it because despite being new to the country, he'd been endowed with the authority to treat her like a criminal? Did she feel because he wasn't British, he didn't have the right? Or because until he opened his mouth he'd been able to pass, to silently position himself within the system like a native, whereas fifty-four years on, she was still being made to feel like a foreigner? Now a foreigner officially.

She said, "Well you won't have to worry about this woman stealing ever again. You'll be happy to know, I'm being deported." [...]

At the till, after she had paid for her items and packed them in the carrier bag she'd brought along, she noticed the security guard was sitting on his barstool again, and realised she'd have to pass him on her way to the exit. She'd decided to just ignore him, but as she approached his perch, he gave her a smile and she was unable to interpret what it was meant to convey. Solidarity? Pity? Glee?

Her pace slowed, but she did not stop. Reflected in his glasses she saw a proud old lady, head held high. Her voice was steady as she spoke: "It's me today, but tomorrow, they'll be back for you."

(994 words)

Beispiellösung

Aufgabe 1

In Yvette Edward's short story "Security", published in 2019, the racially-motivated surveillance of a security guard triggers Merle, a black woman about to be deported after decades in Britain, and causes her to confront him.

As Merle steps inside the shop, she immediately notices a burly, white security guard, who seems alerted by her presence and starts monitoring her every move. Seemingly continuing her shopping, she reflects on her past. Merle recalls arriving in Britain from Jamaica, her work as a caretaker in a home for the elderly and the constant acts of discrimination she had to endure. While having taken those lying down until now, she is surprised that the security guard's surveillance tips her over the edge.

As she moves out of the guard's line of sight, she quickly navigates through different aisles, eventually ending up behind him. Confronting him directly, she is shocked to learn that he himself is an immigrant and eventually warns him that he may soon suffer the same fate as her. (169 words)

Aufgabe 2

The excerpt describes Merle as a 78-year-old woman (cf l. 37) who, since her arrival in Britain after a "six-week boat journey from Jamaica" (l. 27) at the age of 24 (cf. ll. 42 f.), has consistently attempted to assimilate, to fit in and be a part of British society. Self-consciously, she attributes herself the word "church" (l. 42) – painting herself as someone who wants to blend in by being "neat and tidy" (l. 38), even if it means subduing her identity. Furthermore, she is portrayed as careful in her endeavours, even when fueled by rage ("hurrying only as fast as she could manage safely", ll. 78 f.). This awareness of her physical limitations reflects her desire to maintain a dignified appearance and avoid any behaviour that might reinforce negative stereotypes. This picture is complemented by her recalling her past as a care assistant for the elderly, enduring back-breaking and revolting labour (cf. ll. 48–54). Her dedication underscores both her work ethic and her compassion, traits that are often associated with those who seek to assimilate and contribute to their adopted society.

Despite all her efforts, she experiences continued discrimination ("them tell[ing] her they didn't want her black hands touching them, their food, their cutlery and medicine

cups", ll. 56–58). Yet, her resilience is highlighted by her dismissal of said behaviour (cf. ll. 55 f.), as well as her final statement on the matter: "And had she harboured any grudges against them? Nope. She had not" (ll. 67–69). This disposition showcases her willingness to move past the injustices she has faced, indicating her hope for acceptance and a sense of belonging.
Because her experience is marred with persistent discrimination, she immediately notices the security guard profiling her (cf. l. 7). Eventually, this is what "finally [sweeps] her over the edge" (ll. 19 f.), a matter of fact she feels surprised by (cf. l. 11). When confronting him, her actions are purposeful and assertive. She manages to turn the tables on the security guard, a symbolic act of asserting her presence and significance, thus standing up for herself by challenging his assumptions. Merle's dignified response to the security guard's attempt to explain himself is a testament to her courage and refusal to accept being treated unfairly any longer. Her measured words and composed demeanour underline her dignity even in moments of adversity ("a proud old lady, head held high", ll. 135 f.).
(400 words)

Aufgabe 3

<u>The Illusion of Fitting In: Unmasking the Nuances of True Belonging</u>

"Fitting in" and "belonging" may seem synonymous but represent different emotional experiences. While the former indicates superficial adaption, the latter suggests an innate acceptance. In Yvette Edward's short story "Security", the dilemma of Merle – a 78-year-old Jamaican woman who has lived most of her life in England – serves as an illustration of this chasm. This essay argues that "fitting in is not belonging", emphasising that the former often demands superficial adjustments and fear-driven compliance, whereas the latter thrives on genuine self-assurance and courage to maintain one's identity.
A defining issue is the extent to which an individual is willing to modify their behaviour to fit into societal moulds. Merle's 54 years in England were spent in service, toiling as a care assistant. Yet, her continued efforts remain scrutinised rather than noticed, let alone lauded. Merle sacrifices her own identity to meet the biases of others – and still fails. This is also illustrated in the other narratives. When the protagonist meets Laylor in Andrea Levy's „Loose Change," they initially form a fragile connection. But when she realises that the other woman is a homeless immigrant, the narrator's own migration background is thrust aside and she flees, illustrating that fitting in often involves distancing oneself from one's roots. In Shereen Pandit's "She Shall Not Be Moved", the narrator, as a refugee and person of colour, is compelled to show solidarity when the Somali woman is racially harassed, but feels intimidated by majority expectations, affirming that fitting in can be a function of fear or necessity rather than genuine acceptance. In contrast, Samir in Quaisra Shahraz' "The Escape" and the narrator in Jhumpa Lahiri's "The Third and Final Continent" seem to find a semblance of acceptance within their adopted surroundings. In sum, each protagonist demonstrates varying degrees of willingness to modify their behaviour. It is questionable, however, if this acceptance is truly a form of belonging or merely a more comfortable version of fitting in, as each person's efforts serve as mere entry tickets to acceptance.

True belonging then isn't about adapting to social norms but about society accepting individuals for their authenticity. Despite Merle's relentless service, she notes that she remains a foreigner, supposedly ending in her deportation. Adhering to social expectations can thus still leave one excluded. Consequently, her story questions the efficacy of fitting in when it doesn't lead to authentic acceptance. The lack thereof is also shown in "She Shall Not Be Moved". More nuanced, this notion is echoed in "The Third and Final Continent". The protagonist tries to fit in by adhering to cultural norms and so does, with some help and time, his wife Mala. However, they mostly find true belonging not in superficial acceptance but in their relationship with one another. In conclusion, the degree of acceptance by the community is pivotal, not just the individual's acceptance of the community.

Additionally, maintaining one's identity amid the quest for acceptance is crucial, especially for immigrants, as it serves as a touchstone for genuine belonging. Merle is relegated to the peripheries of society, in part because she abandons her connection to her West Indian roots, making her vulnerable to a system that refuses to fully embrace her. In "Loose Change", what keeps Laylor from truly belonging to a country she has always admired is not her insufficient sense of identity but her homelessness, and consequently her lack of money and status. Sharaz' Samir, on the other hand, balances his life in Britain partly with Muslim rituals, creating a hybrid identity that helps him find a sense of acceptance. He doesn't abandon his roots but incorporates them, as does the narrator in "The Third and Final Continent". Their ability to connect with both cultures enriches their lives in a way that transcends a temporary ticket of acceptance. In conclusion, the act of maintaining one's own identity is crucial in creating a genuine sense of belonging.

These short stories' characters illustrate that "fitting in" often requires surrendering one's authentic self in the desperate pursuit of societal acceptance. As Merle's case proves however, external compliance is not a reliable pathway. Similarly, the characters in "She Shall Not Be Moved" and "Loose Change" show how easily community acceptance can turn into rejection based on mere surface-level judgments, further underlining that fitting in is precarious and conditional. Characters like Samir in "The Escape" and the narrator in "The Third and Final Continent" find a more satisfying form of belonging, one that is internally fortified and embraces their unique identities. In doing so, they point the way to an empowering narrative: that true belonging can be achieved when one integrates their original cultural identity with their new environment, thus transcending societal norms and expectations and offering a durable and meaningful connection to both self and the community. (800 words)

eA Aufgabe II mit Beispiellösung

Yohanca Delgado,“The Little Widow from the Capital” (2021, excerpt)

AUFGABENSTELLUNG

1 Sum up the text. (30 %)

2 Examine how the neighbors’ attitude towards the widow is presented in the excerpt. Refer to both narrative perspective and stylistic means. (30 %)

3 On its website *The Paris Review,* a U.S. magazine on literature and culture, has invited readers to contribute to their blog on „Living Together – Communities Today“ and to discuss the statement by author Dean Ornish: „The need for connection and community is primal, as fundamental as the need for air, water, and food.“
Write the blog entry, also referring to the text at hand and materials studied in class, such as the movie *Gran Torino.* (40 %)

Materialgrundlage:

Yohanca Delgado, „ The Little Widow from the Capital “, in: *The Paris Review* 236 (2021), 137–139.

Hilfsmittel:

Ein- und zweisprachiges Wörterbuch der Zielsprache

“The Little Widow from the Capital” (Excerpt) *Yohanca Delgado*

The widow arrived at LaGuardia on a Sunday, but the rumors about the woman who had rented a big apartment, sight unseen, had taken an earlier flight. We had already reviewed, on many occasions and in hushed tones, in the quiet that comes after long hours of visiting, what little we knew about the widow and her dead husband. About her life in the old country, we asked the obvious questions: Were there children? Cheryl heard from a friend who still lived in the Dominican Republic that they had only been married a year when he died. Had her husband been rich? No, our sources in the old country said, poor as a church mouse, with a big family to support out in el campo. Had the husband been handsome? Yes, in a rakish sort of way. And with what we knew we created him in our minds: medium height with a mop of curly hair and an easy laugh, walking down Saona Beach in a white linen guayabera, dropping suddenly to one knee. We ourselves felt a flutter in our hearts.

On the day the widow finally arrived in New York, the rain came in fast, heavy drops that sounded like tiny birds slamming into our windows. She emerged from the taxi with a single battered suitcase and, little-girl small, stared up at our building as the rain pelted her face. Behind us our men and children called out for their dinners, but we ignored them. We would wonder later if she had seen our faces pressed up against the windows, on all six floors, peering out over flowerpots full of barren dirt. We watched her until she made her way out of the rain and into the lobby. Those of us lucky enough to live on the fourth floor squinted through our peepholes or cracked open our doors as the super carried her suitcase to the three-bedroom apartment she was renting. How could she afford it?

The little widow walked behind the super, her gait slow and steady on the black-and-white tiles of the hallway. He was rambling about garbage pickup and the rent. She was younger than we expected her to be, thirty, maybe. The amber outfit was all wrong for the chilly autumn weather. She was from Santo Domingo, but she looked like a campesina visiting the city for the first time, everything hand-sewn and outdated by decades. She wore an old-fashioned skirt suit, tailored and nipped at her round waist, and a pair of low-heeled black leather pumps. Seeing them made us glance down at our own scuffed sneakers and leggings. On her head, she wore a pillbox hat, in matching yellow wool sculpted butter-smooth. She dressed her short, plump body as though she adored it.

Instantly, we took a dislike.

We ourselves had been raised on a diet of telenovelas and American magazines, and we knew what beauty was. We gathered after dinner to laugh at her peculiar clothes. We murmured with fake sympathy about her loneliness, and joked that she might turn our husbands' heads. When we ran into her, though, we smiled and asked her how she was finding New York.

We began to invent stories about the little widow's life: torrid affairs that had driven her husband to die of heartbreak, a refusal to give him children, a penchant for hoarding money – we repeated the tales until we half believed them. The drama of the little widow's previous life became richer and denser, like a thicket of fast-growing ivy. Who did she think she was, anyway? Living alone in that big apartment?

The little widow seemed to understand what we expected of her: she muttered only quiet thank-yous when we held the door open as she struggled with her groceries, or when we helped her up after she slipped on a patch of ice in front of the building and landed flat on her back. As briskly as she could, she composed herself and disappeared, her head bowed low into the collar of her quaint amber coat.

When we heard that the little widow could sew, we started bringing her dresses and pants to hem, mostly because we wanted to know how she lived. The little widow's three-bedroom apartment was laid out like the others, but as she worked, our eyes darted hungrily between her and the contents of her sewing room.

Her hair was curly, dyed reddish brown, and cut short around a pointed chin. When we got to see her up close, we noted that though she did have deep creases at the corners of her eyes, she did not have a widow's peak. Her eyes were a dark hazel, and her pupils so small they looked like pinpricks.

The little widow had wallpapered her sewing room with a cheap burlap. When one of us slipped a fingernail underneath a panel and discovered that the rough cloth was glued on, we crossed ourselves and said a quick prayer for the little widow's security deposit.

On that burlap the little widow had embroidered massive, swaying palm trees, so finely detailed that we could almost feel a salty breeze warm our faces as we stood on her tailor's pedestal. Running our fingertips across the embroidered walls we could feel the braille of her labor; the grains of sand were individually stitched, as if the little widow knew each one. The ocean seemed to ripple and surge as the little widow worked around us in meditative silence, kneeling near our ankles with a pin between her lips. She was so gentle and fluid in her movements, her soft skin creasing like a plump baby's around the pincushion she wore on her wrist.

We liked her in those moments, but even so, we didn't invite her to our birthday parties or gatherings at Christmas, though we knew she was alone in that large apartment, watching the passing of the seasons, just as we did, through black-barred windows. (994 words)

Annotations:

1 **LaGuardia** – New York airport
17 **el campo** – *Spanish:* in the country(side)
21 f. **Saona Beach** – a picturesque beach in the Dominican Republic
22 **guayabera** – a type of shirt commonly worn in areas with a tropical climate
41 **super** – *here:* the caretaker
52 **campesina** – *Spanish:* female peasant
110 f. **widow's peak** – a V-shaped point in the hairline in the center of the forehead
126 **braille** – type of writing for people with impaired eye-sight based on embossed dots that can be felt with the fingertips

Beispiellösung

Aufgabe 1

In Yohanca Delgado's short story "The Little Widow from the Capital", published 2021, anticipation builds among female residents of a New York apartment complex about a new neighbour who is moving in. They learn that she is a widow from the Dominican Republic and speculate about her background and life. When she arrives, they find themselves taken aback by her unexpected youthful appearance and unconventional clothing. To fill in the gaps in their knowledge about her, they concoct elaborate stories. Although they interact with her in a manner that appears friendly, they talk behind her back and maintain a certain distance. The latter is reciprocated by the demure widow. Intrigued by her sewing skills, they start bringing her garments for alterations and are momentarily captivated by her skillful craftsmanship and the décor of her flat. Despite this, they exclude her from their social gatherings and celebrations, even though they are aware she lives alone. (154 words)

Aufgabe 2

The narrative's perspective is a collective but limited first-person point of view, indicated by the use of the pronoun "we" (e. g. ll. 4, 7, 9). This collective voice lends an air of communal observation and judgement, thus emphasising that their thoughts are not isolated ones but shared within their community.
The neighbours' overbearing curiosity is expressed by a number of questions they ask themselves but never the widow herself (cf. ll. 10–18, 43, 81 f.). Neither are means to

truly get to know the new arrival better but instead illustrate how they are gauging her social standing.
Stylistic means like personification also come into play when describing "the rumors [...] had taken an earlier flight" (ll. 2–4) or the rain being described as "tiny birds slamming into our windows", mirroring the neighbours' curious yet aggressive scrutiny of the widow.
The metaphoric statement that "[w]e ourselves had been raised on a diet of telenovelas and American magazines, and we knew what beauty was" (ll. 64–66) suggests that the neighbours' understanding of beauty is ingrained in them as the food they consume, highlighting the source of their judgements and biases. It explains why the widow, with her unconventional style and humble origins, does not fit into their preconceived notions of beauty or acceptability. Accordingly, her self-confidence constitutes an attractiveness that repels them, arguably because of their envy.
"Our eyes darted hungrily between her and the contents of her sewing room" (ll. 104 f.) characterises the neighbours' dominant feeling as an invasive and consuming curiosity, likening them to predators eyeing their prey. The metaphor turns the neighbours' interest into a palpable force, underlining their conflicted feelings of being torn between fascination and a need to feel superior. It reflects the tension between the allure of the unknown and the comfort of the familiar.
In another metaphor the widow's painstaking work is likened to braille (cf. ll. 124–126), suggesting that her labour has a texture, a depth that can be 'read' through touch, thus creating a moment of intimacy and connection between the complex's collective and the widow. This represents a point where the neighbours' come close to appreciating the widow, albeit momentarily, but it also serves as a poignant reminder of the emotional and social distance that still exists, as the tactile closeness does not translate into genuine social inclusion.
The simile likening the neighbours' invented stories about the widow's previous life to ivy (cf. ll. 78–81) depicts them as invasive, suffocating, spreading quickly and sticking in people's minds. It therefore strengthens the image of the damaging and self-perpetuating nature of gossip and preconceived judgements. It encapsulates the essence of the neighbours' relationship with the widow: one that is defined more by their own projections and fantasies than by any genuine understanding or empathy.
Moreover, synaesthesia is used to describe the widow's embroidered walls, saying "we could almost feel a salty breeze warm our faces" (ll. 122 f.). This multisensory description reflects a momentary enchantment with the widow, yet it remains superficial and is not enough to bridge the chasm of their own prejudices and judgmental behaviour.
Consequently, the neighbours' attitude towards the widow is a complex tapestry woven from curiosity, speculation and a desire for social distance to something that remains alien to them. Through narrative perspective and a variety of stylistic means like personification, (rhetorical) questions, metaphors, simile and synaesthesia, the text masterfully captures the essence of this ambivalence. It portrays a community united in its curiosity and its unwillingness to truly welcome an outsider. (579 words)

Aufgabe 3

To what extent can the need for community be considered a substantial necessity?

By stating that "[t]he need for connection and community is primal, as fundamental as the need for air, water, and food", the author Dean Ornish taps into a sentiment that resonates with many. In this blog entry, we will explore its validity by examining it through the lens of Yohanca Delgado's short story "The Little Widow from the Capital" as well as the 2008 movie "Gran Torino".

In the short story, the female neighbours represent a close-knit community. Their curiosity about the young widow reflects an innate human tendency to seek understanding and connection. Likewise, in "Gran Torino", the Christian community, the Hmong neighbourhood and the gangs offer a sense of belonging that contrasts with the loneliness of the main character, Walt Kowalski. In both scenarios, the community serves as a compass for one's identity, providing a sense of place and orientation.

Sometimes, the support system a community provides can be tangible and exceptionally practical. The young widow in the story offers her skills in tailoring, which at least temporarily endears her to her neighbours. Similarly, Walt ends up becoming a mentor figure to young Thao, offering guidance and even material support. This sense of reciprocity underlines the benefits of living in a community –individuals can often rely on their peer group in times of need.

However, Ornish's statement does not account for the human need for autonomy and consequently the freedom of rejecting community. This is exemplified by Walt dismissing his family and church community as well as the young widow maintaining her distance. Neither are obliged to form deeper bonds if they do not wish to do so. It is therefore evident that while being helpful when wanted, community is not necessarily fundamental for survival or happiness.

Additionally, being part of a community can expose individuals to negative influences, like the young widow being scrutinised and excluded, or even endanger their well-being or that of their loved ones, as demonstrated in "Gran Torino". While the Hmong community there provides companionship for Walt, it also introduces him to the darker aspects of society like gang violence, theft and racial tensions.

Lastly, while community possibly provides emotional and sometimes material support, it is not the sole factor for survival. Basic needs like food, water and shelter can also be met independently. This suggests that while social bonds enrich life, they are not as fundamental as air, water or food.

Still, Dean Ornish's statement holds true in many circumstances. Community often provides the emotional sustenance we crave, something that we as a society have been very much reminded of during times of pandemic-induced isolation. It can also offer practical support we sometimes need. However, it is crucial to recognise that this captures an idealistic view of community, one that is not a fundamental truth for everyone. Thus, while community plays a vital role in human experience, it is not as fundamental as Dean Ornish suggests. (495 words)

Stichwortverzeichnis